Breaking Into Acting For Dummies®

Preparing for an Audition

Auditioning can be a stressful experience. Use this handy checklist to help you prepare ahead of time to minimize any possible distractions that could affect your performance. (See Chapter 9 for more auditioning tips.)

- Prepare and pack plenty of head shots and resumes. Staple your head shot to the back of your resume, so you don't lose one or the other.
- Pack a change of clothes in case your outfit gets dirty or torn, or so you can modify your appearance to match the role.
- Take a copy of sides (the pages of a script that you'll be reading from) or the script to practice while you wait your turn to audition.
- Do a final run-through of your monologues to make sure that you have them memorized and are comfortable performing them.
- Confirm directions to the audition location. Also, plan to leave your residence in plenty of time to get to the audition location early.
- Clear your personal calendar for the day of the audition, so you can arrive early and stay late with no worries.
- Make a list of emergency telephone numbers, such as your agent's number and the audition location number.
- Get a good night's sleep.

Taking Clothing Measurements

Casting directors may need your clothing measurements to fit you in a costume. Jot down your measurements and take them to your next audition.

Height: ________	**Females:**	Bust: ________	**Males:**	Suit: ________
Weight: ________		Hips: ________		Shirt: ________
Shoe size: ________		Dress: ________		Inseam: ________
Waist: ________		Blouse: ________		
		Pants: ________		

Breaking Into Acting For Dummies®

Dealing with Frustration as an Actor

The following is a list of suggestions for ways to unwind or rejuvenate your acting dream:

- Meditate or practice Yoga
- Treat yourself to a spa, massage, or a hot bath
- Take a class to overcome your weaknesses as an actor
- Look for a day job that you may actually like
- Participate in non-show business activities, such as sports, volunteering at a hospital or charity, or enjoying a hobby
- Work off some steam — take a karate, boxing, or aerobic workout class
- Start or join a support group with fellow actors
- See a movie, go to a play, or read a good book
- Read a positive-thinking book or listen to motivational tapes
- Browse through one of the trade publications such as *Variety* or *Hollywood Reporter*
- Pursue an additional show business career (writing, stand-up comedy, filmmaking, and so on)
- Take a vacation (It can be as simple as a one-day trip to the beach or a two-week trip to Europe.)
- Take time to develop a plan for advancing your acting career

Deducting Acting Expenses

Be sure to keep accurate records of your acting expenses and consult your tax adviser for specific information about tax deductions. Possible deductions include the following (see Chapter 18 for more tax info):

- Travel expenses to and from auditions (including meals and lodging)
- Admissions to movies and plays (save your ticket stubs)
- Acting classes, workshops, and seminars
- Acting books and magazines
- Office supplies
- Mailing expenses
- Telephone bills, including the cost of an answering machine or service, a pager, or cellular phone
- Union dues
- Head shots (photographer's fees and duplication costs)
- Resume (printing and duplication costs)
- Videotape and DVD rentals
- Television set, VCR, DVD player, and the cost of cable subscription service
- Makeup and clothing specifically used for acting (including dry cleaning expenses)
- Cost of creating and duplicating a demo tape

Item 5446-8.

For more information about Wiley Publishing, call 1-800-762-2974.

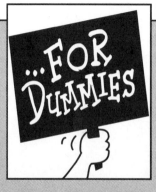

Breaking Into Acting FOR DUMMIES®

Breaking Into Acting FOR DUMMIES®

by Larry Garrison and Wallace Wang

Breaking Into Acting For Dummies®

Published by
Wiley Publishing, Inc.
909 Third Avenue
New York, NY 10022
www.wiley.com

Published by Wiley Publishing, Inc., Indianapolis, Indiana

Published simultaneously in Canada

Library of Congress Control Number: 2002108096

ISBN: 0-7645-5446-8

Manufactured in the United States of America

10 9 8 7 6

1B/SV/QZ/QS/IN

About the Authors

Larry Garrison has been President of SilverCreek Entertainment for more than 20 years. Recently, he executive produced the movie *Like Mother/Like Son,* starring Mary Tyler Moore and Jean Stapleton, for CBS among other projects. He also created and executive produced *Caught In The Act* for NBC with Dick Clark. Larry has also produced segments of *20/20, Good Morning America, Extra,* and other shows. He was an accomplished actor, and he also owned a photography business, shooting celebrities and individuals who were starting out in the industry.

Wallace Wang has written more than a dozen books over the years, including *Beginning Programming For Dummies, Microsoft Office XP For Dummies,* and *Steal This Computer Book.* In addition to writing, he has also performed in theatrical productions and appeared as an extra in several commercials, industrial films, and the film *The Hanoi Hilton.* In his free time, he also performs stand-up comedy, appearing regularly at the Riviera Comedy Club in Las Vegas. He also performed stand-up comedy on A&E's *Evening at the Improv.* His goal in life is to try something new every day just to keep his life interesting. He tries to follow the advice of his friend and fellow comedian, Roy Edwards, who once told him, "I'm not afraid of failing. I'm afraid of living a boring life."

Authors' Acknowledgments

I would like to thank my inspirations:
My daughter and her family — Jaime, Brandon, and Dylan
Lindsay and Dave
My son Sean and Chewie
Shannon Buckley, and my acting mentors the late Lee Strasberg and Vera Vlosova

My sister Stephanie along with Ed, Brian, Courtney, and Chris
My sister-in-law Susan
My angels — Mom, Dad, and my brother Jim
My friends Gayle, Sherwood, and Joey
My partner Wally Wang

And Rocke and Debra and Ben and Belinda

My friends and business associates Iris and Bubba
My agents Matt Wagner and William Gladstone
And thanks to Scott Brazil (Director/Producer) who has been my partner with my company in film and television for more than 20 years. Because of your belief in me and this project, hopefully many people will achieve their dreams. Thank you and God Bless!

—Larry Garrison

I would like to thank the many people who had nothing to do with this book but still played an influential role in my life in some form or another:

All the friendly folks at the Riviera Comedy Club, located at the Riviera Hotel & Casino (`www.theriviera.com`) in Las Vegas: Steve Schirripa (who appears in HBO's hit show, *The Sopranos*), Don Learned, Bob Zany, Gerry Bednob, Bruce Clark, and Kip Addotta. The Riviera Comedy Club is one of the best places to work because of the tireless efforts of Lynn Snyder, the comedy club manager; and Patricia Weber, the Entertainment Supervisor.

Another big round of thanks goes to Kent Brisby and Ginger Lily Lowe (`www.asianstorytheater.com`), Brendon Fox (`www.theglobetheatres.org`), and Larry Lapidus (`www.lapidusphoto.com`) for their valuable information and advice.

Patrick DeGuire also deserves thanks — not because he helped with this book (he didn't) but because he helped me form Top Bananas Entertainment (`www.topbananas.com`), our company devoted to providing clean, quality stand-up comedy to people who aren't drunk. Additional thanks must also go to Chris (the Zooman) Clobber, Leo (the man, the myth, the legend) Fontaine, Judy (the love goddess) Tenuta (`www.judytenuta.com`), Freddie King and

Terry Sanchez at Twin Dragons, Mitzi Shore at The Comedy Store (`www.thecomedystore.com`), and Mark Ridley at The Comedy Castle (`www.comedycastle.com`) in Detroit (actually, Royal Oak).

Thanks also goes to my co-author, Larry Garrison, for his wonderful sense of humor in the face of adversity.

Final thanks go to Cassandra (my wife) and Jordan (my son) and Bo, Scraps, Tasha, and Nuit (our cats) for providing my life with lots of interesting tasks that usually involve something coming out of one end of the cat or the other.

—Wallace Wang

Dedication

We dedicate this book to our wonderful families and friends who have inspired us to follow our dreams. May every actor and individual know that success equates to luck, timing, and longevity, coupled with desire. Learning the business of acting, or anything that one aspires to, will lead you to your goal. Don't let anyone tell you that you cannot be a success.

Publisher's Acknowledgments

We're proud of this book; please send us your comments through our Dummies online registration form located at www.dummies.com/register/.

Some of the people who helped bring this book to market include the following:

Acquisitions, Editorial, and Media Development

Project Editor: Alissa Schwipps

Acquisitions Editor: Natasha Graf

Copy Editors: Christina Guthrie, Patricia Yuu Pan

Editorial Manager: Jennifer Ehrlich

Editorial Assistant: Nívea C. Strickland

Special Help: Tina Sims

Cover Photo: PHX-Hagerstown

Production

Project Coordinator: Nancee Reeves

Layout and Graphics: Scott M. Bristol, Jacque Schneider, Jeremey Unger

Proofreaders: Laura Albert, Andy Hollandbeck, Angel Perez, Carl Pierce, TECHBOOKS Production Services, Inc.

Indexer: TECHBOOKS Production Services, Inc.

Publishing and Editorial for Consumer Dummies

Diane Graves Steele, Vice President and Publisher, Consumer Dummies

Joyce Pepple, Acquisitions Director, Consumer Dummies

Kristin A. Cocks, Product Development Director, Consumer Dummies

Michael Spring, Vice President and Publisher, Travel

Brice Gosnell, Publishing Director, Travel

Suzanne Jannetta, Editorial Director, Travel

Publishing for Technology Dummies

Andy Cummings, Acquisitions Director

Composition Services

Gerry Fahey, Vice President of Production Services

Debbie Stailey, Director of Composition Services

Contents at a Glance

Cartoons at a Glance

By Rich Tennant

"I know it's a Furby, Ronald. Just work with it until we can get a skull."

page 277

The 5th Wave
By Rich Tennant
STAND-UP COMEDIAN MAKING TRANSITION TO TAX ATTORNEY

"Hey – what's the deal with all these statutes? Hey – what's the deal with all these books? Hey – what's the deal with the Bar Exam? Hey – and what if I don't pass it...?"

page 233

page 7

"Well, I don't like to brag about myself, but I've got a little friend here that has a few stories I think you'll find interesting."

page 41

"Excuse me! Witch number three, your line is also 'Hail,' not 'Whatever'."

page 137

"I know you're all classically trained actors, but I don't think the public's ready for Titus Andronicus performed by the cast of Stomp."

page 85

Cartoon Information:
Fax: 978-546-7747
E-Mail: richtennant@the5thwave.com
World Wide Web: www.the5thwave.com

Table of Contents

Introduction

Acting can be one of the most glamorous, exciting, lucrative, and totally unpredictable careers in the world. While other people trudge off to routine jobs pushing paperwork, sitting in office cubicles, or fighting each other just for an office with a window in it, actors may be performing on stage one day, appearing in a film or television show the next, and flying around the country (and the world) the following day all the while getting paid to pretend to be somebody else. If acting sounds like the type of work you'd like to do, then this book can help you pursue your dreams.

No matter how much (or how little) acting experience you may have, you can start pursuing an acting career right now — no matter where you happen to live — and this book shows you how.

About This Book

Although acting may seem exotic and enticing, it can also be terrifying and frustrating as well — but only if you don't know what you're doing. Naturally, this book can't guarantee that you'll succeed as an actor, but by following the information in this book, you can increase your chances of success immensely whether you're a beginning actor or someone who already has plenty of experience performing on stage or in front of the camera but may need help in pushing your acting career up to the next level of success.

Specifically, this book can help you break into the world of show business that includes acting in movies, television, and stage plays. You'll discover what casting directors look for, figure out how to prepare yourself for those all-important auditions, and find out how to take control of your acting career so you can succeed as quickly as possible.

Acting is more than just about talent; it's a business, as well. By showing you the business of acting, this book gives you information that many actors either overlook or simply don't know where to find. Written in plain English with plenty of information that both novice and experienced actors can use, *Breaking Into Acting For Dummies* can be your guide and reference for succeeding as an actor.

How to Use This Book

You can use this book as a reference to help you get started in the wild world of acting or find out more information about a particular aspect of acting.

- If you want a complete look at getting into acting, then read this book from cover to cover. You'll gain a full understanding of acting as a business and acting as a craft.
- If you want to find out about a particular topic, just flip to that chapter or section and read away! The chapters in this book are designed to stand alone — you don't need to read one chapter as a "requirement" before moving on to the next.

Conventions Used in This Book

To help you pick out information from a page, we use the following conventions throughout the text to make elements consistent and easy to understand:

- Any Web addresses appear in `mono font`.
- New terms appear in *italics* and are closely followed by an easy-to-understand definition.
- Sidebars, which look like text enclosed in a shaded gray box, consist of information that is interesting to know but not critical to your growth as an actor.

Foolish Assumptions

We assume a few things about you. For starters, you have an open mind and believe in yourself. Also, we assume that you're

- Mentally stable and know why you want to go into acting. (If you want to go into acting for money or attention, you really need a book like "Greed For Dummies," or "Getting the Attention the World Owes You For Dummies" instead.)
- Ready to jump into areas of life that may be completely new and unfamiliar to you.
- Willing to explore, to take risks, and to trust that you have the ability to do whatever you want to do — if you really want to do it.

How This Book Is Organized

To help you find the information you need, this book is divided into several parts, where each part focuses on a specific aspect of acting.

Part I: Figuring Out the Business of Acting

This part of the book gives you background information on how the world of show business works and what roles the different people in show business may play in your acting career, from producers and casting directors to agents and business managers.

Part II: Packaging and Marketing Yourself

In this part of the book, you find the two standard promotional tools that every actor needs: head shots and resumes. Plus you'll discover what kind of additional skills you may need to embark on an acting career.

Part III: Taking Your First Steps into Show Business

This part explains how to find work, how to conduct yourself during an audition, how to get an agent, and how to promote yourself to the show business industry.

Part IV: Scoping Out the Markets

The chapters in this part of the book focus on specific acting opportunities in movies, television shows, theater, commercials, and voice-overs. Part IV also explains how to get work as an extra and break your child into acting.

Part V: Managing Your Money as an Actor

Managing money is a skill that many people desperately need to acquire, and actors are no exception. So this part of the book explains how to avoid typical con games that prey off actors' vulnerability, get a job that pays the bills and still allows you time to pursue auditions, and save and invest money to protect you during those inevitable times when your acting income may plummet (or jump) dramatically.

Part VI: The Part of Tens

This part of the book provides tips for improving and succeeding as an actor and ways to act just for fun or on a part-time basis. You'll also find ten popular myths about show business that you need to avoid so you can succeed as an actor.

Icons Used in This Book

To help you remember the important points of each chapter, this book marks certain paragraphs with helpful icons. Some icons highlight useful information; others offer shortcuts to help you break into acting more quickly and easily; and other icons wave a red flag in your face to warn you about some of the possible dangers that could sabotage your acting career.

Tip icons highlight useful information that can save you time or money in helping you pursue your dream of acting.

This icon highlights useful ideas or information that you may not want to forget. By flipping through this book and looking for all the Remember icons, you can quickly read the most important information in each chapter.

Watch out! A Warning icon flags certain traps or pitfalls that can slow down, delay, or actually hurt your fledging acting career.

This icon spotlights important acting-related terms that you're likely to hear when hanging around other show business people.

Where to Go from Here

If you're serious (or just plain curious) about acting as a career and you have no experience whatsoever, start with Chapter 1 to grasp the basics of the wonderfully wacky world of show business that you're about to join.

If you have some acting experience, you may want to skim through Parts I and II and jump right into deciding how to market yourself or into exploring the different types of acting jobs you could start investigating.

Of course, not everyone may want to pursue acting full-time, so for readers who are considering acting just part-time or as a hobby, take a look at Chapter 22. That chapter reveals the abundance of opportunity available to anyone who sees acting as just a really cool hobby that allows them to express themselves in public without getting arrested.

Consider this book as a gentle guide that you can browse through, skim, and even ignore as you want. Just remember to keep your sense of humor and enjoy your life right now, no matter what your dreams may lead you toward — and you'll always be happy no matter what amount of success you may ultimately achieve.

The purpose of acting (or any career) isn't just to make money. The purpose is to have fun, and armed with the information in this book, you can have fun as you break into the exciting and unpredictable world of acting.

Part I

Figuring Out the Business of Acting

The 5th Wave
By Rich Tennant
©RICHTENNANT
LITTLE-KNOWN FACT: Most of the movie stars' handprints in the cement sidewalk in front of Grauman's Chinese Theater were put there AFTER the cement had dried!

In this part . . .

Many talented actors don't succeed in show business because they forget the first rule: Show business is a *business.* So this part of the book gives you a brief understanding about the business details behind the world of film, television, and theater. By understanding the needs and desires of the people who control the money, you can better understand your role in the larger scheme of show business as an actor.

The business of acting is simple. You help others make money, and they'll help you make money. But first, you have to figure out how show business really works, and that's what this part of the book is all about.

Chapter 1

Opening the Door to Show Business

In This Chapter

- Succeeding in show business
- Understanding how show business works
- Preparing yourself for an acting career

Nearly everyone fantasizes at one time or another about being a star. Who wouldn't love to see his or her name on a big-screen marquee or experience the thrill of bowing before an audience that's giving a standing ovation just for you?

For many people, the idea of becoming a star in show business will always remain just a dream. But with the help of this book, you can be one of those few who turn their dreams of acting into reality.

Before you begin, you need to understand the two sides of show business. On one hand, you have the "show," which means learning how to act and includes the glamour and fame that comes from being a star. On the other hand, you have the "business," which includes the money and the negotiations that make a profit for everyone involved. The business side also means treating acting as a business, so you can get paid to act. If you remember nothing else from this book, at least remember this: *Acting is a business.* The more you treat acting like a business, the more likely you'll be to succeed.

In this chapter, you get a quick peek at what you need to succeed as an actor, whether you live in London, Los Angeles, or Lima, Ohio. You can see how actors market themselves by using a head shot and a resume and how persistence and determination are the real secrets that can help you break into show business faster than you may think. If you ever thought that you could be an actor, you can. And this chapter gives you a brief introduction to that wonderful world of show business.

Understanding the World of Acting

If you want to succeed in show business as an actor, you need to learn how to act (duh). But you also need to be familiar with the business side of show business.

Every year, thousands of hopefuls flock to Los Angeles and New York. And every year, thousands of these same hopefuls wind up disappearing into obscurity. The reason is simple. Many aspiring actors embark on their career without knowing how show business works. So before you quit your job, pack up your bags, and move to Hollywood or Broadway to become tomorrow's next big star, take a sneak-peek behind the production curtain in Chapter 2. Then take a look at Chapter 3, which introduces you to the movers and shakers of show business who can open doors for you.

What You Need to Succeed

If the thought of spending years studying acting, working in bit roles, and getting paid sporadically (if at all) depresses you, maybe acting isn't for you. On the other hand, if you truly enjoy acting for the sake of acting, the previously mentioned obstacles will be nothing more than minor nuisances on your way to success — whatever form that success may ultimately take.

Every successful actor has to have two skills. One is a certain amount (but not necessarily a lot) of acting talent, which usually comes from a combination of natural ability and constant training. The second, and perhaps the more important skill, is knowing how to market yourself as a product.

As an actor, you're a salesperson, and the product that you're selling is you. In order to sell yourself to the people in position to pay for your product (you as an actor), you need a head shot (so people know what you look like), a resume (so people know what experience and skills you have), and the necessary talent to wow a casting director when you audition for a role.

An attention-grabbing head shot

Talent and determination can increase the odds that you'll succeed in show business, but until people know who you are, you're just another face in the crowd. Because you can't possibly introduce yourself to everyone who may be able to advance your career, you have to use a head shot instead.

A *head shot* is a photograph that acts as your calling card by displaying your face for others to see when you can't be present physically. Your head shot should capture your best physical features in order to make casting directors and agents say to themselves, "I've got to meet this person!"

Because head shots can be such a crucial promotional tool, you absolutely must have the best head shot possible, which means finding the best photographer and developing a specific image for your head shot to project. In Chapter 4, you can find out how to choose a photographer, what to wear during your photography session, and how to look your absolute best, so that your head shot highlights your unique personality.

A five-star acting resume

While your head shot projects your physical characteristics, a resume lists the acting experience and unique skills behind your attractive face. After seeing an actor's head shot, casting directors often study an actor's resume to see whether that actor has the ability to perform in a particular role.

A good acting resume answers any questions a casting director may have about an actor's ability to play a certain role and supplies enough evidence to convince a casting director to choose you. Chapter 5 discusses ways to create an award-winning resume, whether you're a complete novice, a seasoned veteran, or someone in-between. (Psst, Chapter 5 also shows you what to put on your resume and what to leave off to increase your chances of making a great first impression.) By knowing how to create and present your acting experience and skills in the best light possible, you can use your resume to help you land roles again and again.

Polished talent

Everyone has some talent for acting (think of the last time you called in to work and pretended to be sick so that you could take the day off). Even if you have astounding natural acting talent, you may still want lessons or coaching to nurture and further develop that talent (see Chapter 6 for more information on improving your acting skills with training). Here are some of the different ways to polish your acting talent:

- Majoring in drama in school
- Attending an acting class or workshop
- Working with an acting coach
- Learning on the job

If you're serious about becoming an actor and you're already in school, you can't get any better training than performing in your high school or college drama department. Not only does such exposure give you an idea how much fun (and how much of a pain in the neck) acting can be, but it can also teach you all the technical details necessary to put on a play, ranging from creating backdrops and building sets to sewing costumes and marketing the show.

If you've already graduated or just want to jump right into the world of acting as soon as possible, you can choose from plenty of acting workshops, classes, and coaches available for varying prices. Once again, some acting teachers have better reputations than others, and some charge outrageous amounts of money while others are more reasonable. Chapter 6 gives you tips on how to pick a workshop or acting coach that's right for you.

The best way to develop your acting skills is to keep looking for acting roles wherever you can find them, whether they're lead roles in small plays or bit roles in larger productions. The more experience and knowledge you can gain by acting in a real role and watching others perform, the more you'll discover about the world of acting that no class or coach can ever duplicate.

Taking Your First Steps in Show Business

How did big stars like Julia Roberts, Tom Hanks, Robert Redford, Sandra Bullock, Bruce Willis, and Angelina Jolie break into show business? They all started as beginners. So as an aspiring actor, you too can follow in the footsteps of the most successful actors in the world if you figure out what to do first and how to get started. Who knows? Within a few years, people may be clamoring for *your* autograph.

Marketing yourself

Some people just happen to be in the right place at the right time when some Hollywood or Broadway producer spots them and suddenly decides to turn them into a star. Then again, some people win a million bucks in the lottery, too, so you don't want to base your future on blind luck.

Unless you happen to become an overnight success (ignoring the fact that most overnight successes actually take ten years or more to happen), you'll find that succeeding in acting requires persistence, dedication, and perseverance.

Perseverance means overcoming every obstacle that threatens to get in your way and blazing your own trail to success. Because you can never rely on blind luck or fate to bring you success, you have to actively hunt out success yourself. Chapter 7 lists different ways that you can promote yourself in the world of show business and jump-start your career right now — wherever you happen to be.

Finding your first ally: An agent

Although you certainly can work as an actor for years without an agent, an agent can be crucial in finding obscure roles that you may never hear about otherwise. An agent can also introduce you to casting directors who may be looking for someone just like you (if they only knew where to find you) and handle the business end of your acting, such as making sure that you get paid on time and making sure that you get paid as much as possible for your work.

Because an agent can help your acting career enormously, Chapter 8 explains how to find an agent and how to keep an agent happy, so he or she will be happy to look for work and negotiate big contracts for you.

Showcasing your talent: Auditioning

The process of looking for an agent can teach you negotiating and cold-calling skills. Auditioning can teach you how to think and react quickly in unfamiliar environments and situations.

Because an audition (like a first date) can be your first (and sometimes only) chance to showcase yourself, Chapter 9 explains how to maximize your chance of creating the best impression possible during every audition you attend. Chapter 9 includes tips for what types of clothes to wear, how to prepare for any audition, how to behave during an audition, and what to expect during an audition.

The Many Ways to Make Money as an Actor

Starring in the next Broadway hit or Hollywood blockbuster can make you rich beyond your wildest dreams, but what many actors don't know is that you can make money as an actor in a variety of other ways as well, some of which can make you equally wealthy and famous, too. Here they are:

- **Film and TV:** Although you may not automatically star in the next box office smash or have your own sitcom, you don't want to overlook the traditional acting routes of film and television. Chapter 10 explains the feature film and television market, so you can use your knowledge to break into these highly lucrative markets right away.

- **Commercials:** Appearing in a commercial can be another great way to get exposure, gain valuable acting experience, and possibly make a lot of money at the same time through the magic of *residuals* (also known as royalties), which is money actors receive every time their commercials appear on national television. John Travolta got started in television commercials, which ultimately led him to television and, finally, feature films. See Chapter 11 for more information on breaking into the commercial acting market.
- **Theater:** Don't forget this time-honored tradition! Chapter 12 explains this prestigious acting market and what you can expect when performing in a play.
- **Voice-over acting:** Watch any Saturday morning cartoon, animated feature film, or animated TV show (such as *The Simpsons*), and you'll soon realize that many actors can make a great living just by acting with their voices alone. Best of all, voice-over acting relies strictly on talent and not on looks, which means that actors of all ages, backgrounds, and nationalities can find a wealth of opportunities open to them — no matter what their age or appearance may be. Go to Chapter 13 for more on the hidden but lucrative world of voice-over acting.
- **Extra acting:** Although being an extra won't necessarily make you rich and famous, Chapter 14 shows you how to use extra acting to help yourself break into show business from the inside. After you start working as an extra, you can peek behind the scenes to see how film and television acting works. You can also make invaluable contacts with directors and other actors who may be able to help you pursue your dreams of acting.
- **Roles for children:** In case you have children, you may want to get them into show business as well. So take a peek at Chapter 15 to see what types of acting opportunities may be available for your son, daughter, nephew, or niece. With a little bit of luck, your child may be able to earn his or her own college money by appearing in commercials, films, TV shows, commercials, or theater.

Managing Money (A Little or a Lot)

As a beginning actor, you have to figure out how to juggle acting, earning a living, and handling your money all at the same time. To help you keep your money (and avoid losing it on show business scams that promise you success but only take your money and run), make sure that you read Chapter 16. Con artists prey on actors, so this chapter can expose the more common con games and help you avoid wasting time and money on these scams.

Until you start earning a steady income from your acting career, you'll most likely need a day job to provide you with a reliable source of income. Chapter 17 explains different types of jobs suitable for actors who may need to take off for an audition in the middle of the day. Chapter 17 also provides tips for looking for a job that provides the most flexibility and income, so you can focus your efforts on becoming a working actor.

Acting is a completely unpredictable business. One moment you're flooded with work, and the next few months (or years) may bring you no work at all. That's why many aspiring actors pursue a second career. Not only does this choice provide a solid financial foundation so that they can live halfway decently, but it also gives them enough financial security so that a single rejection isn't emotionally or financially devastating. If you're too busy worrying about paying your rent this month, you probably won't have enough energy to focus on becoming a better actor.

Finally, Chapter 18 offers tips for managing your money wisely, from saving and investing your hard-earned cash to living frugally on a budget. We also give you some tips on ways to live cheaply (or even rent-free).

Knowing What to Expect from an Acting Career

At the very least, acting can expose you to interesting people, situations, and environments that you might never see otherwise. You'll figure out how to face and conquer your fears of speaking before an audience, how to use your body and voice to present yourself to others, how to develop a thick skin to handle the inevitable criticisms that you'll receive from less than adoring fans, and how to develop social and negotiating skills when searching for work and working with your fellow actors.

Oh, and by the way, you may make a little money on the side from acting as well.

If your purpose for acting is to get rich, you should probably start a business, work for a Fortune 500 company, or become a lawyer instead. Many different paths to riches are much more reliable than acting. If your purpose for acting is to get noticed, you don't need to be onstage or in front of a camera. You need to see a therapist to understand what emotional needs are lacking in your life. Go into acting because you want to become an actor. Any other reason for becoming an actor is ultimately pointless and self-defeating.

No matter what your age, your occupation, or your appearance, you can break into acting at any time from anywhere. It all boils down to your own desire, drive, and persistence. Combine those traits with the information in this book, and you can discover how to blaze your own trail to success in the wonderfully wacky, weird, and slightly surreal world of acting.

Chapter 2

Discovering How Show Business Really Works

In This Chapter

- Figuring out the business of show business
- Peeking behind-the-scenes at the creative process

Being an actor is just one part of show business. This chapter gives you a chance to peek behind the scenes of show business, so you can better understand how the entire process of creating a film, television show, commercial, or play works. You can also figure out how you, the actor, fit into the larger scheme of the world of entertainment.

The Business of Show Business

First and foremost, show business must create, develop, and present shows that people want to see. Whenever the show business industry forgets this simple rule, they tend to produce expensive bombs that flop and waste millions of dollars in the process (while also tainting the careers of everyone involved in the flop).

Paradoxically, although the show business industry has no problems lavishing millions of dollars on actors, producers, writers, and directors who have a history of working on blockbuster hits, these same show business executives are extremely reluctant to risk any money on unknown talent. (An unknown actor often has to struggle for years in low-budget productions that are more receptive to newcomers. Gradually, as the actor gains more experience, he or she can get the more visible and lucrative roles and, from the general public's point of view, suddenly be "discovered.")

That's why breaking into show business can seem so intimidating and difficult. Until you can make money for someone else, few people will be interested in you. Agents may turn you down, casting directors may tell you no, and even acting coaches (who you pay) may tell you that you're lacking talent in some area or another. Given all this discouragement, does an aspiring actor have any hope to make it in show business?

Obviously, the answer is *yes.* Show business may like working with established stars who can (almost) guarantee them money, but the world of film, TV, and theater devours talent as quickly as talent scouts can find them. Every year, newcomers break into the ranks of show business, and every year, the public celebrates the new faces until the next new celebrity comes along.

Taking It "From the Top" — It All Begins with an Idea

Show business is a world of dreams. Before a theater can sell tickets, before an actor can audition for a role, and before anyone builds a set or designs costumes, someone somewhere has to have an idea first.

Ideas for TV shows or films are often "ripped from the headlines" — newspaper or magazine articles, or true-life stories based on current events. Other times ideas emerge from a poem, short story, novel, a writer's dream, a cartoon, a song, or a play.

An idea by itself may be interesting, but it won't be marketable or useful in any way. So the next step in creating a show is to turn a raw idea into a script.

When someone buys the rights to a story (such as a current-events, true-life story), they purchase the *option* to that story. An option guarantees that no one else can work with the people who sold you their story. Options typically last for a limited time period, such as one year. If the person holding an option to a story hasn't produced the story within that time period, they can renew the option or let it expire, so someone else can buy it.

Selling an Idea

Everyone has an idea for a good story, but what really counts is the way the story is told. In the world of film, a writer writes a script and tries to market it. In the world of television, people usually create a *treatment* instead of a full script. The treatment includes a short description of the story and the characters involved, and typically ranges from one to six pages in length.

Sometimes, studios or production companies pay enormous amounts of money for a treatment — with no guarantee that the final script, based on that treatment, will be any good. Other times, a studio may pay a minimal amount of money for a treatment and wait for the entire script to be completed before spending any more money.

In many cases, several writers may work together to put words to an idea. Sometimes, writers may create a script in hopes that someone will buy and produce that script (called a *spec* script), and other times, a production company may hire writers to create a script from a story idea that they already own.

If you can write, you can increase your chances of breaking into show business. Many actors got their big break by writing their own script to star in, such as Sylvester Stallone with *Rocky* and Matt Damon and Ben Affleck with their film *Good Will Hunting.* Other actors have written one-man shows that they perform in theaters, which is an excellent way to showcase your talent for agents and casting directors. (Chapter 7 has more tips on how you can showcase your talents and get recognized in the business.)

Just because a studio either options or purchases the rights to a script doesn't necessarily mean that the script will ever get produced. The screenplay for the film *Platoon* circulated around various studios for over ten years before someone finally made it into a film.

Producing a Script

After a production company or studio buys the rights to a story idea, the next step is to produce the script, which is the responsibility of the producer. (Many producers run their own production companies and work with studios, but if a studio has an idea that they want produced, they may hire the producer who optioned the rights to the project.)

Producing a script involves several processes:

- **Hiring a director:** The producer hires the director. The director and the producer may then work together to hire the rest of the production crew, such as a costume designer or choreographer.
- **Polishing the script:** Scriptwriters often rewrite the script several times, sometimes for valid reasons to strengthen the story and sometimes for trivial reasons, such as to accommodate a major star who wants a certain role expanded or altered before he or she will agree to play the role.
- **Scouting out locations to film scenes:** The producer, along with several assistants, may scout locations for filming.

- **Finding and booking a place to rehearse:** The director, an assistant, or the stage manager takes care of setting a rehearsal schedule. In film and television, rehearsals take place on the set. In theater, rehearsals may take place anywhere, usually because the actual set or theater isn't available yet.
- **Setting a shooting or rehearsal schedule:** In film and television, the director and producer may collaborate on defining a shooting schedule. In theater, the director and stage manager may set a rehearsal schedule.
- **Establishing a budget:** The producer is responsible for estimating the cost of producing the film, television show, or play. (A producer may also hire a *unit production manager* to help with this task as well.) He or she must consider the cost of the shooting locations, actors' salaries, costumes, catering, travel and lodging expenses, special effects (a fire or a snow storm, for example), and so on.

  Budgets are often divided into above-line and below-line costs. *Above-line costs* make up the expenses for the creative people including the major actors, director, and producer. The *below-line costs* are for the technical people needed, such as lighting technicians, makeup artists, and costume designers.

- **Storyboarding each scene:** For a film, an artist sketches out the way each scene will look, a process known as *storyboarding*. By seeing a sketch of a scene, a director can tell whether filming a scene from a specific angle will work. Finding and fixing problems on a storyboard is infinitely faster and less expensive than trying to fix the problem during filming or after the film has already been shot.
- **Auditioning actors to play the various roles:** Every speaking role, from the major starring roles to the smallest roles where the actor may just say one line, must be filled.

Stretchin' that production dollar

Because a production's budget only goes so far, the director and producer always look for ways to cut costs without sacrificing quality. One such way is to cut corners on the set. For example, instead of building an entire log cabin, they may just build a front façade and cleverly mask the sides with additional scenery or film from certain angles, so that no one will notice that three walls are missing. Not only do they save money this way, but they also save time in construction.

Another common cost-cutting method is shooting films out of sequence. If the beginning and end of a film take place in the same location, such as in Singapore or on the deck of a cruise ship, the director films all those scenes at the same time before moving to a new location and a new group of scenes. That way the entire film crew doesn't have to visit the same location twice (and avoid additional traveling expenses) just to film two different scenes in chronological order.

Going into Production

After the script has been developed, the project is considered *green lit* when it moves into production. Production involves building sets and designing costumes. Also during the production phase, actors are measured and fitted for costumes, introduced to their fellow actors, and put through rehearsals to learn their lines and practice their movements on the stage or in front of the camera.

As an actor, one of the most important aspects of going to production is the beginning of rehearsals. In general, rehearsals go through three phases:

- **A dry rehearsal:** This first phase is designed to acquaint the actors with their roles and their lines. Dry rehearsals usually take place at a table where all the actors read the script while making any suggestions or changes.
- **The walk-through:** After the actors are familiar with their lines, they get acquainted with their positions on the stage or set. During this time, actors usually rehearse in their street clothes and may or may not be on the actual set where they will actually perform. The purpose of the walk-through is to discover any logistical problems, such as finding that some actors don't have enough time to exit off the stage and change into a different costume before their appearance in the next scene.

  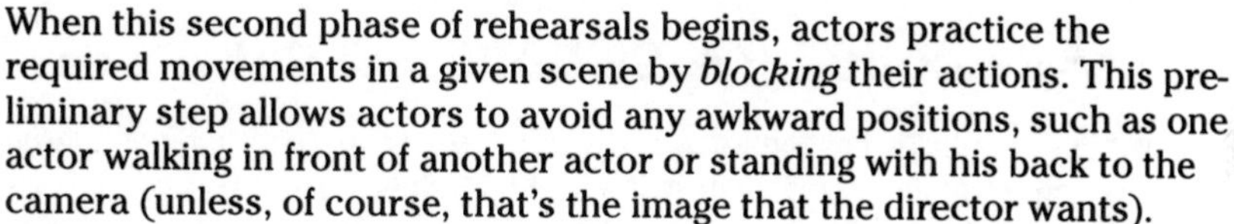
  When this second phase of rehearsals begins, actors practice the required movements in a given scene by *blocking* their actions. This preliminary step allows actors to avoid any awkward positions, such as one actor walking in front of another actor or standing with his back to the camera (unless, of course, that's the image that the director wants).
- **The dress rehearsal:** During this final phase, actors rehearse on the actual set while wearing the costumes that they will wear during the show. The actors and director have a chance to spot any additional problems with costumes and set design, such as doors that don't open properly, dresses that prohibit certain movements among the set because of their bulk, or lights that cast shadows across an actor's face. On a film set, actors who look and dress similar to the stars act as stand-ins for the stars, so the camera crew can adjust and focus their cameras before the real stars show up.

  Note: In stage plays, actors rehearse much longer and more often than they would do for a film, television show, or commercial. In film and TV, actors may be lucky to get even one rehearsal before the cameras start rolling, so it's a good idea to have your lines and movements ready before you show up on the set that day.

It's Showtime!

The time for rehearsals always runs out too quickly before showtime. That's when the actors perform for real in front of a live audience or in front of the camera.

Showtime is the pinnacle of all that the cast and crew have worked for. So as an actor, you must try especially hard at this stage to behave professionally, which means showing up on time, being prepared, and doing your job to your best ability. If you do anything that threatens to disrupt a show, you can always be fired at any time.

Sometimes, the best stage actors never make the transition to film and television, while film and television actors may not do as well on the stage as they do in front of the camera. The reason is because film, television, and theater all require different types of acting skills for performing in different environments.

When performing on many TV shows, such as situation comedies (sitcoms), actors usually perform in front of a live audience while the cameras are rolling at the same time. That way the studio can record the audience's laughter on a *laugh track* to play back when the show finally airs.

The collaborative nature of show business

Show business is a collaborative business. Although an actor may stand alone in the spotlight, he never would've gotten there without the combined work of a writer, director, producer, and costume designer (among other people). When starting a project, everyone tries to surround themselves with the best possible people for the job because the better other people do their job, the better you look in doing your job. Having a small role in a blockbuster hit is infinitely preferable to having a starring role in a bomb that becomes the butt of jokes for years to come.

Naturally, working with other people can never be completely harmonious. Sometimes people have minor disagreements that can be settled with a little bit of talk and compromise, and sometimes major stars clash egos with major directors or producers, creating a war-like atmosphere for everyone involved on the set. Sometimes perfectly good projects are abandoned because the people involved can't get along, despite everyone having excellent qualifications for doing their jobs.

So when any project is being developed, finding the right people to work on it is only one problem. Getting everyone to work together toward a common goal can create a completely different set of problems. As an actor, do your best to make sure that you're not part (or the source) of any problems, and you increase your chances of working with the same people again in the future. Given a choice between working with an actor who nobody can stand or someone more likeable and easy to work with (hopefully you), guess which actor most people will hire for the job?

For films that use special effects, the actors may be required to express intense emotions in a close-up with the camera while staring at nothing at all. During post-production, the director adds in the special effects, such as a computer-generated dinosaur leaping out at the actor or a volcano suddenly erupting in the distance.

An actor may have to respond to another actor who may not appear on camera. Rather than require this other actor to stare at nothing, it's common courtesy to read your lines off camera to make it easier for the actor on camera to respond to a real person rather than to an imaginary one. If you're the one on-camera, the other actors may not be as courteous, and you may find yourself trying to react all by yourself while staring at a camera and a blank wall.

Cleaning Up in Post-Production

Post-production occurs after the initial filming of a movie, TV show, or commercial is completed but before the final film or tape is shown to the general public.

Although post-production is a process associated with film and TV, a sort of post-production occurs in stage plays as well. After the initial performance, the actors, director, and writer may alter lines or entire scenes in the script from one show to the next in an effort to fine-tune the show, depending on the audience's reactions. If you feel that a certain line doesn't work or needs to be changed, consult with the director or playwright before changing your lines.

During post-production of a movie or a TV show, the director may cut out entire scenes or dialogue, add music (called *scoring*), and add special effects and sound effects. If the sound quality is poor in certain scenes, the actors may be asked to watch the film of themselves and dub in their own dialogue — a process known as *looping*. Sometimes, a director may ask another actor to loop in dialogue. So in the final film, you may appear, but another actor's voice is coming out of your mouth.

In rare cases, the director may reshoot unsatisfactory scenes (an expensive process, especially if the scene was shot in a distant location like Russia or aboard a nuclear aircraft carrier) or shoot entirely new scenes to help the continuity of the film.

During post-production, an entire scene that you appeared in may very well get cut and wind up on the cutting room floor. That's show business. (Of course, if you buy the DVD version of a film, you can often see the cut scenes. Sometimes, though, the cut scenes are so out of place that even the DVD version won't show them.)

Post-production can radically change the mood of a film, depending on how the director cuts and edits it. That's why you see so many films marketed as the *director's cut,* which is usually slightly or drastically different from the final cut that the studio ultimately released.

After all the cuts and edits have been made, the final product is often reviewed and approved by many different people before it's released to the public. Who does the viewing and approving depends on the kind of project. For example, before a TV commercial can appear on the air, the client must approve it. If the client doesn't like the TV commercial, it may never be aired. To test an audience's reaction to a film, studios usually offer special screenings to *test audiences.* Depending on the reaction of the test audiences, certain scenes may be dropped or new ones added.

Distributing the Product

After the director finishes editing a film, TV show, or commercial, and the finished product is approved, the final step is distribution.

Films can go through as many as six stages of distribution (outlined in the following list). Some films are designed specifically for distribution in the pay-per-view, television (often called a *made-for-TV* movie), or video and digital video disc (DVD) markets only.

- **Stage 1 — Initial release or *first-run:*** The film appears in major movie theaters across the country. Studios often release a film near a major holiday weekend, such as the Memorial Day weekend, to take advantage of the holiday crowds to maximize profits.
- **Stage 2 — Secondary release or *second-run:*** The film appears in smaller theaters.
- **Stage 3 — Overseas release:** During a film's first- or second-run, the studio may also release the film to overseas markets.
- **Stage 4 — Pay-per-view:** When the film is no longer showing in theatres, it may be sold to a cable pay-per-view network.
- **Stage 5 — Rental:** The film becomes available to rent on videotape and DVD.
- **Stage 6 — Television broadcast:** The film may be sold and broadcast over one of the major television networks.

At each step of the way, the actors involved with that particular film receive *residuals* (also known as royalties). (See the sidebar on residuals later in this chapter.) Therefore, it's in the actors' best interests to create a quality product, so as many people as possible will want to pay money to see it.

The magic of residuals

Acting is a job. The biggest difference between working in an ordinary job and working as an actor is that as an actor in film, television, and commercials, you may get paid many times for doing a job once. The first time, you get paid for doing your job; after that, you may get paid each time your part of the show is broadcast again. Each time that a commercial runs on the air, a TV show is rerun, or a film is broadcast on pay-per-view, television networks, or in overseas markets, you get a *residual* (or royalty).

Residuals are money paid to you for the privilege of broadcasting your performance on film or tape over and over again. Your agent usually negotiates the exact percentage of your residuals, although for smaller roles, you may receive no residuals at all.

As an actor, you strive for a speaking role because the more lines you speak, the more likely you'll qualify to earn residuals and earn the highest possible percentage for your residuals. For popular films, TV shows, and commercials, it's possible to earn a comfortable living off residuals alone.

Right before a film appears in theaters, the film's major actors often appear (at the studio's expense) on local and national radio and television shows to promote the film. Studios also compile short previews, called trailers, to run before movies in theaters to generate interest in the upcoming film. Studios often make deals or tie-ins with book publishers, toy companies, and fast food restaurants. The book publishers sell a novelization of a screenplay, the toy companies sell action figures of the major characters, and the fast food restaurants give away plastic cups or toys related to a film. By licensing out a film's characters, a studio can reduce its financial risk and earn back as much money as possible before a film is even released. Many actors may also earn extra money by licensing their likeness to action figures, comic books, or video games as part of any tie-ins that studios may have made with other companies.

By the time a film finally appears in the theaters, many of the actors could already be busy working on other projects.

Television shows follow a different distribution cycle from films. TV shows are usually broadcast once and then rerun one or more times. If a television show is popular, it may be sold into *syndication,* which means that it may be broadcast in a local or regional market. Each time a syndicated show appears on the air, the principal actors receive *residuals.*

Special distribution circumstances apply to theatrical productions as well. For example, if a stage play is particularly popular, it can run for several years, providing long-term employment for all the actors involved. During this time, the play may travel around the country or even the world.

The real secret of show business

The real secret of show business is that nobody can predict the next blockbuster hit. Even the most experienced and talented directors and actors have had their share of horrendous flops in projects that initially looked like sure-fire hits. Likewise, every year an unknown actor or director suddenly breaks through with a blockbuster hit that nobody thought had much of a chance.

So when dealing with agents, casting directors, producers, managers, and other actors, always remember that no one knows for sure what will sell in the future. Everyone can give you advice and tips for succeeding as an actor, but nobody knows for sure who will succeed and who won't. The actor rejected today may turn out to be the superstar of tomorrow.

In rare cases, a film may be shot, edited, and made ready for distribution only to find that the studio never releases it at all due to legal or other obscure reasons.

Chapter 3

From Agents to Unions: Introducing the Movers and Shakers of Show Business

In This Chapter

- Knowing who's boss (the producer)
- Knowing who's boss on the set (the director)
- Working with the writers
- Getting in good with the casting directors
- Realizing your agent's role
- Hiring other people to manage your life and your finances
- Knowing your role as an actor
- Utilizing unions

You may have heard the old saying: *It's not what you know; it's who you know.* Show business, like any business, depends on people.

This chapter introduces you to the different people in the world of show business and what they do so you can better understand how your own role as an actor fits into the chaotic world of show business.

Producers: The Champions of Every Project

Show business is full of great ideas, but nothing happens until a producer takes the initiative to turn a good idea into a finished product. Producers are responsible for guiding a project from a raw idea or script to a finished film, play, TV show, or commercial. Producers spend the most time on a project and often risk losing money or their reputation if the project never gets completed (or gets completed poorly). So the overriding goal of a producer is to create a quality product that's both marketable and profitable as quickly and inexpensively as possible.

Basically, producers do the following:

- Search for and obtain the rights to a story or script that has the potential to be both interesting and profitable.
- Get money to finance the project. (The money can come from a studio, a production company, individual investors, the producer's own bank account, or wherever the producer can get it.)
- Hire a director and writer to work on the project.
- Audition actors and ultimately help decide which actors to cast.
- Oversee the filming, taping, or rehearsals of a film, TV show, play, or commercial.
- Supervise the editing of the project.
- Work with studios or distribution companies to market and distribute a project.

Producers also have the less than enviable job of soothing frayed egos and dealing with problems that may occur between the director and stars on the set. When directors and stars can't agree on the way a project is developing, one or both of them may threaten to walk out of the project (or actually do it), citing creative differences. Sometimes, the producer has to replace the director or star, and sometimes, the producer can convince the warring parties to stick together long enough to finish the project (and hopefully do a great job despite any professional or personal disagreements between them).

Until you're a big star, you may work on a project without ever talking to the producer. When you're on a set and you have a problem, talk to the line producer or one of the line producer's assistants. While the producer takes care of the overall details of finishing a project, a *line producer* worries about the day-to-day details of getting a project completed, such as telling you what time to return to the set the next day and helping you with any problems involving your costume.

Directors: The Bosses on the Set

After the producer, the director is usually the second most powerful person involved with a project. Directors typically do the following:

- Help the casting director decide which actors to hire for the major roles
- Control the creative aspects of the set, including lighting, background design, and camera angles
- Work with the actors on a daily basis to shoot the various scenes in the script
- Polish the final film prior to its official release

The lighting and set designers may create the actual backgrounds, but the director has the final say on whether to alter the look, add more lighting, or film the set from a particular angle. The director determines the overall mood and tone of the final production. The actors' roles comprise just one of many pieces that the director has to juggle when completing a production.

After shooting a film, the director (along with the producer and, occasionally, the writer and an actor or two) remains with the project in post-production, where scenes may be cut or rearranged and sound effects and music added. In some cases, the director may need the actors to dub in their dialogue in scenes where the existing dialogue doesn't sound right due to technical difficulties, an airplane flying overhead at the wrong time, or any number of problems.

On a set, any number of things can go wrong, from light bulbs burning out to costumes being torn. Every problem that delays the production is likely to fall on the director to fix, so, as an actor, do your job, stay out of everyone else's way, and be flexible. If you do, the director will remember you as an actor who's easy to work with, which increases the chances that the director will want to use you in the next project he directs.

Writers: The Idea Makers

No project gets done without a script, so every project relies heavily on the people who write (and rewrite) those scripts. Basically, writers convert a bunch of ideas (good or bad) into a cohesive script that tells a compelling story with interesting characters that (hopefully) the general public will want to pay money to see.

Writers may write a script from an original story, an existing story (such as a novel, poem, or short story), or an idea given to them by a director, producer, or another writer. No matter how a writer starts with an idea, the final result should be a script that a director can use to tell the beginning, middle, and end of a story and that a producer can use to generate interest (and money) to get the project rolling.

Sometimes, writers write an entire script in hopes of selling it, which is called writing a script on *spec* (short for speculation). As an alternative, or in addition to writing spec scripts, many writers hire themselves out to work on various projects.

Many directors and producers write their own scripts to prevent someone else from messing up their original vision for their story. Actors sometimes write scripts so that they can create roles specifically to showcase their talents.

In the world of theater, the writer (known as the *playwright*) wields enormous power, sometimes equal to that of the director. A director rarely changes a script without the playwright's approval, and the playwright may also be involved in casting and rehearsals.

In rare cases, a producer may actually start filming before the script is even finished. On television sets, writers may write (and rewrite) scripts right up until the time of taping (and then they may rewrite the scene afterwards for another take as well).

The Studios: The Ones Who Make It All Possible

Studios represent the business end of show business. Studios typically provide the following for a film or television project:

- Financing to get a project started or completed
- Sets and production facilities (such as cameras, editing equipment, and even food services)
- Marketing and distribution to advertise a project

Getting a job in a studio — whether you're working as a security guard, a janitor, or a secretary — is an excellent way to meet people and learn about show business from an insider's point of view. (See Chapter 17 for more information on gaining experience from an acting-related job.)

Studios are in the business to make money, so on any given day, a studio may rent out its facilities to various productions shooting a film, a TV show, or a commercial. If you're on a set where another production is filming, stay within the confines of your own set and don't go sight-seeing on a different set because you'll only get in the way (and then you may get two different directors or producers mad at you).

Financing a project

Every film or television project needs money. Although a producer can raise money from a variety of sources — including individual investors — many projects eventually need the financial resources of a studio. (Occasionally, studios even collaborate with each other to share the costs and risks of a project, such as Twentieth Century Fox and Paramount Pictures did with *Titanic.* That way, if the project bombs completely, neither studio loses too much money as a result of diversifying their risks.)

When a producer tries to convince a studio to invest money in a project, the producer is said to be *pitching* the idea or script to the studio. Pitching a project involves convincing the studio to help get the project completed. Getting a studio to agree to fund a project is still no guarantee that the project will ever get done. Sometimes a studio may decide to kill a project for political reasons (maybe the new studio executives don't want to complete any projects started by the previous corporate executives), and sometimes studios kill a project because they think it's going to bomb so they want to cut their losses.

Sometimes, big stars and directors may invest their own money into a project to ensure that the project gets made and to earn a bigger share of the profits. Kevin Costner invested his money to get *Dances with Wolves* completed, and George Lucas put in his own money to finish *Star Wars.*

Although studios have millions of dollars in resources, they can't finance every possible project. Instead, they must selectively choose which projects they think will succeed and pass on those projects that they think won't make money. (Of course, every studio has passed on projects that turned out to be blockbuster hits, which only goes to show you that nobody can predict who or what will hit it big tomorrow. Just ask the people at Universal Studios who thought *Star Wars* wasn't worth financing.)

When a studio commits to starting a project, that project is said to be *green-lighted.*

Marketing and distributing a project

After a studio has created a project, the next step is marketing and distributing. The premiere of every film involves advertising in magazines, on television, and in previews shown before currently running films. After a film is released, the studio may also pay for the principle actors to publicize the film on television and radio talk shows.

If a studio thinks that a film is really bad, it'll try to cut its losses by eliminating most of the marketing budget. So if you ever appear in a really awful film, take heart that at least you got paid, got some experience, and did your best in your role. Then worry about going out and getting your next role that will hopefully put you in a blockbuster hit the next time around.

Through their marketing and financial power, studios can ensure that a film appears in as many theaters as possible. Without the backing of a major studio, a film may appear in a few cities or in the smaller (and less profitable) independent theaters (although in rare cases, positive word of mouth can boost a film from the independent theater circuit to the wider mainstream theater market).

During the initial release of a film, the studios earn the majority of the ticket sales. The longer a film plays (which, in show business terms, means that the film has *legs*), the more the theater gradually earns from ticket sales. If a film is doing poorly, theaters will yank that film to make room for a new film or for an existing film that's doing well.

Besides marketing and distributing a project to theaters, studios may also market and distribute films to television and cable networks, foreign markets, and the home entertainment market consisting of videotapes and DVDs.

If a film or TV show has any tie-ins (such as books, action figures, or video games), the studio may negotiate the licensing fees for these as well. In some cases, a film may make more money through foreign or television network distribution than they do during the initial run in theaters.

Casting Directors: The Gatekeepers

Casting directors may work directly for a single production company, or they may freelance and work for several production companies on a temporary basis. Casting directors do the following:

- Analyze a script in order to break down the roles to determine the types of actors needed
- Audition actors
- Choose several potential actors for each role

Although casting directors sometimes advertise open casting calls in newspapers, more often they print a list of roles available and the type of people they want for each role, such as a young housewife or a tall basketball player. They then send this list of available roles to a company, such as one called *Breakdown Services* (`www.breakdownservices.com`), which gets paid to distribute this list to various agents. (***Note:*** Such Web sites give you information about the company; they don't provide breakdown lists of available roles.)

Before sending out the breakdown of the available roles for a script, a casting director may contact agents or managers to interview actors who may be particularly suitable for a certain role. Casting directors may browse through the *Academy of Players Directory* (`www.acadpd.org`), which displays head shots of different actors, or they may spot a particularly interesting actor in a commercial, play, or film and contact that actor's agent or manager directly. So many roles may already be filled before your agent even gets the breakdown list.

Next, the casting director sets aside time to audition actors for all the different roles. Auditioning roles for a commercial may take a day or more, while auditioning roles for a major TV show, film, or play can take several days to several weeks.

After viewing an endless parade of actors for each particular role, the casting director calls back a handful of actors for a second look. Casting directors have the power to choose the actors they want to callback, but they don't necessarily have the power to pick any one particular actor. The final actor chosen for a role is often based on the decisions of several people, such as the director or, in the case of TV commercials, a representative from the advertising agency.

After one actor has been chosen for a particular role, the remaining roles are often filled based on how good an actor looks compared to the actor already chosen for another role. For example, if a TV commercial has already cast a tall redhead for the role of the mother, the actor chosen to play her son will likely look like he could actually be her son and isn't likely to have a completely different hair color and ethnic background.

Because many casting directors freelance, you're likely to run into the same casting director over and over again. Be cordial to the casting director! In the world of show business, people tend to have long memories. So if you treat someone with disrespect, don't be surprised if, sometime in the future, they treat you with disrespect in return.

Agents: Your Door to Show Business

In the world of acting, the actors are the commodity, and the agents are the sales people. An agent acts as a middleman between you and anyone who wants to hire you for your acting skills. (See Chapter 8 for more details about finding and working with an agent.)

Agents can

- Help you find an acting job
- Negotiate your contracts (hopefully to get you as much money as possible)
- Make sure that you get all the money owed to you, even if it comes from a rerun of a TV show you did 20 years ago

Even the best, most powerful agent in the world can't get you an acting job. The best an agent can ever do is point you in the direction of the people who can hire you for an acting role.

Personal and Business Managers: The Guiding Forces Behind the Scenes

Agents can help an actor find a job, but managers provide advice to an actor:

- *Personal managers* offer career advice by mapping out a long-term plan to help the actor pick the types of roles that will (hopefully) increase the actor's appeal.
- *Business managers* (who are usually accountants) offer financial planning advice and handle the actor's money by investing it (hopefully wisely), saving enough for the actor's retirement, and making sure that all the actor's bills are paid on time, so the actor can focus on acting.

A manager can perform invaluable services, such as helping you find an agent or helping you decide when to dump your current agent and who to choose as a new agent. But these services may come at a hefty price — typically 15 percent of an actor's income.

In case you're wondering whether you need a manager, the answer is *no* — not right away. After you start landing roles on a regular basis, you may want a personal manager to suggest which roles you should take to further your career and which roles you should reject to avoid killing your career. When you start earning sizable chunks of money on a consistent basis, you may want a business manager to handle your money, which includes paying your bills and investing your income so you can (hopefully) retire comfortably when your acting career starts to slow down.

Be careful when you give control of your money to another person. Unscrupulous business managers often steal millions from their clients before their theft is discovered (if ever). In general, keeping control over your own money is a good idea.

Actors: The Talent in Front of the Spotlight

The ultimate job of an actor is to perform onstage or in front of a camera. Sounds easy, right? It can be, but performing is only part of the actor's job. Some of the other tasks that all actors must master include

- Studying and improving their acting skills
- Figuring out how to market themselves
- Knowing how to audition
- Being able to act reliably and consistently

To even get a chance to perform, an actor first needs to learn the craft of acting, which can mean taking acting workshops, improv classes, voice lessons, or hiring an acting coach. An actor must be able to improve his or her acting skills so well that acting appears flawless and natural even though it may be artificial and rehearsed.

Of course, developing the best acting skills in the world is useless if nobody knows you exist, so the second job of an actor is figuring out the business of acting, which involves reading trade papers to find out about possible acting roles, contacting agents and convincing them to sign you on as a client, promoting yourself, and auditioning in front of casting directors over and over again until finally landing a role.

After an actor gets a role, the final job of the actor is to show up on time, perform, and listen to the director. As an actor, you bring a script to life and turn stage directions and dialogue into the illusion of a compelling story that others will want to watch.

When one acting job is over, your job as an actor starts all over again with taking classes, marketing yourself, and (hopefully) landing another role, so you can keep learning and gaining valuable experience as an actor.

Knowing how to act is just one part of becoming an actor. If you don't know how to act or you don't improve as an actor, you may never land a role. Likewise, all the acting talent in the world is useless if you don't market your self to the people who can hire you.

Besides knowing how to act, actors should also develop these additional work habits:

- Be on time
- Be prepared

- Be reliable
- Be easy to work with
- Be willing to do whatever it takes to get the job done

Show business has no set rules. You can break every rule in show business and still succeed. Likewise, you may follow the best advice and guidelines from the experts and yet never succeed at all. The best way to increase your odds of success is by possessing etiquette and professionalism. *Etiquette* means that you treat everyone with the proper amount of courtesy and respect. *Professionalism* means that you do your job as efficiently as possible to the best of your ability at all times.

Unions: An Actor's Best Friend

Because so many studios, producers, and directors exploited the desperation of actors in the early days of show business, actors banded together and formed unions to protect themselves. The various actors' unions have increased pay for actors (including lucrative residual payments — also known as royalties — for reruns and broadcasts in different countries), protected actors' rights to work in clean and sanitary working conditions, restricted the time limits that actors can be expected to work each day, provided legal counsel, and even offered health and retirement plans.

Although a union's main job is to protect your rights and ensure that you're paid fairly, unions also offer a variety of other services that can make your quest for an acting career much simpler. Many unions offer seminars and workshops to help their members find work; they maintain bulletin boards where actors can post classified advertisements, buying or selling various items or advertising the availability of rooms or apartments; and they furnish libraries where members can borrow and study scripts. As a union member, you may qualify for a whole range of additional benefits, including credit union membership, health insurance, pension plans, and even access to a retirement home. So be sure to find these things out when you're applying for membership and take advantage of whatever services your union offers.

If you're just getting started in acting, you may not want to join any union right away because joining the union effectively eliminates you from working on non-union productions. As a beginner, you may want to get experience working in the more numerous (but lower paying) non-union productions first. You don't have to join a union to work as an actor, but the highest-paying and most prestigious acting roles almost always go to union members, so when you've reached a point where you can vie for those roles, joining a union is a wise thing to do.

Be prepared — when you decide to join a union, the cost to join may be fairly expensive, usually over $1,000. Also, after joining a union, you must pay dues regularly (probably semi-annually), but the regular dues are much less expensive than the initial union membership dues. The regular dues usually run $100 or more, depending on how much you're actually earning as an actor.

If you are aware of a union production that's breaking a union rule, call the union (even if you're not a union member) and ask them to investigate this problem. The unions are your friends, so treat them with respect and don't be afraid to ask for their help at any time during your acting career.

In the world of entertainment, the main union is the *Associated Actors and Artists of America*, also known as the *Four A.* Within the Associated Actors and Artists of America are several branches that cover specific fields of acting. The three most popular actors' unions are

- The Screen Actors Guild (SAG)
- Actors' Equity Association (AEA, also known as Equity)
- American Federation of Television & Radio Artists (AFTRA)

Working at a union's office, either as a volunteer or paid employee, is an excellent way to meet actors, writers, casting directors, and producers.

The Screen Actor's Guild (SAG)

The *Screen Actors Guild* (`www.sag.org`) covers actors primarily involved in films (both commercial films and industrial films). In addition, SAG also maintains a list of agencies that have agreed to follow SAG guidelines for working with actors.

Don't ever sign up with a non-SAG affiliated talent agency, or you may not be treated fairly. A non-SAG agent likely won't hear of the higher-paying union roles available, either.

One of the first major goals of any actor in film or TV should be to get into SAG. This process is often referred to as "getting your SAG card" (and, yes, you really do get a membership card).

The most common way to join SAG is through a clause known as the *Taft-Hartley Act,* which allows non-union members to work up to 30 days on a union production. Officially, union productions can only hire union members, but because that would prevent new actors from ever breaking into show business, the Taft-Hartley Act gives newcomers a way to become a union member.

The de Havilland decision

In the mid-1940s, studios dictated the roles that actors could play. Actors often had to change their appearance for different roles and appear in less-than-satisfactory roles that could potentially damage an actor's fledging career. If an actor rejected a particular role, the studio could "suspend" that actor from working. Because actors were under contract to work for one particular studio, studios essentially dictated the future of an actor's career.

Even worse, studios would often extend an actor's contract against his or her will, effectively enslaving that actor to that studio. After appearing as Melanie Hamilton in *Gone With the Wind,* actress Olivia de Havilland rebelled against the restrictions in her contract and wound up getting a six-month suspension from Warner Brothers Studio as a result.

So Olivia took Warner Brothers Studio to court to fight for her right to choose her own roles. After three years, the courts decided in Olivia's favor and ruled that she could leave her contract with Warner Brothers. This court battle became known as the "de Havilland decision," and it forever changed the way actors and studios worked together.

After the courts allowed Olivia de Havilland to get out of her contract with Warner Brothers, other major film stars began using the de Havilland decision to justify getting out of their contracts as well, further strengthening the role of the then-fledgling Screen Actors Guild.

Today, actors regularly work for different studios and have the freedom to choose their roles at any time. Of course, judging from some of the roles actors have chosen, they still manage to appear in bombs every now and then, but at least now they have no one to blame but themselves.

Other ways to become a member of SAG and get your SAG card include

- Providing proof that you're wanted for a role in a SAG-recognized production.
- Providing proof that you've already worked on a SAG-recognized production.
- Providing proof that you've been a paying member of an affiliated Four A guild (such as Equity or AFTRA) for at least a year and that you have had at least one role as a principal performer with that union. (If you're already a member of another actors' union, you won't have to pay the full union dues to join SAG.)

Getting your SAG card is no guarantee of employment, let alone fame or money. The large majority of SAG members earn less than $7,500 a year.

Actors' Equity Association

The *Actors' Equity Association* (www.actorsequity.org), which is also known simply as Equity, covers actors who perform in theater. (The British branch of Equity offers its own Web site at www.equity.org.uk, and you can find the Canadian branch of Equity at www.caea.com.)

Equity is the oldest of all the actors' unions (formed in 1919) and began as a way to counterbalance the power producers held over actors. Actors in theater often got paid marginal wages (if they got paid at all), were forced to endure horrible working conditions, never got paid extra for working on holidays, had to make or buy their own costumes, and could be forced to attend unlimited numbers of rehearsals for any length of time — all without any pay, of course.

To protect its members, Equity forced producers to post sufficient advance funds to guarantee salaries and benefits, established minimum salaries and pay for rehearsal time, and even established rules forbidding producers to force actors to work in any theater that discriminated against audience members because of race, color, or creed (later modified to include gender, sexual preferences, and political beliefs).

Like SAG, Equity has also established guidelines for how agents should treat actors. When looking for an agent, call your local Equity office and ask for a list of Equity-franchised agencies. (A publication called *The Ross Reports* also lists agencies, so be sure to check both lists in case one list is more current than another.) Then, only contact those agencies.

Three common ways to become a member of Equity include

- Providing proof that you're wanted for a role in an Equity-recognized production company
- Working for up to 50 weeks in Equity productions (known as the Equity Membership Candidacy Program)
- Providing proof that you've been a paying member of an affiliated Four A guild (such as SAG or AFTRA) for at least a year and that you've had at least one role as a principal performer with that union

After you join Equity, never work on a non-Equity production, or else you could be fined and lose your Equity membership. Equity may allow its members to work in non-Equity productions that are sponsored by charities or religious organizations, but make sure that you get written permission first.

In some small cities, Equity productions may be scarce. If Equity work is limited in your area, you may want to delay joining the union until you can be sure of getting more steady Equity work.

American Federation of Television & Radio Artists (AFTRA)

As the name implies, the American Federation of Television & Radio Artists (`www.aftra.org`) covers anyone involved in television, radio, and broadcasting — which includes entertainment programming, industrial programming, and educational media, such as software distributed on CD-ROMs.

At the time of this writing, AFTRA and SAG are separate unions, but they may eventually merge to better serve actors who work in both film and television.

Unlike SAG and Equity, AFTRA is considered an open union, so you can join simply by paying an initiation fee. However, like both SAG and Equity, AFTRA also establishes guidelines for how agents are supposed to treat actors, so only deal with AFTRA-franchised agencies after you join to ensure that you get treated fairly.

Just because you can join AFTRA at any time doesn't mean that you should. You can buy membership into AFTRA, get an AFTRA job, and then apply for membership in SAG or Equity. However, membership in any union means you can't work on non-union productions, so you need to decide when the time is right for you to join any union.

Part II

Packaging and Marketing Yourself

"Well, I don't like to brag about myself, but I've got a little friend here that has a few stories I think you'll find interesting."

In this part . . .

As an actor in the world of show business, you're selling your looks and your talent. No matter how beautiful or handsome you may look or how much acting talent you may possess, you're not going to be successful until you can sell yourself to an agent or casting director.

This part of the book talks about ways to market yourself as an actor with your head shot, resume, and training. As an actor, you want to make yourself look like the most talented actor for every role you audition for. Until you land a role, agents and casting directors can only know you through the way you market yourself, so the better you present yourself, the more likely you'll be on your way to becoming a professional actor.

Chapter 4

Making a Great First Impression with a Head Shot

In This Chapter

- Understanding the purpose of a head shot
- Taking a look at different head shot styles
- Shooting your head shot
- Printing and distributing your head shot
- Pinpointing head shot problems

As an actor, you're in business for yourself, and your product is you. What you're selling is your acting ability, but what you're advertising is your look and appearance. Of course, to get potential buyers interested in purchasing your services as an actor, you need to catch their interest first.

In this chapter, you discover the characteristics of a good head shot as well as how to use your head shot as a marketing tool to grab an agent's or casting director's attention and make them remember who you are.

Introducing the Head Shot: An Actor's Calling Card

Ideally, you want to meet casting directors and agents face-to-face like a door-to-door salesman, but that isn't always possible. So until cloning becomes feasible, the next best solution is to rely on head shots.

A *head shot* is a close-up photograph of yourself that you submit along with your resume to agents and casting directors, so they can evaluate you in your absence. (Find more info on putting together a five-star resume in Chapter 5.) Essentially, your head shot is an advertisement that shows the best features of you as the product.

Your head shot (sometimes called an "eight-by-ten" or a "resume shot") should be 8 inches wide and 10 inches long. The photograph should be black and white and should focus on your face and hair, reflecting what you honestly look like. A good head shot

- Makes you look natural. (Deliberate posing can make you look phony.)
- Shows you smiling, relaxed, and friendly.
- Shows you looking directly at the camera.
- Makes someone say to themselves, "I'd like to meet that person."

It's important to update your head shot during your acting career to reflect the way you look now (as opposed to three years ago when you might have gotten your last head shot taken). Also, every time you make a major change in your appearance, such as cutting considerable length from your hair or dying your brown hair blonde, you should get new head shots to reflect your new look.

A head shot serves two main purposes:

- To get an agent interested in representing you. As a beginner, this is the main purpose of your head shot. A good head shot can attract the attention of an agent and make him or her want to sign you on as a client.
- To get a casting director interested in calling you in to an audition. The casting director usually receives head shots from your agent. After you audition, your head shot also helps the casting director remember what you looked like and what he or she liked about the way you acted and looked.

The most common head shot captures your face and part of your shoulders, as shown in Figure 4-1. This actor isn't wearing distracting jewelry, and her makeup is conservative and flattering. (***Note:*** In general, men should stay away from makeup, while women should apply makeup sparingly. You want to look natural in your head shot, so makeup shouldn't be obvious.) She's looking directly at the camera, and her hands aren't covering or obscuring her face. In general, the actor appears relaxed, is smiling, and looks natural.

Perhaps the most critical element of a head shot is your eyes. Your eyes should draw a viewer in, which is why you should always look directly at the camera and not off to the side. You also want to avoid wearing sunglasses or striking a pose in which you're winking.

Dressing up in costume, drastically changing your hair style just for your head shot, wearing excessive jewelry, or making a face for the camera will only distract others from seeing who you really are (and also from hiring you for a role). Figure 4-2 shows an example of a poor head shot that does nothing to highlight the actor's natural features. (Note the sunglasses that mask part of the face, the excessive jewelry that distracts from the actor, and the unusual clothing that interferes with rather than highlights the actor. When casting directors and agents see this type of a head shot, they don't want to call you in for an audition. They want to call the police.)

Figure 4-1: A standard head shot.

Figure 4-2: Definitely a poor head shot.

Although the standard head shot is effective in most cases, you may want to have different head shots taken if you plan on auditioning in different markets, such as theatre or television commercials.

Examining Variations on the Standard

Not all head shots are equal. Depending on what type of acting you want to pursue — for instance, commercials, theater, or film — you may need a different type of head shot for each market (or multiple head shots for a single market). For example, one head shot may show a glamorous view of yourself for theater auditions, while a second head shot may show a simpler yet bubblier version of yourself for commercial auditions. You may also want to get different head shots to project different "looks" when targeting the same markets. For example, you may have a nerdy look, a business look, and a tough-guy look in three different head shots all targeted for the television commercial market. You can improve your chances of landing a role by submitting the head shot that best matches the type of person casting directors need for a certain role.

Beginners or actors with limited funds should stick with one general head shot. As you get more experience (and hopefully more money), you can invest in multiple head shots to help you market and target yourself for specific roles.

The commercial head shot

Commercial head shots especially need to emphasize an actor's smile (showing your teeth because you may have to audition for a toothpaste commercial one day) and the upbeat, cheerful side of your personality. In the world of commercials, people are bubbling over with enthusiasm all the time because they've just discovered that their brand of toothpaste is the only one recommended by four out of five dentists, or that the new brand of cat food that they bought provides 15 important vitamins and minerals for their cat.

As a result, the perkier, happier, and more bright-eyed and bushy-tailed you can appear in a commercial head shot, the better. Your commercial head shot should radiate a feeling of unbridled cheerfulness that makes advertising agency executives want to jump up and shout, "Yes! This person is the one I want to represent my client's hemorrhoid cream this year!"

Your commercial head shot needs to show you as a typical, happy consumer. Men should keep their hair trimmed to a reasonable length and keep facial hair to a minimum. Women should look attractive without going overboard and looking too glamorous. Teenagers and younger actors should fit in the current style of their generation. If your commercial head shot makes you look too radical, you may limit your potential for certain roles.

When shooting a commercial head shot, make sure that you don't wear any clothes that display a corporate logo or name. After all, wearing a shirt with the Coca-Cola logo stitched across the front won't do you any good if you have to audition for a commercial being developed by Pepsi.

One type of head shot that's popular in the commercial industry is the *composite,* which crams several different images of you together on one 8 x 10 spread to give casting directors a quick way to determine how you may look in different settings. Generally, composites are used to capture different expressions and ways of dressing, such as showing you in an athletic pose, a professional pose (like a lawyer or a doctor), a family-type pose (either as a parent or a student, depending on your age), and a classy, more elegant pose in a tuxedo or gown. The main purpose of a composite is to show the range of characters and looks you're comfortable portraying.

Because of the number of photographs needed, composites can be expensive. Only shoot composites if your agent requests them. In recent years, composites have fallen out of favor with many agents and casting directors (although that could change at any time). In many cases, a standard or commercial head shot is sufficient for casting directors to see what you look like.

The theatrical shot

Unlike a standard or commercial head shot that captures your everyday look, a theatrical head shot can capture a specific quality that you want to project — such as a sexy, sophisticated look or a thoughtful, introspective look. Also, with a theatrical head shot, you can emphasize a certain type of character, whether it's a crafty villain or a confused, bumbling, everyday man. (If you can play a crafty villain and a bumbling person, consider getting two head shots that reflect both of these characters. That way you can choose which head shot to use when auditioning for a particular role.) Just make sure that if you project a certain image, you can also act well enough to support that type of a character, or else the real image you'll project will be a bumbling amateur who doesn't know what he's doing.

The clothes you wear for a theatrical head shot can be more varied than a standard head shot, too, depending on the image you want to emphasize. For example, you may want to wear a suit or an evening gown. (And if you're a man wearing an evening gown, you'll really project a certain image, although that kind of image may not necessarily get you any work.)

For theatrical work, you may want to get two head shots. One head shot may show you in a more dramatic, contemplative pose, while a second head shot may show you in a happier, more light-hearted mood. If you're auditioning for a tragedy or drama, you can use your more dramatic head shot. If you're auditioning for a comedy, you can use your upbeat head shot.

Because a commercial head shot captures you in a bright-eyed, enthusiastic look, you may be able to use your commercial head shot as your second theatrical head shot and vice versa.

Creating the Perfect Head Shot

Your head shot may be the first (and, in many cases, the only) impression casting directors get of you, so your head shot needs to present you at your best. To get the best head shot possible, you need the following:

- You all by yourself, looking neatly groomed and well rested. (Leave the kids, pets, relatives, and friends at home.)
- Clothes that fit, are currently in style, and won't distract from your face.
- The best head shot photographer you can find.

Hiring a professional photographer

A professional photographer is a must. Unless one of your friends or relatives is a professional photographer, don't even consider having them take your picture. Trying to save money by using a disposable or digital camera and having your friend take the picture is pointless because a poor head shot will ultimately cost you when nobody takes you seriously as an actor.

Of course, not all professional photographers are equal, either. What you need is a professional photographer who specializes (note the emphasis on *specializes*) in theatrical or commercial shoots.

The best way to find a photographer is through word-of-mouth. Ask your fellow actors for recommendations. If a particular agent is interested in representing you, ask the agent for a list of several photographers he or she trusts and recommends. If you already have an agent, ask to scan through the head shots of other actors that your agent represents. Not only can you get a rough idea of the types of head shots this particular agent prefers, but you also get a chance to look for actors who may look similar to you, so you can see what your competition's head shots look like. You can also scan the classified ads of various trade publications, such as *Back Stage* (`www.backstage.com`), to find ads for photographers who specialize in head shots.

Before hiring a photographer from an ad, get a referral from someone who trusts and likes that photographer's work. If you choose a photographer at random, you have no idea what that photographer's work may be like or even if that photographer has any happy customers at all.

Make a list of four or five professional photographers that you're interested in working with. (If you consider too many photographers, you'll simply take up too much time and likely wind up confused with all the different choices.) Call your top five candidates and make appointments to meet them in person. (Sometimes, after making a few phone calls, you may decide to eliminate one or more photographers because they're rude, unhelpful, annoying, and so on.) Ask to meet each photographer at his or her studio.

Even the best photographer in the world isn't right for you if you don't feel comfortable working with that person. Talk with the photographer and get a feel for the photographer's personality and how he or she works. You're essentially conducting a job interview for a photographer, so don't be afraid to ask lots of questions. You want to find the photographer who can capture your best look at a cost you can afford.

Some questions to ask a photographer include the following:

- How much will a head shot photography session cost?
- How much time will the photography session take? (Typical sessions last from 2½ to 3½ hours, longer if you plan on changing in and out of several outfits.)
- How many rolls of film will the photographer shoot?
- Are any 8 x 10 prints included in the cost? (Many photographers toss in one or two prints as part of the cost.)
- Will you be allowed to change into different outfits during the photography session?
- Does the photographer offer any extra services for an additional price, such as a make-up artist?

- How long until you can see your proof sheet? (The *proof sheet* contains miniature versions of all the pictures captured on film.)
- Who keeps the negatives — the photographer or you?
- Does the photographer offer any guarantees or refunds if none of the head shots are acceptable? (Typically, photographers offer guarantees or refunds if the head shots have technical imperfections, such as being out of focus. They may not offer similar guarantees or refunds if you just don't like any of the pictures.)

Price isn't always a measure of quality. The cheapest photographer may not be the worst, and the most expensive photographer may not be the best. Although price is important, keep in mind that a great head shot will more than pay for itself in the long run, and saving money on a poor head shot will only hurt your chances of getting agents or casting directors interested in you.

Some photographers may charge you a low price for your head shot photography session, but then charge an outrageous price for printing your head shot. You're usually better off choosing your own printing service to duplicate your head shot rather than relying on a photographer to do so because the photographer will charge more.

Be sure to ask to study the head shots that they've taken of other people. Do these head shots impress you? (If you don't like the head shots that the photographer's done for others, you probably won't like any heads shots that the photographer may do for you.)

Some photographers may display a picture of a famous celebrity to give the illusion that this celebrity had his or her picture taken by that photographer. Anyone can buy a picture of a celebrity and hang it on the wall, so don't let photographs of famous people influence you into choosing any particular photographer.

Don't let any photographer try to rush you into making a decision. Your head shot is one of the most crucial stages in your acting career, so you need to take the time to choose the photographer you like best.

Before you leave, be sure to take a close look at the photographer's studio. Is it attractive and organized or ugly and sloppy? Also, make mental notes about the photographer. Does the photographer spend time answering your questions, or is the photographer more interested in getting you to commit now? Does the photographer have time to focus on helping you evaluate his or her work, or does the photographer seem rushed and busy? Make mental notes and jot down your first impressions on the train or when you get back to your car. Your notes can be helpful reminders when the time comes to hire the photographer of your choice.

Picking the right look

When you finally decide on one particular photographer, the next step is a *consultation meeting*. This meeting gives you a chance to ask the photographer questions regarding your clothes, makeup, what types of look you want to capture, and so on. This consultation is crucial. Don't let the photographer start snapping pictures until both you and the photographer completely understand what you hope to accomplish during your photography session.

You can use your head shot to project an *image* (look and personality) that uniquely defines you and emphasizes your natural special qualities. For example, a head shot for someone like Goldie Hawn may emphasize her perky personality and bubbly smile, and a head shot for someone like Pamela Anderson may focus more on sex appeal.

Choose your clothes with care. Thong bikinis, eye-dazzling patterns that look "busy," clothes that look dated, and clothes that resemble Halloween costumes are a no-no. In general, solid colors are best, but avoid all-white or all-black clothes. All-white clothes tend to "wash out" your face, making your face harder to see, and all-black clothes tend to give you a sinister, foreboding look. Stay away from clothing or jewelry that could reflect light. During your consultation, ask the photographer for advice on how to best portray yourself to others. You want your head shot to project a special quality that uniquely identifies you and that instantly separates you from everyone else.

If you have an agent, also ask him or her for recommendations on the type of "look" you should capture for your head shot. An agent can help you define the type of look that works best for you. (Keep in mind that two different agents may think that you should emphasize two entirely different looks, so whatever look an agent suggests for you, make sure that you're comfortable with that choice.)

If you don't yet have an agent, ask friends and relatives what qualities they like best in you, and use your own judgment, too. Some common types of looks consist of the following:

- **Alluring, sexy, and sensual:** Think of the face — not any other body part — of every centerfold you've ever seen.
- **Romantic and caring:** This type of person inspires love (not lust) in others, such as the girl (or boy) next door.
- **Business person:** The typical person you'd expect to see working in a bank or insurance agency.
- **Commanding and powerful:** Someone used to ordering others around, such as a military general or CEO.
- **Funny-looking, nerdy character:** Think of the stereotypical image of a jock or computer nerd.
- **Mommy or Daddy:** Picture a housewife or father.
- **Traditional:** Someone with a conservative, middle of the road look.
- **Sporty outdoor-type:** This athletic, healthy person looks at home camping, jogging, or swimming at the beach.
- **Elegant and sophisticated:** The kind you expect to see at the opera or in the back of a limousine.

If your head shot projects a certain look, don't be surprised to find agents and casting directors only considering you for roles that take advantage of that particular look. For example, if your head shot projects a sexy look, you may be cast only in steamy roles.

To help you get an idea of the type of look you want to project, look at other actors' head shots. If you can, get a copy of the *Academy of Players Directory* (`www.acadpd.org`), which displays head shots for many of the big stars in show business. By studying the head shots of the stars, you can see what features you like and what may work for you as well. As another alternative, type "head shots" into your favorite search engine (such as *Yahoo!* or *Google*) and browse through the Web sites that display head shots from different actors to see what kind of pose and look you like in other actors' head shots.

When people look at your head shot, they should be able to identify a characteristic of your unique personality. If different people look at your head shot and come away with different impressions of what type of person you are, your head shot may not be doing its job. (Unless, of course, it's getting you work.)

Making the most of your photo session

After your consultation, the final step is your actual photography session. This session will capture the way you look for others to see for months (or even years) to come, so make sure that you're as relaxed and comfortable as possible.

Give yourself plenty of time to travel to your photography session, bring all the clothes you plan to wear (and keep them organized so you can find what you want right away), bring any makeup you want to use, and (most importantly) be happy. If you just broke up with your boyfriend or girlfriend, your face will express those emotions, and they probably won't help you capture a very good head shot. In these cases, it's probably best to reschedule your photo shoot rather than capture a poor head shot.

Don't bring anyone along to your photography session. You need as few distractions as possible, and a friend (however well-meaning) will likely only get in the way.

During your photography session, the photographer may suggest different poses and help you relax by telling jokes, asking you questions, or talking about nothing at all. The point is to capture that split second when your look is absolutely perfect for a head shot, so cooperate with your photographer.

Getting Your Head Shot Ready

Within a few days after your head shot photography session, your photographer will provide you a *proof sheet* that contains miniature versions of all the pictures captured from your head shot session. Study each image carefully and decide which one you want to use for your head shot.

Don't be afraid to ask your photographer to recommend the best images. If you have an agent, make sure that your agent reviews the proof sheet before you choose any particular image for your head shot.

After you've chosen a particular image for your head shot, the next step is to get your head shot printed, so you can start distributing it to anyone who may help advance your acting career. When getting your head shot printed, you need to decide whether to put borders around your head shot, what text to include on your head shot, and what type of finish you want on your head shot.

Adding (or eliminating) borders

A border acts like a frame that centers and focuses attention toward your face. Some people prefer borders; others prefer head shots without borders. Ask your agent which style he or she prefers because all styles are considered acceptable.

A head shot has three common border styles:

- White borders around all the edges (as shown in Figure 4-3a)
- No borders at all (also known as a *bleed* because your picture appears to "bleed" across the entire page, as shown in Figure 4-3b)
- A white border just at the bottom of the head shot (as shown in Figure 4-3c)

a.

b.

c.

Figure 4-3: Three common border styles for a head shot.

Including your name and contact info

Your name normally appears at the bottom of your head shot, as shown in Figure 4-4a and b. Some actors even have their name printed directly over the bottom of their head shot, as shown in Figure 4-4c. However, this option can make your name hard to read against the background of your head shot. The name on your head shot should be the name you plan to use, whether it's your real name, nickname, or a made-up stage name.

a.

b.

c.

Figure 4-4: Three different styles for displaying your name on a head shot.

Consider printing your name in the lower right-hand corner and your agent's name in the lower left-hand corner of your head shot. That way, if the head shot gets bound in a book, your name appears farthest from the binding and is easier to find and read.

You can't use the same name as a famous celebrity, even if your real name happens to be Tom Cruise or Julia Roberts. That's because no one wants to think that the "real" Tom Cruise or Julia Roberts is appearing in a film when it's really an unknown actor with the same name. So before printing your name on hundreds of head shots, check with the Screen Actors Guild and Actors' Equity to see if your real name or stage name is already taken. If so, you may have to change it slightly, such as using your formal name (Thomas Cruise instead of Tom Cruise), an informal version of your name (such as Julie Roberts instead of Julia Roberts), or adding or dropping a middle name or initial (such as Samuel Jackson instead of Samuel L. Jackson).

A printer can offer different fonts for printing your name, but the simpler the font you use, the better, because you want to draw attention to your face and not to the weird font you used to display your name. (And if you choose a particularly bizarre font, such as a script or calligraphy font, your name may be hard for someone to read.)

In addition to your name, you may also want to consider putting one or more of the following on your head shot:

- Your cell phone, pager, or answering service number
- Your agent's name and phone number

Putting contact information on your head shot has advantages and disadvantages. The main advantage is that if your head shot ever gets separated from your resume, a casting director or agent can still know how to reach you.

Without such contact information printed on your head shot, a casting director may love your look but have no way to reach (and hire) you for a role.

The biggest disadvantage of putting contact information on a head shot is that the information becomes obsolete if you change one of your numbers or if you change agents. Then you'll be stuck with useless headshots and will have to pay to have new ones printed.

One way to avoid dating your head shots is to print your contact information and agent's name on the back. That way, if the information changes, you can still use your head shots and just cover up your old information with a sticker that displays your new information.

Never have your home phone number printed on your head shot. You never know who may get a hold of your head shot, and anyone can use your home number to find your home address.

Choosing a finish for your head shot

You can choose from three types of finishes for your head shot:

- Glossy
- Matte
- Semi-gloss

Glossy gives your head shot a "shiny" look and tends to reproduce well in newspapers. A matte finish gives a flatter look, and a semi-gloss finish is (obviously) a cross between glossy and matte. The finish of your head shot is mostly a matter of personal preference and what may be currently fashionable at the time. Depending on the printer you choose, the cost for different types of finishes may vary.

At the time of this writing, the latest trend was a matte finish without borders (a *bleed*). A matte finish tends to reproduce well (and then you can use a glossy finish on any duplications you make), and a bleed tends to focus attention on your face and not on any artificial borders around your face.

Duplicating your head shot

After you've decided on borders, how to display your name, and the finish, your last step is getting your head shot duplicated in the familiar 8 x 10 format.

Although you can pay your photographer to duplicate your head shot, you usually save money by hiring the services of a professional printer instead. Call different printers, ask for recommendations from other actors, and shop around for the best price and service. As with a photographer, don't go by price alone. Just because a printer quotes you a low price doesn't necessarily mean that the printer is bad, and a high price doesn't necessarily guarantee that the printer is good.

To help yourself decide on a printer, consider the service and the quality of reproduction that each printer offers. Ask the printer for a sample copy of a head shot, so that you can evaluate the quality of the head shot both in terms of the way the head shot looks and the quality of the paper that the head shot is printed on. You may also want to have a handful of head shots printed by each printer, so you can evaluate the quality of the reproduction. After you choose a printer, ask if the printer can keep your head shot on file so they can quickly print up new ones at a moment's notice.

Printers may use two common ways to reproduce head shots:

- Lithographed prints
- Photo-reproduced prints

Many mail-order printers offer lithographed prints, which allow you to buy vast quantities of duplicate head shots at an extremely low price, such as 500 copies for $80. Photo-reproduced head shots look much sharper, but they cost much more — typically $1 per head shot. Although photo-reproduced head shots are more expensive, the price can be worth it because they'll only make your head shot (and ultimately you) look more attractive.

If you're trying to use a head shot to get an agent, don't get too many head shots printed up, because your agent may ask that you get new head shots anyway. (When an agent asks a client to get new head shots, the problem is often because the actor's current head shots don't reveal the actor's most marketable features, whether it's sex appeal, a winning smile, or a likeable and trusting look.) Otherwise, you may wind up getting stuck with a lot of obsolete head shots that you won't be able to use (unless you want to line the bottom of your bird cage with them).

Head shots should be in black and white. Color head shots are expensive and rarely used. If you really want to draw a casting director's attention to a particular color in your hair, skin, or eyes, list those colors in your resume and save your money to buy black and white head shots instead.

Be careful about retouching or airbrushing your head shot. If you have an absolutely perfect head shot that's marred by a pimple or a dirt speck on your cheek, go ahead and have that flaw removed. But don't remove wrinkles, birthmarks, or anything else that truly appears on your face. Retouching should be used to improve a natural head shot, not create an artificial version of who you really are. If possible, have the negative etched directly rather than having your head shot airbrushed because etching tends to be harder to notice than airbrushing.

Publicizing Your Head Shot with a Twist

Everyone needs a standard 8 x 10 head shot. However, you may also consider printing your head shot in a variety of other sizes and forms, such as postcards, business cards, and Zed cards.

- Postcards are especially useful as thank-you notes (and don't forget to include your contact information on these post cards, too!). Not only are they inexpensive to mail, but, by displaying a miniature version of your head shot, they also put your name and face in front of a casting director for a second time.
- Printing your head shot on business cards is a great way to promote yourself. Carrying around and handing out business cards is quick and easy — not to mention inexpensive as well.

- *Zed cards* (a sheet folded in thirds where each third of the page displays a different picture and look of an actor) are often used for print work, such as modeling in catalogues or advertisements. Because a Zed card displays several different pictures of you, you can provide a variety of poses and looks for someone to see, such as a business executive look, a tasteful one-piece bathing suit look, and an outdoor look.

Whatever type of additional photographs or formats you decide to buy, use them to promote yourself at all times. Remember, if people don't know who you are, they'll never take the time to find you to hire you for anything. So use your promotional materials to put your name and face in front of as many people as possible.

Distributing Your Head Shot

Give your head shot to anyone (reputable) who asks for it. Besides casting directors and agents, you never know if your bank teller's second cousin's best friend may wind up getting your head shot to the right people who may eventually hire you.

If you have friends who own a business, ask if you can sign a head shot, promoting the business, and have your friends hang your head shot for customers to look at. If you submit a press release to a newspaper or magazine, be sure to include your head shot in case the newspaper or magazine wants to publish your photograph. In general, the more people who see your head shot, the better.

By getting into the habit of distributing your head shot, you constantly remind yourself that you're an actor willing to promote yourself every day. Head shots don't do you any good if they stay in the bottom of your desk drawer.

Avoiding Problems with Head Shots

Your head shot provides the first impression that most agents and casting directors get of you. Make a great first impression, and you get a chance to make a second impression, which can lead to that all-important callback (or better yet, an actual role in a production). But if you make a poor first impression with your head shot, you may never get a chance to audition for any roles, even if you're the best actor in the world.

Most photographers are happy to recommend the photographs that they think will make your best head shot. The advice of your head shot photographer can often spare you the embarrassment of getting stuck with awful head shots.

Is that really you?

The most common complaint among casting directors is meeting actors who don't look anything like their head shots. Often, the head shot portrays a young, glamorous actor who looks like he or she could play a supermodel or a body builder. Yet when the casting director finally meets that actor in person, in walks a bent-over, 50-year-old actor with dark shadows under the eyes, wrinkles scratched across the forehead and cheeks, and an entirely different hair color and style.

A head shot is meant to represent how you look today – not how you wish you really looked or how you used to look 20 years ago. If your own friends and relatives have trouble recognizing you in your head shot, you need to get some new ones made.

Some of the more common problems with head shots include

- **You look younger (or older) than you really are.** Whether you like it or not, you will get older, and your face will change as a result. As a general rule, you should get new head shots every few years to reflect any subtle changes in your appearance. Perhaps the most common mistake actors make is using a favorite head shot for too long.
- **Your hair color and/or style is dramatically different.** In general, every time you change your appearance, you should get new head shots — whether you change your hair color, style your hair differently, or get hair implants. When casting directors review head shots, they're looking

for someone they can use right away, not someone who needs to get his hair colored or styled again just to look like his head shot.

- **The background draws attention away from your face.** The main focus of a head shot should be your face. As a general rule, if the background or the clothes you're wearing draw more interest or seem more prominent than your face, you need a new head shot.
- **Your face doesn't look like your head shot.** Depending on the angle the photographer shoots you, sometimes your face in a photograph doesn't look like your face in real life. If your jutting nose or other prominent facial feature isn't clearly seen on your head shot, agents and casting directors alike will be in for a rude surprise when they see that missing facial feature suddenly seem to sprout on your face when you show up in person.

Your head shot doesn't match your personality

A head shot needs to let agents and casting directors know what kind of person you are. If your head shot promotes one look but your real-life personality projects an entirely different look, you're going to confuse agents and casting directors. For example, if your head shot makes you look like a business executive but you commonly dress and act like a flower child, your head shot obviously isn't accurately reflecting your personality.

To fix (or avoid) these types of head shot problems, ask your fellow actors, your agent, and your friends and relatives what kind of a person they see you as being. Try to get as many opinions as possible, and make sure that the people you're asking are honest and not just trying to flatter your ego. If you see yourself as a seductive temptress, but your friends and agent see you more as a chubby little tomboy, you may seriously need to evaluate yourself and what you want your head shot to project to others.

It won't do you any good to lie to yourself and use a head shot that represents who you fantasize you are rather than who you really are. Fantasy is what Halloween costumes are for. Reality is what head shots are for.

Don't be "cute" or "funny" (or naked)

Sometimes, to attract attention, actors may try to use a "cute" or "funny" head shot that usually isn't cute or funny. For example, they may make funny faces, dress up in outlandish costumes, or pose in front of something silly like a Mickey Mouse statue or a clown.

If a head shot doesn't conform to the standard that the show business world expects, your head shot will likely be tossed within seconds into the nearest wastebasket, never to be seen by anyone ever again. If you're the silly and playful type, your head shot should convey that personality in your eyes, your posture, and your smile. If you're just trying to get attention by looking silly, the only attention you'll get will be having an agent or casting director remember you as one of the many aspiring actors whom they never seriously considered for a role.

Sometimes, actors feel that an overtly sexy pose (such as a woman appearing topless) may get the attention of an agent or casting director. Although this type of head shot probably will get somebody's attention, that person probably won't be thinking about hiring you as an actor.

Once again, if you're a sexy person, let your head shot project your image as a sex kitten or hunk. If your head shot captures your personality properly, you won't need to display your private parts to do that for you.

Show business has no set rules, so a "cute" or "funny" head shot really could grab the attention of a casting director or agent. If you're willing to take that risk, be aware that you may actually be hurting your chances of success rather than helping them.

Technical problems: You look great but your head shot still stinks

You may look exactly like your head shot, and your head shot may perfectly reflect your unique personality. Yet your head shot still won't be perfect if it isn't free from a variety of technical problems that could make your head shot a liability instead of an asset.

Some common technical problems include head shots that are out of focus, blurry, or too light (or too dark). A head shot needs to portray your face clearly so casting directors can see what type of look you present.

Don't use any picture for your head shot unless it's 100 percent perfect, both artistically and technically. Trying to distribute a head shot that's less than perfect is just a waste of everyone's time (and your money). Ultimately, the best head shot will be the one that gets you the most work.

Chapter 5

Creating a Five-Star Acting Resume

In This Chapter

- Making up your acting resume to look like a star
- Highlighting the important info
- Knowing what not to put on an acting resume
- Comparing resumes: veterans versus novices

Casting directors only care about one thing: Are you right for the part? So, they aren't looking for career objectives, salary requirements, or whether you worked at a Fortune 500 company for the past five years. They're looking for evidence to justify whether you may be the right actor for a particular role. This chapter shows you what to include (and what to exclude) from an acting resume as well as how to create an impressive acting resume when you have little acting experience.

A typical *resume* lists a job applicant's previous employment, experience, education, and so on. You don't need a typical resume. You need an acting resume. An *acting resume* focuses exclusively on acting and establishes your credibility as an actor by listing your acting experience and training. Your acting resume should promote you as an actor, show agents and casting directors that you're serious about being an actor, and have the necessary training, skills, and/or experience to do the job if hired.

Be sure to include a cover letter when you mail your resume and head shot to an agent. See Chapter 8 for more information on creating an attention-grabbing cover letter.

Tackling the Basics of Creating a Resume

Creating an impressive-looking acting resume isn't hard. You can choose from a variety of ways to put your resume together — all of which are correct. But if the content and appearance of your resume is sloppy, hard to read, and disorganized, you come across as a sloppy, disorganized actor. Make sure that your resume is easy to read, neatly organized, and loaded with experience that's especially appropriate for a particular role. Doing so makes you look your best.

A typical acting resume appears in black ink against a plain white background. An acting resume should fit on one side of a single page that measures 8 x 10 inches, so it can fit neatly on the back of your head shot (discussed in Chapter 4). That way, if someone is impressed by what she sees in your head shot, she can flip it over and read about your experience as an actor (and vice versa).

Be sure to trim your resume to the exact same size as your head shot, so that the paper doesn't get torn, bent, or frayed. Also, a resume that's larger than your head shot may be hard to file and may be distracting when someone looks at your head shot and sees the extra width and length of your resume sticking out underneath.

Some actors glue their resumes to the back of their head shots. Unfortunately, glue tends to lose its adhesiveness with age, which can cause your resume to separate from your head shot. To avoid this problem, use staples instead (preferably on all four corners). Make sure that your resumes are stapled to your head shots *before* you get to an audition because casting directors frown on actors who pester them for a stapler. For added insurance, carry a miniature stapler with you for those rare occasions when you forget to staple your resume to your head shot, or if your resume detaches from your head shot.

Although you can hire someone to type or print your resume, you can save a lot of money by creating your own resume with a word processor or desktop publishing program. (If you don't have access to a computer, borrow a friend's computer and printer or rent a computer and printer somewhere.) By storing your resume on a disk, you can quickly customize, update, and print your resume at any time.

To add a little visual spice to your resume, try one or both of the following:

- **Quality paper:** Use a durable bond of paper because your resume will likely pass through several hands. If you use paper that's too thin, your resume will likely tear and fall apart.

Consider printing your resume on slightly off-white paper to make your resume look just a bit different.

- **A variety of different fonts, type sizes, and type styles (such as bold or italics):** Just remember that if you use too many fonts, or if you choose really bizarre-looking fonts, your resume may be harder to read.

You may want to use a yellow (or any other colored) marker to highlight those areas of your resume that you want to emphasize. For example, if you're up for a part in a comedy, highlight your most impressive comedic acting experience and training.

A good resume (and a great head shot) can help open doors for you. But after that, it's up to your talent, your looks, and a little bit of luck to help you land a role.

Identifying the Info to Include

The top of your acting resume should include the following information:

- Your name.
- A phone number (other than your home number) where you can be reached. If you have an agent, include his or her name and phone number instead.
- Your physical characteristics (optional).
- Your membership in any of the acting unions, such as *Screen Actor's Guild* (SAG), *American Federation of Television and Radio Artists* (AFTRA), or *Actor's Equity Association* (AEA). Check out Chapter 3 for more information on joining acting unions.

Follow up your vitals with your experience and knowledge as an actor. The bulk of your resume should list:

- Any acting experience in film, television, or theater. (The more, the better; and the more current, the better, too.)
- Your college degree if it's related to drama.
- Your acting training, including workshops, coaches, and classes.
- Any special skills you have that may come in handy for an acting role (such as knife-throwing or snowboarding).

Even the most impressive resume is useless if you don't audition well. Ultimately, what decides whether you get a role isn't what you've done or how your head shot looks, but how you audition. (See Chapter 9 for tips on auditioning.)

Your name, union membership, and contact information

The most impressive resume won't do you any good if casting directors don't know how to reach you. So the most important information that you need to include is your up-to-date contact information in a prominent place on your resume — usually at the top of the resume.

Your contact information should include your name as it appears on your head shot (if you're using a stage name, use your stage name rather than your real name) and a phone number, so casting directors know how to reach you. If you have an agent, list your agent's name and phone number instead of your own phone number. If you don't have an agent, list your cell phone number, an answering service number, or your pager number.

Never list your home phone number or address on your resume. You never know who may see your resume, and you want to make sure that the wrong people don't get hold of your home number or address.

Keep your contact information up to date. If you change phone numbers or agents, print new copies of your resume with this latest contact information and destroy all copies of your old resume. The easier casting directors can find and contact you, the easier it is for them to hire you.

If you belong to any of the actors' unions, be sure to list that information on your resume, too. Union membership lends credibility to your acting career, and casting directors know that if your contact information is out of date, they can always contact the appropriate union to track you down, if necessary.

When listing your union membership, you can use the union initials, such as *SAG* (for Screen Actor's Guild), *AFTRA* (for American Federation of Television and Radio Artists), and *AEA* (for Actor's Equity Association) to save space and look more professional.

Your physical description

Because a head shot only shows your face in black and white, casting directors may look to your resume to find out more about your physical appearance that your head shot can't tell them. Your physical description, should you choose to include it, should list the following:

- Height
- Weight
- Eye color
- Hair color

If you decide to include your physical characteristics, highlight your particularly striking features by listing them with descriptive adjectives, such as flaming red hair or brilliant blue eyes.

Unless you have particularly striking eyes or unusual height, you may consider omitting the physical description of yourself altogether. Many actors leave their physical characteristics off their resumes because being of average height and weight isn't likely to help you and may actually limit you in case the casting director really wants someone shorter or skinnier. If you have an agent, ask for your agent's advice on whether to include your physical characteristics.

Don't lie about or exaggerate your physical characteristics. If your weight changes drastically, print new resumes that list your new weight. If you've recently dyed your hair blonde, print up new resumes and list blonde as your hair color. Your resume must accurately portray who you are today, not how you were three years (or even three days) ago.

Eye and hair color can be especially important for certain kinds of commercial work. For example, a shampoo commercial may want to hire two blondes and two brunettes, so if they've already hired the two blondes, you may get the role just because you're a brunette.

No matter what your physical characteristics may be, eventually, you'll find a role that's just perfect for someone like you.

Your acting experience and education

Initially, you need to list every available acting experience you've ever had, just to fill up your resume. Eventually, as you gain more experience, you can selectively choose the more impressive roles and eliminate the less important or trivial ones, such as your bit role as a butler in a community theater or your appearance in a play put on by your college drama department.

Even if you have experience in television commercials, never list them on your resume. If your resume says that you once did a commercial for Hertz rental cars (even if it was ten years ago), another car rental company like Avis may be reluctant to hire you for its ad campaign. Instead of listing specific commercials, play it safe and just create a commercial section on your resume, saying, "Commercial list available on request."

When listing your film, television, and theater experience, include the following four items for each role:

- The name of the film, play, or television show you were in
- The role you played
- The type of role you played (lead role, featured role, supporting role, or a recurring role)
- The studio name, television network, theater, or director you worked for

A *lead role* is considered a starring role. A *featured role* is a co-starring role, where you may have played a large role but weren't necessarily the main character. A *supporting role* is usually a small role where you had some acting and speaking parts (unlike an extra, who has no speaking roles whatsoever). On television shows, you may also have a *recurring role,* which means your character pops up from time to time in a few episodes of a regular show.

If you played a lead role, you may want to emphasize that on your resume. If you played a minor role but worked for a major director like Steven Spielberg, you may want to emphasize your work experience with Steven Spielberg rather than mention that you had a supporting role. If you appeared in a particularly prestigious theater, you may want to mention that theater name instead of the type of role you played. In general, include whatever looks most impressive. Again, your agent (or someone else knowledgeable in the industry) can give you additional advice on what to highlight.

Under your theater credits, be sure to identify any roles where you were an understudy rather than the principle performer. Nobody will fault you for being an understudy, but people may get upset if your resume gives the impression that you played a major role when you really didn't.

Be sure to include information about your college education if your degree is in an acting or performance-related field such as drama, broadcasting, or public speaking. If you didn't major in an acting-related field, don't bother listing your college history because no one cares if you graduated from Harvard or Yale in engineering or English literature. An education in acting shows that you've studied acting, but actual working experience beats education every time.

Your knowledge of special skills

Sometimes, an actor who knows how to juggle or sky-dive lands a role simply because no other actor possesses the special skill necessary for that particular role. So in a separate section of your resume, be sure to list all the unique skills that you can do extremely well. Here are some common types of skills that may come in handy:

- **Foreign languages:** Only include this information if you speak the language (or languages) fluently. (Two years of high school Spanish doesn't count.) Also, be sure to list any accents that you can do, such as a Southern or a British accent.
- **Athletic skills:** You may list skills, such as martial arts, sky-diving, juggling, skiing, fencing, gymnastics, horseback riding, or riding a unicycle.
- **Artistic skills:** Perhaps you can play a musical instrument, know how to create an ice sculpture, or have experience with ballroom dancing. If you can sing, list your vocal range such as alto, tenor, and so on.
- **Unusual skills:** This skill set can include pretty much anything. Some examples are shuffling cards like a card shark, trick shooting with a pistol, twisting balloons into animals, or impersonating a celebrity.

If you list any special skills, make sure that you can do them extremely well. For example, if you only took one year of karate classes, you probably wouldn't want to list *Martial Arts* on your resume as a special skill. However, if you're close to getting a black belt in karate, you can probably get away with listing it.

Avoiding Resume No-Nos

Your acting resume is meant to highlight your acting experience and qualifications, so don't list anything on your resume that detracts from your acting career or experience. Here are some items to avoid listing:

- Your age. If you list a specific age, casting directors may only cast you in roles for people your exact age. Let your appearance define your age range (some actors can be 35 and still play the part of a 21 year old).
- Previous jobs that have no relevance to acting. (Does any casting director care to know that you spent last summer working as a fry cook for a fast food restaurant?)
- Education not related to acting.

- References. (Who you know is less important than how well you act.)
- Salary requirements.
- Career objectives.

You want to list only your acting credentials on your resume, but make sure that you don't exaggerate or lie about your background. If you do, it'll eventually catch up and hurt you in the long run.

Many actors, especially novices, may be tempted to exaggerate their accomplishments. Don't fall into this trap. If a casting director discovers that you exaggerated your accomplishments, you may possibly lose out on a role. At the very least, you become highly suspect in the eyes of the casting director, which will only hurt you for any future auditions that the casting director may be involved in.

Many actors exaggerate their past experiences because they falsely believe that doing so makes them look more credible and professional in the eyes of a casting director. Casting directors know that everyone has to start out as a novice and that even the biggest stars were once beginners with no credits, too. So don't be ashamed of how little you may have accomplished so far, instead, revel in the fact that you're a "fresh talent."

Even worse than exaggeration is outright lying. Although people may stretch the truth a bit when creating a corporate resume, lying on an acting resume can get you in serious trouble in show business. If you lie about performing in a film, casting directors can often verify your claims by either watching that film or asking others who were involved in that film.

One of the most popular show business Web sites is the *Internet Movie Database* (`www.imdb.com`), which allows anyone to search a film to find out about an actor's, director's, or producer's previous experience. If you list a film credit, make sure that it's real, or else someone can easily find the truth with just the click of a mouse. Lying simply brands you as an untrustworthy actor, and if a casting director can't trust you to tell the truth about your acting experience, why should he or she trust that you'll be able to act in a role?

Casting directors are people, and most people respect honesty (even if they're not always very honest themselves). If you lie and get caught, you're liable to hurt your career worse than any amount of lying would've been able to help it.

Examining Sample Resumes

Your acting resume should evolve as you train and gain experience in the biz. Just as you should update your head shot every time your look changes, you should update your resume every time you land another good role.

This section takes a look at what credits you should highlight on your acting resume as a beginner, as an intermediate, and as a veteran actor. Use the samples in this book to serve as a guide for creating your own beginner's acting resume. Then, when you land that first big role, you can get this book out again and update your resume, using the intermediate actor's example. Then, when you finally hit it big and are on the verge of becoming a major celebrity, you can take this book out one more time and use it to put together your veteran actor's resume. After that, you'll be so famous that casting directors and producers will be knocking your door down to offer you roles, and you won't even need to bother with a resume anymore!

There are no fixed set of rules for creating a resume. Use these examples to stir your imagination and creativity. The most important part about creating a resume is to make your resume look impressive whether you use specific words, highlight words in bold face or unique fonts, or rearrange your skills and experience so it appears you have the exact background and skills needed for the current role you're auditioning for.

The beginner's resume

If you're just starting out in acting, the hardest part of making up a resume can be figuring out how to fill up a blank page when you have absolutely no acting experience whatsoever.

To make a beginner's resume fill an entire page, use plenty of white space to separate text and display all text in a large type size, such as 12 or 14 point. You may also want to include your physical characteristics to help fill up space.

Be sure to include any acting experience you have — no matter how small the part. Whether you performed a bit role in a community theater or appeared in a student film or a public access television show, that's acting experience and you should include it on your resume until you can list something more noteworthy. Any type of acting job, however trivial, shows agents and casting directors that you at least have some experience performing in front of an audience.

Figure 5-1 shows Nancy Novice's acting resume. Notice how Nancy uses a large (but reasonable) font size to fill the page with text. Also, notice how Nancy doesn't have much acting experience, but she still includes minor work in theatrical productions as well as supporting roles in small films. Nancy's resume does a nice job of highlighting all the performance-related training she's received (including ballet and ballroom dancing — skills that may come in handy when auditioning for a part in a musical).

Nancy Novice

(555) 123-4567

Height: 5' 5" Eye color: Bright blue
Weight: 120 lbs. Hair color: Strawberry blonde

Acting Experience

Theatre:

*Played the Rabbit in the Idaho State University Children's Story Theatre production of Alice in Wonderland.

*Played the Maid in the Meadowlake Performing Art Center's production of The Black and The White.

Film:

*Played the Supporting Role of Unsuspecting Swimmer #1 in Attack of the Rabid Piranhas.

*Played the Supporting Role of the Orphan Girl in Homeless in Happyland.

Education

*Received a Bachelor of Arts degree in Theatre from Idaho State University.

Training

*Attended an acting workshop lead by Lee Strasberg.

*Took voice and speech lessons from Mike Taylor's School of Dictation.

*Received improvisational training from The Groundlings Improv Troupe.

*Practiced ballroom dancing at the International Dance Academy of Barstow.

*Practiced ballet dancing at Fresno Dance Academy.

Special Skills

Ice Skating, Swimming, Water-Skiing, Snorkeling and Diving, Skateboarding, Snowboarding, Snow Skiing, Horseback Riding, Typing, Gymnastics, Ballet, Ballroom Dancing, Yoga, Fluent French, Southern Accent, Guitar, Singing, Driving a Manual Transmission, Sailing, Miming.

Additional Experience

*Worked as a mime entertaining visitors at Water World.

Figure 5-1: A beginner's resume must often emphasize training and special skills in lieu of actual acting experience.

Note: The sample resumes shown herein are included for demonstration purposes only and are not the actual or true resumes of the individual resume's holder. Further, the names used herein are fictitious and any relation to any person living or dead is purely coincidental.

Every actor was a beginner at one time, so the lack of actual working experience doesn't matter as much as the way you handle yourself at an audition (see Chapter 9). Even beginners can compete against veteran actors and land a role, especially in the film, television, and commercial market where looks can override any acting experience you may (or may not) have.

The intermediate actor's resume

An intermediate actor generally has at least one or two fairly impressive acting credits or a long list of minor credits that demonstrates that he has been getting acting work on a regular basis.

The resume for an intermediate actor is usually a combination of acting experience and training. The top portion of the resume lists your acting experience, and the bottom portion of your resume lists any classes or additional training you may have taken. Because an intermediate actor has more impressive roles to highlight than a novice actor, the training and special skills portion of the resume can be shortened.

Figure 5-2 shows a typical intermediate actor's resume. Notice that an intermediate actor most likely has an agent and is a member of one or more of the actors' unions. Also, under each acting category (film, television, theater, and so on) Ian lists his most impressive credits first because those are likely to catch someone's eye.

As you gain more working experience, you'll need to start trimming your educational and acting credits, starting with the less prestigious ones. For example, you may have taken both a television commercial workshop and an acting class from a famous acting coach. If you only have room on your resume to list one of them, which one should you keep? The answer is both *and* neither, depending on circumstances.

For example, if you're auditioning for a commercial, dump the acting class listing and keep the television commercial workshop credit. If you're auditioning for a film role, dump the television commercial workshop credit and keep the acting class listing. The point is to list the credits that will help convince a casting director that you have the necessary skills and experience to win the current role.

Ian Intermediate

SAG/AFTRA/AEA

Height: 5' 7"
Weight: 142 lbs.
Eyes: Emerald Green
Hair: Strawberry Blonde

Silent Partner Agency
Agent: Bertha Bedrock
666 Sunset Blvd.
Los Angeles, CA 90120
(213) 555-6924

Acting Experience

Film:

- **Blackhawk Down:** Played Lt. Smith (Featured Role); directed by Ridley Scott.
- **Friday the 13th, Part 192:** Played Jason's therapist (Supporting Role).

Television:

- **Friends:** Played Jake (Supporting Role).
- **General Hospital:** Played Dr. Jones (Recurring Role).

Theatre:

- **Romeo and Juliet:** Played Mercutio at Pasadena Playhouse.
- **The Importance of Being Earnest:** Played Merriman at Meadowlake Performing Arts Center.

Industrial Films:

- **Telemarketing Can Be Fun:** Played Bill (Lead Role).

Training

- Acting workshop with Lee Strasberg
- Improvisational training at Second City in Chicago
- Dance lessons at the Arthur Murray Dance School
- Comedy classes at the Top Bananas Comedy Club in San Diego
- Voice lessons with Donald Maxwell

Special Skills

- Singing (Tenor)
- Dancing (Tap, Jazz, and Swing)
- Riding a Unicycle
- Juggling
- Gymnastics
- Martial Arts
- Scuba Diving

Figure 5-2: An intermediate actor's resume is often a balance between acting experience and training.

The veteran's resume

A veteran actor is someone who has plenty of acting experience and can afford the luxury of minimizing or eliminating training skills altogether. A veteran actor often has two or more impressive credits and a handful of lesser known credits.

Unlike a novice's resume, a veteran actor's resume heavily emphasizes past acting experience in film, television, and theater. Training is still important, but when casting directors and agents see that you've spent the last five years performing on Broadway, in a blockbuster film, and as a recurring character on a hit television situation comedy, they'll tend to assume that you must know what you're doing with or without any training listed on your resume.

Because veteran actors need to emphasize the variety of acting experience, their resumes may need to list the acting roles into separate categories:

- **Theater**

  Veteran actors with extensive theatre credits often subdivide their experience into three categories: Broadway, Off-Broadway, and Regional (as shown in Figure 5-3).
- **Film** (list any Industrial Film credits in a separate category)
- **Television**

If you've appeared in commercials, include a separate section labeled *Commercials,* but don't list the commercials you've appeared in. (That way, you have a fair shot at getting the part in a soda commercial even if you've previously appeared in an ad for a competing soda.) Instead, let the casting director know you have commercial experience by saying, "Commercial list available on request." (See Figure 5-3.)

As a veteran (or even an intermediate) actor, you may want to tailor your resume to emphasize specific skills when auditioning for certain parts. For example, when auditioning for a theatrical part, you may want to list together all your Broadway experience and experience in Shakespearean plays. Just be sure to list other types of theater credits as well, so people don't think that all you can do is Shakespearean plays.

When you're auditioning for a theatrical or film role, print a separate version of your resume that includes your acting coach credit because casting directors and agents may be impressed by the reputation (or actually know) of your acting coach. When you audition for commercial work, keep your commercial workshop credit and dump your acting coach credit.

Vinnie O. Veteran

SAG/AFTRA/AEA

Height: 6' 2"	Agency of the Mobsters
Weight: 202 lbs.	Agent: Sammy "The Bull" Vittario
Eyes: Brown	619 Second Avenue, #6
Hair: Black	New York, NY 10016
	(212) 555-1456

Theater

Broadway	Grease	Danny Zuko	Carnegie Hall
	Hamlet	Hamlet	Italian Arts Theater
	Dr. Doolittle and the Rabid Puppy	Dr. Doolittle	Royale Theater
Off-Broadway	The Death of a Vacuum Cleaner Salesman	Billy Slowman	Greenwich Village Performing Theater
	Godzilla: the Musical	Simon Darkstar	Tokyo Arts Center
Regional	The Life of a Cat	Maxwell	Findlay Theater
Film	Santa Claus vs. the Martians	Santa Claus	Embassy Pictures
	Jaws	Captain Fourlimbs	Director/Steven Spielberg
	Jaws 2	Captain Threelimbs	Universal Pictures
	Jaws 3D	Captain Twolimbs	Universal Pictures
	Jaws 4: The Revenge	Captain Onelimb	Universal Pictures
	Jaws 5: Sharks in Outer Space	Captain Nolimbs	Sleazy Productions
Television	E.R.	Dr. Malpractice	Featured Role/NBC
	Friends	Johnny Balestrari	Recurring Role/NBC
	Will and Grace	Bookie	Supporting Role/NBC
	Starship Jupiter (CBS Pilot)	Captain Monocle	Lead Role/CBS
	Guys in the 'Hood (UPN Pilot)	Gangster #1	Supporting Role/UPN
Commercials	List available upon request		
Training	Acting Workshop with Lee Strasberg		

Figure 5-3: A veteran actor's resume emphasizes actual working experience.

Figure 5-3 shows a typical veteran's resume. Vinnie is auditioning for a theatrical role — you can tell because his theater experience is listed first and he lists his famous acting coach in the Training section. (See the following section for advice on how to organize your resume according to the part you're auditioning for.)

Customizing Your Resume for the Part

By tailoring your resume for specific roles, you can show the casting director that you've done similar roles before and are fully qualified for the current role as well.

If you don't have experience in a particular category, such as television, then don't create an empty Television category on your resume because doing so will just highlight your deficiency in that area. Your resume should emphasize your strengths, not highlight your weaknesses.

The order that you list your acting experience depends on the type of roles you want. For example, if you're auditioning for theatrical roles, you may want your resume to list your theater experience first (refer to Vinnie O. Veteran's resume in Figure 5-3).

In the world of theater, list your special skills selectively. Two of the most important skills to include (if you can do them well) are singing and dancing because those skills can help you get cast in a musical. Don't forget to list any additional skills that you can perform onstage, such as juggling, riding a unicycle, fencing, or gymnastics.

Unlike theater resumes that should only list those special skills you can do on stage, film and television resumes should list all the unique skills you possess — whether it's mountain climbing, pole vaulting, or alligator wrestling. You never know when any of your special skills may come in handy for a film or television role, so don't be shy about any of your abilities.

If you're auditioning for an Oscar Wilde comedy, for example, you may want to create a separate resume that emphasizes all your comedy experience in film, television, and stage along with any improv or comedy workshops that you may have taken. If you don't have enough comedic roles to fill out a resume, it's okay to list some of your other more impressive credits even if they have nothing to do with comedy.

Chapter 6

Training to Improve Your Acting Skills

In This Chapter

- Auditioning like a pro for any part
- Perfecting your performances
- Staying in shape
- Getting attention with an unusual skill

On rare occasions, someone may suddenly be discovered to be a naturally gifted actor who skyrockets to stardom literally overnight. Of course, every week, someone is lucky enough to win the multimillion-dollar jackpot in a lottery, too. If you want to leave your future up to fate and just hope that you get to be one of the lucky ones, that's fine. But you're better off taking control of your life and developing your skills to become the best actor possible.

Just knowing how to act isn't always enough, though. So this chapter discusses other types of training, such as auditioning and special-skills training, that can help increase your chances of success. Although no amount of training can guarantee success, the more training you get, the better your chances are of landing that next important audition.

Mastering the Art of Auditioning: Taking Classes

The most important skill every actor needs to learn is how to audition. (See Chapter 9 for detailed auditioning advice.)

For many actors (including novices and veterans alike), auditioning can be a terrifying process because they don't know what to expect. Although each audition can be a learning process, it can also be a missed opportunity if you allow nervousness or lack of preparation to interfere with your audition. So the more familiar you become with the whole auditioning process, the more comfortable you become when performing in any unfamiliar situation that may occur during your audition. To help you get comfortable auditioning, take an auditioning class.

Benefiting from an auditioning class

For a beginning actor, an auditioning class can teach you basic etiquette for how to behave at an audition and what to expect at different types of auditions. For veteran actors, auditioning classes can provide a chance to practice dealing with the unexpected, such as when the casting director asks you to improvise a scene or audition by using an entirely different script from the one you thought you were supposed to read.

Auditioning classes are typically run by battle-hardened veteran actors who've made numerous mistakes during their careers of attending auditions, and now they're willing to pass their wisdom on to you. Sometimes, auditioning classes may be run by current or former casting directors who've seen actors make numerous mistakes and want to share their tips on what they look for in actors and how they've seen actors mess up an audition. Ask your fellow actors for their recommendations on the different types of auditioning classes and instructors available.

To get students used to the auditioning process, most auditioning classes focus on making students practice auditioning and pointing out what they're doing right and what they're doing wrong. The idea is that the more you practice auditioning (even if it's just in front of an instructor and your classmates), the more comfortable you'll ultimately feel during a real audition.

Advancing your auditioning skills

Some auditioning classes and workshops focus on improving cold reading, on-camera techniques, scene study, and monologue training.

Succeeding at cold reading

Quick! Act like you're a mother of five who just found out that her husband lapsed into a coma at work while you're busy preparing a birthday party for your youngest child. Not easy is it? Yet, that's exactly the kind of unexpected direction you may get at an audition when a casting director asks you to perform a *cold reading* from a totally unfamiliar script to see how well and how accurately you can play a role with almost no time to think, rehearse, or analyze the script.

Because most actors panic when faced with the unexpected, cold reading workshops can teach you how to adapt quickly to any changes and still remain confident and competent as an actor.

Good cold reading skills come in handy both at an audition and on the set of a situation comedy where writers commonly rewrite the script based on the audience's reaction to the jokes. Then, the actors need to learn these new changes in time to shoot the scene over again. Learning how to deal with this type of sudden pressure during an audition can help you handle it during an actual acting job.

Improving your on-camera techniques

Many auditioning classes teach on-camera techniques to help actors look their best through the camera's point of view.

On-camera techniques can show actors what not to do, such as never looking directly into the camera because on film or tape, the actor may appear to be breaking through the imaginary *fourth wall* and staring right at the audience. (Then again, for some films or television shows, the director may want this type of effect.) Other types of on-camera techniques actors can learn are how to perform an intensely emotional scene in a close-up (where you may be talking to nobody but the camera and feeling kind of foolish while you're doing it), how to *cheat* towards the camera so your profile appears more visible, and how to *block* your movements so that you never block another actor from the camera.

For film and television, the way you look in person doesn't matter so much as the way you look on camera. If you don't look good on film or videotape, the quality of your acting can be irrelevant. The best actor doesn't always get the role. The actor who looks the best on camera (and auditions well) for a particular role often gets the role.

Studying scenes

Similar to cold reading is *scene study and analysis.* Before an audition, you can often get a copy of the *sides* (a few pages of the script) that you can study ahead of time. Interpret the sides incorrectly and you may play a serious scene with humor. Because humor probably isn't what the casting director wants to see, the casting director may just dismiss you with a polite, "Thank you," leaving you with no clue as to what you did wrong.

Learning how to study a scene can help you understand the possible motives behind a character, what subtext the character may be trying to communicate, and what goals the character is trying to achieve. Knowing this information can help you give different interpretations of a particular role.

Scene study also comes in handy when you're on a film set, shooting scenes out of order. By knowing how your character is supposed to feel, look, and behave in each particular scene, your overall acting performance will look realistic.

Maximizing your monologue

Besides teaching how to analyze a scene to help you get the maximum amount of clues for how to portray a character, many classes also teach *monologue training.* (A monologue is a long speech presenting the words or thoughts of a single character.)

Taking a monologue class gives you the opportunity to practice your monologues and receive feedback from your instructor and fellow students. They can offer you suggestions for what works and what you need to improve before your next audition. Getting such feedback now can be invaluable later because during an audition, you rarely get any feedback at all from the casting directors. Because you won't be able to drag your acting coach to all your auditions, you need to learn how to deliver and perform a monologue to the best of your abilities before you start performing that same monologue during an actual audition.

A good instructor can also help you choose the best types of monologues to showcase your talents. A monologue that's perfect for one person may not emphasize the strengths of another actor so it's important to learn both how to deliver a monologue effectively and choose the best monologue for emphasizing your talent and skills.

Improving Your Performing Skills

Like any skill, you can always learn something new about acting. Theater actors often take film and television acting classes to learn how to act for the camera, and film and television actors often take theatrical acting lessons to learn how to project their character portrayal on a large stage.

At the basic level, an acting workshop can teach you the fundamentals about acting. On a more advanced level, a workshop or coach can suggest ways to fine-tune your existing acting skills as well as spot and improve your weaknesses. At the very least, an acting workshop can help you keep your acting skills sharp if you happen to be between jobs at the time.

An acting workshop of any kind can help an actor at any stage of his or her career. However, the quality of instruction can vary drastically, depending on the background knowledge and personality of the acting instructor or coach. Before signing up for any acting class, get referrals from fellow actors and sit in on a class to study how the instructor works. The best instructor for you is simply the person who can teach you the most in the shortest amount of time, regardless of any impressive credentials that person may or may not have.

How to find an acting class, workshop, or coach

Finding the right acting coach for you can be almost as frustrating and time-consuming as finding the right mate. Flip through the classified ads in the back of any trade publication, such as *Variety* or *Backstage,* and you can make a quick list of the more prominent acting coaches available in your area.

But just because someone advertises in a major trade publication doesn't guarantee any measure of competency. So do your homework first and call to find out the cost for each workshop or class, the qualifications of the teacher, the typical number of students per class, how the class may be structured, and whether you can observe and audit a single session for free. That way, you can determine whether the teacher's style and class format is compatible with your way of learning.

Also, talk to agents and your fellow actors and ask for their recommendations on who the better acting coaches may be in your town. Taking lessons from a highly respected acting coach can lend credibility to your resume, especially when you're first starting out and don't have any work experience.

Some of the many different classes available to improve your performing skills include stand-up comedy workshops, improvisation classes, speech and accent coaching, and singing and dancing lessons.

Stand-up comedy workshops

Situation comedies can be an extremely lucrative role for television actors, so many actors take stand-up comedy workshops. These types of workshops teach actors the basics in writing and understanding the structure of a joke along with learning how to deliver and perform a joke in front of a live audience.

Although many stand-up comedy workshops are designed for novices interested in pursuing a career in stand-up comedy, actors can benefit by learning to perform onstage by themselves with only the material they wrote themselves. Most actors are terrified of being onstage without the support of a script or actors. Stand-up comedy workshops can help actors overcome this fear, which can translate into more confidence onstage, in front of the camera, and during auditions.

Talent scouts often scour comedy clubs in large cities such as Los Angeles and New York, looking for new talent to fill roles in upcoming situation comedies. If you can project a likeable personality onstage and make people laugh in a comedy club, chances are good that you can also project a likeable personality on-camera and make people laugh in the studio audience and at home.

Improvisation classes

Auditions can be unpredictable places. Sometimes, a casting director may be interested in you and suddenly ask you to improvise by performing a completely different scene or character. Because you can't plan the unexpected (otherwise, it wouldn't be the unexpected now, would it?), you can do the next best thing and figure out how to adapt to the unexpected by taking an improvisation (or *improv*) class. An improv class can teach you to think quickly and logically on your feet, so you can appear calm and confident even during the most unusual situations that may pop up.

Improvisation also helps actors develop a sense of play and spontaneity that can improve their acting skills, too. The more relaxed and confident you appear at an audition, the more you can concentrate on your acting to help you land a role.

If you're planning to act in theater, plan on the fact that you (or some other actor) may forget some lines in the middle of a crucial scene. Rather than just stand paralyzed with fear, by taking improvisation classes, you can learn to adapt to this terrifying situation and make it work for you.

Speech and accent coaching

No matter where you're from, you likely have some sort of regional accent. In some cases, you may have a distinctly pronounced accent. Although accents can be helpful in landing you certain roles, knowing how to lose your accent can help you qualify for even more roles. Someone with a thick Southern accent may be perfect for a film that requires a Southern character, but that same actor is going to have a mighty tough time trying to convince a casting director to let him play the lead role of Hamlet with that same accent.

Besides taking classes to help you lose your existing accent, you may also want to take classes to help you develop different dialects. The more accents you can speak, the more acting tools you can bring to a particular character portrayal.

Knowing how to switch to different types of accents can be particularly useful if you plan on doing *voice-over acting.* (See Chapter 13 for more info on voice-over acting.)

Besides accent coaching, many actors take speech classes to help them learn how to pronounce certain sounds and words correctly. If you have trouble saying certain letters such as *R's,* run to a speech therapist right away. Even if your speech is easy to understand, a speech instructor can still help you fine-tune your speech to make it as clear as possible.

Many actors take yoga or meditation classes to help them learn how to regulate their breathing. Knowing the proper way to breath can help you relax and project your voice clearly.

Singing and dancing lessons

Singing lessons can improve your chances of landing a role in a musical or in some commercials. Seasoned actors often take singing lessons to continue improving their voices. Beginning actors may take singing lessons just to expand their ranges of available skills.

Even if you never land a singing role in your entire acting career, learning how to sing can, at the same time, teach you how to breathe, how to project your voice, and how to modify your voice to achieve different intonations. And all these skills help improve your overall delivery as an actor.

Consider taking dance lessons in addition to voice lessons. At the very least, dance lessons can teach you how to move gracefully. If you take enough dance lessons, you can confidently audition for roles in musicals that require elaborate dance routines. Some actors even specialize in specific types of dancing such as jazz, ballet, swing, or ballroom dancing to better their chances of landing a role.

Developing Physical Fitness Skills

You can't work if you're too sick, so staying healthy is very important. In order to stay healthy, you need to keep your body in shape. Besides maintaining a regular exercise program, you may also want to learn some additional physical skills that may one day help you land a role.

Choose a skill to learn because you enjoy it, not because you think that it may help you get a role. Any skill you learn should be fun because there's no guarantee that any skills you learn will ever help you land a role in anything.

To develop greater strength and flexibility in your body, consider a gymnastics or Yoga class. Many action films and TV shows make generous use of the martial arts and the various weapons associated with self-defense, including fencing, boxing, and archery. Although a director will likely use stunt people to perform the more dangerous stunts involved in fight scenes, any actor who can appear believable while performing a fight scene will be more in demand than another actor who can't even throw a punch without looking like a wimp.

Practicing a sport can be a great way to stay in shape, relax, and develop a potentially marketable acting skill at the same time. Although most people can look halfway decent playing baseball or football, faking other types of sporting skills, such as skiing (water and snow), scuba diving, sky-diving, skateboarding, horseback riding, or motorcycle racing, isn't as easy.

When listing any physical fitness skill on your resume, make sure that you can do that particular skill at a near expert level. Nobody wants to see a beginner throw a karate kick when they could watch a black belt throw a karate kick instead. (Flip to Chapter 5 for more advice in creating a five-star acting resume.)

Improving Your Unique Skills

The most important unusual skills to develop are those that other people can see or hear. Think visually. If you can do back-flips while juggling a chainsaw, a poisonous rattlesnake, and a hand grenade, you have a visually interesting skill that won't fail to grab someone's attention. Of course, your skills don't have to border on the extreme or the bizarre. Sometimes, they can be as simple as knowing how to speak a foreign language fluently or how to play a musical instrument, such as a piano or a harp. In general, the more skills you can perform well, the more talent you have to help convince a casting director to choose you.

Knowing how to ride a unicycle on a tightrope may be an interesting skill, but, ultimately, the most important skills that can help you succeed as an actor are business and acting skills. Business skills can teach you how to market and promote yourself as an actor, and acting skills can help you do a great job after you land a role (which could then lead to landing additional roles).

Part III
Taking Your First Steps into Show Business

"I know you're all classically trained actors, but I don't think the public's ready for Titus Andronicus performed by the cast of Stomp."

In this part . . .

Every major star whom you see in film, television, or theater started as a beginner. So this part of the book explains the first steps that you need to take to enter the wildly chaotic world of show business.

Your first step into show business involves finding ways to promote yourself and find your own work so you can gain valuable acting experience. Your next step is to find an agent to represent you who can help you look for work and also perform the crucial job of negotiating your contract for you after you do get work.

You also need to understand and master the skills of auditioning. As soon as you can succeed at auditions on a regular basis, you'll be well on your way to establishing your career as an actor.

Chapter 7

Getting Seen by the Industry: Promoting Yourself

In This Chapter

- Getting work on your own by using actors' unions and other resources
- Using your resume and the Internet to put yourself on the market
- Showing off your talents

One way to get noticed is to show up at enough auditions and be such a good performer that casting directors can't fail to take note of your talent and skill. Unfortunately, show business has plenty of talented actors. So showing up to enough auditions still may not guarantee that you land a role, let alone become a working actor.

Rather than waiting to be discovered (which means that you could be waiting the rest of your life), a better approach is to work towards promoting yourself. The more you promote yourself, the more likely you'll create your own big break that may turn you into a star (or at least into a successful, working actor).

This chapter explores ways to get yourself noticed by agents, casting directors, and other people involved in show business.

Looking for Your Own Work

Getting an agent can be a major milestone in your acting career (see Chapter 8), but an agent alone is still no guarantee that you'll get work. When many actors get an agent, they get lazy. Instead of hustling to find work for themselves, they wait for their agents to find it for them. If they don't yet have an agent, they still don't look for work because they think that they need an agent first to get it. So whether you have an agent or not, you must continue to look for work on your own.

Looking for work on your own isn't easy, but it's better than never having the chance to work at all.

Use the actors' unions

Membership into one of the actors' unions doesn't guarantee you a job, but the unions make an effort to help their many members find work all the time (refer to Chapter 3 for more information about actors' unions). If you're already a member of an actors' union, call your local union branch (listed on the various actors' union Web sites such as `www.sag.org`, `www.aftra.org`, and `www.actorsequity.org`), and they can provide you with a job hotline that you can call periodically to find out about acting opportunities that may be suitable for you.

Because the various actors' unions often conduct seminars or workshops for actors, drop by the union offices on a regular basis and network with other members to share acting and auditioning tips or upcoming audition information.

The unions are there to help and protect their members, so don't be afraid to contact them for any type of information or help that you may need. If they can't help you, they can often point you in the direction of someone who can answer your questions.

Network to stay in touch

If you don't belong to an actors' union, network with fellow actors by exchanging information about available auditions.

Your fellow actors will likely hear of auditioning opportunities that you won't know about (and you may hear of auditions that they don't know about). So to increase your chances of getting an audition, share information with other actors you trust so you can help each other.

Scan trade publications

Some the best ways to find work are through advertisements in trade publications and on show business-related Web sites.

One of the most useful trade publications for actors is *Backstage* (www.backstage.com), which offers regular columns that list the latest film, television, and theater work available, mostly in the Los Angeles and New York areas but occasionally in other cities as well. Some of the listed work is union work, some is non-union work that often includes some amount of pay, and a large number are student films or plays with little or no pay available. Still, any type of work is preferable than doing nothing at all because you'll be getting valuable acting experience, showcasing your talents for casting directors and agents, and meeting different people who may become top actors, directors, writers, or producers sometime in the future.

Two other show business trade publications, *Variety* (www.variety.com) and *Hollywood Reporter* (www.hollywoodreporter.com), are more concerned with covering the business end of show business and rarely advertise work for aspiring actors. You may still want to browse through these publications, though, because they often list the latest projects going into production that may have a role that's just perfect for someone like you.

Browse the Internet

Besides reading the trade publications, use the Internet. Many Web sites list auditions for both union and non-union acting work; tips and resources for becoming a better actor; and employment opportunities for day jobs within the show business industry, such as receptionists, script readers, Web designers, and even film crews. By browsing through the following Web sites periodically, you may find both acting work and a day job.

- The Acting Depot (www.actingdepot.com)
- The Hollywood Creative Directory (www.hcdonline.com)
- Acting Resources (www.madscreenwriter.com)
- Actor's Update (www.actorsupdate.com)
- AboutSpeech.com (www.aboutspeech.com)
- ActorNews (www.actornews.com)
- Acting Goldmine (www.actinggoldmine.com)
- Acting World (www.actingworld.com)
- Hollywood Actor (www.hollywoodactor.com)
- Eperformer.com (www.eperformer.com)
- The ActorSource (www.actorsource.com)

Finding the proverbial day job

Although most actors would rather spend their time looking for acting work, sometimes, you have to find a job in a hurry to help you pay your bills. If you're going to do temporary, part-time, or full-time work, you may as well work in show business where you can make potentially useful contacts to help your acting career.

For actors looking for temporary work, The Acting Depot (`www.actingdepot.com`) provides a list of temporary agencies that specialize in placing temporary workers inside talent agencies, studios, and production companies.

If you're looking for part-time or full-time work in the show business industry, visit Showbiz jobs.com (`www.showbizjobs.com`) where you can look for a job in a variety of different fields, including data entry, graphic arts, film production, and internships.

Many of these Web sites are run by individuals who do their best to provide accurate and useful information for actors, but be careful. The information on these Web sites may not always be up to date or may not always be accurate.

Contact casting directors on your own

Too many actors just wait for an audition in the hopes that they may land a role. Instead of just waiting for auditions, go out and create your own opportunities! And the best way to create your own opportunities to audition is to contact casting directors yourself.

By contacting casting directors on your own, you can increase the chance that you can get a particular role without having to attend an open casting call or through an audition arranged by an agent.

The best way to contact a casting director is to mail your head shot and resume to him or her and ask for a general interview. Because you're trying to get a casting director to remember you out of the thousands of other actors he or she may know, give the casting director a reason to call and remember you.

For example, if you know that a particular casting director tends to cast comedies, write a funny cover letter or modify your resume to show your experience in comedies. If a particular casting director has cast you in a role before, mention that fact, too.

In addition to sending mailings to casting directors, try dropping by the casting director's office in person. If you happen to be on a studio lot for an audition, stay on that lot after your audition and look for casting directors' offices where you can drop off your head shot and resume. Just make a quick introduction, such as, "Hi, I'm John Doe. I just finished auditioning for a new show on NBC, and I'd like to introduce myself." If you're lucky, the casting director may ask you to perform a monologue on the spot (so be ready). Otherwise, you might be able to schedule a general meeting later. But at the very least, you've put your face in front of another casting director.

Always respect other people's time. Be brief and be ready to leave politely if asked. You want casting directors to remember you for your talent and ability, not because you're a nuisance.

When meeting a casting director, the goal is to get them to agree to let you arrange a general meeting with her. Sometimes, casting directors set up open auditions and publicize this for anyone to appear, but other times, an actor can arrange a private general meeting on his or her own.

The general meeting won't necessarily lead to a role right away, but by letting the casting director know who you are and what you're capable of doing as an actor, the casting director may later find a project with a role just for someone like you. Rather than notify talent agencies of that particular role, casting directors may first contact the actors whom they think may be right for the part. If the casting directors know about you, they may contact you to try out for the role long before it becomes available to the rest of the actors in various talent agencies.

After a casting director casts you for a role, be sure to write a thank-you note and send a gift as a small token of your appreciation, such as a basket of fruit or a bouquet of flowers. You may also want to periodically mail news of your latest acting roles to any casting director who may have chosen you in the past. Doing so can keep your name and face fresh in that casting director's memory in case he or she needs someone like you for an upcoming project.

Advertising Yourself

Businesses advertise because they know that advertising brings them customers. Because acting is a business, actors often advertise themselves to attract the notice of agents and casting directors.

The simplest ways to advertise are to carry your head shot, resume, and business cards with you everywhere you go. You never know when you may meet a potential agent or casting director at the airport or in a restaurant.

You also don't know who may know a particularly powerful agent or casting director, either. Your bank teller may be the cousin of Steven Spielberg. Your mailman may be good friends with the wife of the hottest celebrity. The guy behind the counter at your favorite fast food restaurant may be ready to quit and start working at a high-powered talent agency tomorrow. You never know who you may meet and when, so be ready to promote yourself with head shots and resumes at all times.

Besides passing out head shots and resumes (which can get expensive, but you can consider that the cost of doing business), look into creating your own Web site. Many companies offer free Web site hosting where you can post your head shot, resume, and list of recent accomplishments for everyone to see. Although casting directors probably aren't going to search the Internet at random for actors to evaluate, a Web site can just be an additional advertising tool that you can use to promote yourself. That way if you do catch the attention of a casting director, you can suggest the casting director visit your Web site to learn more about you.

Put your Web site address on your resume and business cards so that people who want more information about you can find it as easily as clicking on their mouse. (Be sure to update your Web site periodically to give it a fresh appearance, rather than a stale, static Web site that hasn't changed in the past three years.)

If you land a particularly high-profile role, post that information in an ad in one of the trade publications where everyone in show business can see it. Also consider mailing out post cards, announcing your latest achievement. If you send out enough post cards to casting directors and agents saying something like, "See Jane Doe starring in *Attack of the Killer Mushrooms* on CBS at 9 p.m. this Thursday," you're bound to get someone who'll watch and look at your acting performance.

To show you how outrageous some actors can get in advertising themselves, one actress had her name and phone number plastered on a billboard in Los Angeles for several months. Sometimes, outrageous stunts don't get you anywhere, and sometimes, they may become a legend in their own right. As long as you try to promote yourself in a way that's legal and non-intrusive, people in show business will at least admire your chutzpah.

Showcasing Yourself

Getting noticed is half the battle of show business, so take every advantage to showcase your talents as much as possible. Here are some ways that you can showcase your talents:

- **Participating in acting showcases:** Many acting classes and workshops offer a special showcase night on the final day of class. During these showcase nights, the acting instructor invites agents and casting directors to evaluate the students for possible representation or consideration in future projects.

  Actors often band together and put on a special showcase night of their own by renting a theater and performing monologues or scenes from plays. With enough actors inviting agents and casting directors to the showcase, the bulk of the audience can be important show business people specifically there to evaluate the talent of all the different actors. Because the agents and casting directors have the opportunity to evaluate a large number of different actors (rather than just one), you increase the odds that agents and casting directors will actually show up.

  Casting directors may hold their own cold reading showcases, so be on the lookout for those, too.

- **Putting on a one-man show:** This option allows a single actor to tell a story while portraying several different characters during the course of the show. Because you're the only actor seen and you get to play a variety of different roles, any agents or casting directors who attend your show can't help but notice and evaluate your talent.

  When putting on a one-man show, you have to play the role of producer, director, writer, actor, and sometimes marketing director, too. Producing a one-man show that's interesting and can attract the attention of show business people isn't necessarily easy, but the showcase opportunities can be tremendous and can definitely be worth the time and effort required.

- **Writing and starring in your own screenplay:** Sylvester Stallone skyrocketed to fame after writing and appearing in *Rocky,* and Matt Damon and Ben Affleck boosted their acting careers immensely by writing and appearing in *Good Will Hunting.*

- **Writing your own stage play:** Create a play and hire your fellow actors to perform in it. That way, everyone gets a chance to showcase his talents, and you get experience producing and writing a play. Some people find that playwriting and screenwriting can be more interesting than acting. Although playwriting and screenwriting can be just as tough to break into as acting, you may find that you enjoy it more or that you have a natural talent for writing. Some celebrities, such as Woody Allen and Steven Martin, have managed to become both actors and writers, so you may want to pursue this dual career like they did.

- **Developing a stand-up comedy act:** When searching for actors to appear in situation comedies, casting directors often scour the comedy clubs. The theory is that teaching stand-up comedians to act is much easier than teaching an actor how to perform comedy. Actors, such as

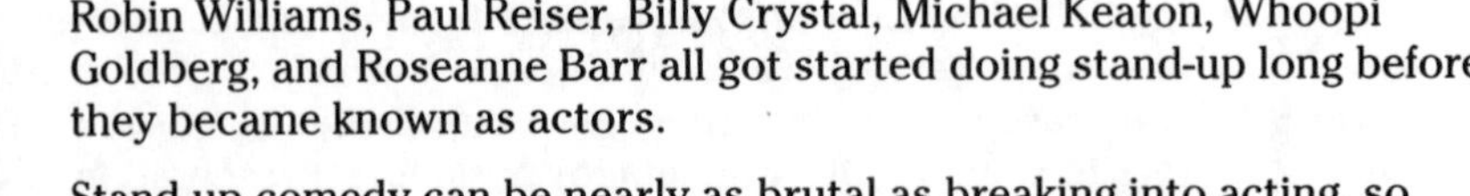

Robin Williams, Paul Reiser, Billy Crystal, Michael Keaton, Whoopi Goldberg, and Roseanne Barr all got started doing stand-up long before they became known as actors.

Stand-up comedy can be nearly as brutal as breaking into acting, so don't look at stand-up comedy as a quick way to break into acting. Rather, look at acting as the next logical step to take in your stand-up comedy career.

No matter how you decide to promote yourself, the important thing is to keep actively working to advance your own acting career because nobody — not your agent, your manager, your spouse, or your parents — will have as much interest in your success as you. The more time you spend trying to land the higher paying, higher profile acting roles, the greater your chances that one day you'll be able to work full-time and support yourself comfortably as a professional actor.

Chapter 8

Finding and Working with an Agent

In This Chapter

- Finding potential agents
- Choosing the right agent
- Knowing when and how to leave your agent

Although you can often find acting roles without the help of an agent, full-time working actors need an agent eventually. An agent can help you find auditions and negotiate contracts for you, freeing your time to focus on studying acting, going to auditions, and actually working as an actor. Agents hear of nearly all the top (read: the more lucrative and prestigious) roles before the general public hears about them. If you don't have an agent, you may miss out on auditions that are just perfect for you — if you only knew where those auditions were being held.

Your agent can greatly influence your acting career, so you need to find the best possible agent for you who meets your personal acting needs. When looking for an agent, you want to find someone who wants to represent you and who you're comfortable working with.

In this chapter, we discuss agents — from why you need one to how you convince one to represent you and your acting career. We also give advice on how to tactfully fire your agent if things aren't working out.

In New York, a beginner can get started working without an agent. But in Hollywood, everyone from beginners to veterans needs an agent because attending auditions for the more lucrative union markets without agency representation is nearly impossible.

Getting the Ball Rolling

The process of getting an agent is actually fairly simple. (The hard part is convincing an agent to agree to represent you.) To get the ball rolling, you first need to compile a list of potential agents. Next, you have to contact all those agents to see whether they'd be interested in representing you.

Discovering potential agents

One way to discover potential agents is to contact unions to request lists of franchised agents. Working with a franchised agent is best because he or she has agreed to follow union guidelines for working with actors.

Never consider an agent who isn't franchised by one of the actors' unions. Non-franchised agents can theoretically do anything that they want, which usually means that a non-franchised agent is more likely to be a con artist than a legitimate agent.

Even if you don't yet belong to an actors' union, you can always call the union to ask whether a particular agency has been approved by the union. Sometimes, new agencies pop up after the union prints its list of franchised agents, so an agent who isn't on the union list could possibly be from a franchised agency after all.

Contact the following unions for lists of franchised agents (you may need to pay a nominal fee for this list to cover the union's postage and handling expenses):

- **Screen Actor's Guild National Office**, 5757 Wilshire Blvd., Los Angeles, California 90036-3600; phone 323-954-1600; www.sag.org
- **Actor's Equity Association National Office**, 165 West 46th Street, 15th Floor, New York, New York 10036; phone 212-869-8530; www.actorsequity.org
- **American Federation of Television and Radio Artists National Office,** 260 Madison Avenue, New York, New York 10016-2402; phone: 212-532-0800; fax: 212-532-2242; www.aftra.org

Although you should hunt for an agent by contacting each one on the union-franchised list, don't overlook these additional ways of finding an agent:

- **Accessing *Academy Player's Directory.*** You can access the directory online at www.acadpd.org and view different actors and the names of the agencies that represent them.

- **Buying a copy of the *Ross Reports*.** This is a monthly publication that lists union franchised agencies around the country. The Ross Reports may list a new union franchised agent that the union's own list may not include yet.
- **Asking for referrals from reputable and respected show business people.** Referrals make introducing yourself to an agent easy because the referral (hopefully) comes from someone the agent trusts and respects. An agent who hears about you through one of his currently working clients is more apt to meet with you than if you were a total stranger.
- **Showcasing for agents in an acting workshop or class.** Acting instructors often have relationships with agents, so part of their courses may promise you a chance to showcase in front of an agent. This opportunity gives an agent a chance to snare any new, promising talent before another agent can do so.
- **Demonstrating your acting skills in an actual play.** If you're currently appearing in a play, invite agents to the play you're in and be sure to leave complimentary tickets for them at the ticket booth. If an agent likes what he sees in your performance, he may later invite you in for an interview.
- **Landing an important role.** Perhaps the easiest way to get an agent is to land a fairly major role without an agent's help. After you land a role, you can contact potential agents and inform them that you need an agent to negotiate your contract. Anytime an actor dangles the prospect of guaranteed money in front of an agent, you can bet that even the most reluctant agents suddenly are eager to meet you right away.

If you had your head shot printed as post cards, be sure to mail out your post cards to prospective agents when you invite them to evaluate you in a play.

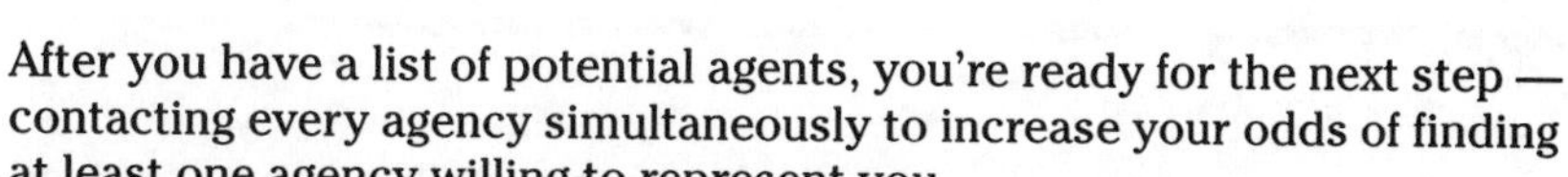

After you have a list of potential agents, you're ready for the next step — contacting every agency simultaneously to increase your odds of finding at least one agency willing to represent you.

Contacting potential agents

When contacting potential agents, mail them three items:

- Your head shot (so an agent knows what you look like)
- Your resume (so an agent can evaluate your experience and training)
- A one-page cover letter (to introduce yourself to an agent)

Your whole goal at this point is to get an agent to agree to meet with you in person to evaluate you as a potential client. So your head shot should capture an agent's eye (see Chapter 4 for details on head shots), your resume should demonstrate your seriousness in getting experience and training as an actor (see Chapter 5 for info on creating an acting resume), and your cover letter should do the following:

- Introduce yourself and your most impressive acting experience.
- State that you're seeking representation.
- List any additional reasons why that agent should be interested in you. (If possible, list the name of someone reputable who recommended you to that particular agent.)

See Figure 8-1 for a sample cover letter.

Dear Mr. Smith,

I am interested in representation with your agency as a film and television actor. I recently appeared in the musical version of *The Towering Inferno* and recently appeared in the non-union film *Liars and Thieves: the Making of a Law Firm.*

As you can see from my enclosed head shot and resume, I have been enrolled in Loren McCall's eight-week course "Acting in Film" and have also completed Robert Mitchell's "Cold Reading" workshop.

I trust that my head shot and resume can give you the chance to evaluate my abilities, skills, and experience. I will call early next week, so that I may possibly schedule an appointment with you.

Sincerely,

Your Name Here

Figure 8-1: A typical cover letter lists your latest accomplishments to attract an agent's interest.

Always make sure that you get the correct spelling of an agent and the agency along with the correct address, too. Nothing looks worse than misspelling an agent's name or mistaking an agent for a man when she's really a woman and vice versa.

To improve your chances of getting an agent as soon as possible, mass mail your package (head shot, resume, and cover letter) to every union-franchised agent. Then, after a one week waiting period, start contacting each agency to ask for an appointment.

Send your package through ordinary mail. Sending your package by overnight or courier service may draw attention to your package initially. But after the receptionist opens the package and stacks your head shot and resume in a pile, the prospective agent won't know whether your package arrived by registered mail, overnight mail, or Pony Express.

To save money on postage and insure that your package arrives safely to a potential agent's office, consider dropping by and handing your package to the receptionist (or, if possible, to an actual agent). This delivery option gives you a chance to establish a friendly relationship with the receptionist or meet the agent in person. (Then again, you may just get the receptionist or agent angry or annoyed at your unannounced presence, so make sure that you don't interfere with anyone.)

Calling for an appointment

Give the agent plenty of time to receive and evaluate your package. Wait a week or so from the time you mail your package, and then start calling each agent to request an appointment.

Usually, the best time to call agents is at the end of the day when they aren't likely to be too busy. The mornings are usually the most hectic because the agents are likely to be making or taking phone calls from casting directors, producers, and studios. By calling late in the afternoon, you increase the odds that you won't make a nuisance of yourself.

When you call an agent, you probably won't get the agent directly, but the agent's receptionist instead. The receptionist generally serves double duty. He or she performs the routine office duties, such as answering the phone, typing letters, and mailing packages and, at the same time, serves as the unofficial screener, gatekeeper, and bouncer for the agent. Be nice to this receptionist because the receptionist may one day become an agent or (more immediately) may have the power to "accidentally" drop your package in the trash before the agent ever sees it, if you're particularly rude and obnoxious.

When you reach the receptionist, briefly state your name, explain that you recently sent your package, and ask whether making an appointment to talk with an agent about representation would be possible. Your greeting should sound something like this:

> "Hi, my name is John Doe, and I mailed Mr. Agent my head shot and resume last week. I'm seeking representation and would like to schedule an appointment to see Mr. Agent."

The range of responses you may get include

- **"I'm sorry, Mr. Agent is not interested."**

  This option is often followed by the harsh sound of the telephone hanging up in your ear. If an agent isn't interested in you, you may want to try again at a later date, such as three or six months later. You may have called at a bad time for that particular agent.

- **"I'm sorry, Mr. Agent is not looking at new talent at this time."**

  If you get this response, ask when the agent plans to be looking at new talent and make a note to call back and resubmit your package at the specified date.

- **"I'm sorry, Mr. Agent is not available right now."**

  Ask what time you should call back, and call back again at that time. If the receptionist gives you a vague time to call back, such as next week, ask for a specific date when you should call. If the agent or receptionist seems to be in a hurry, suggest a possible date, such as, "May I call back next Tuesday?" You may have to be persistent with an agent until you get that final yes or no.

- **"Yes, Mr. Agent would like to schedule an appointment with you."**

  Make sure that you get the exact time and date of the appointment and the address to the agent's office. If an agent (or the agent's receptionist) suggests a time or date that won't work out for you, don't be afraid to ask for an alternate date. But after you accept an appointment, clear out your schedule to make absolutely sure that nothing else like a doctor's appointment or your day job schedule interferes with that appointment.

The seasonal nature of agents

No matter what, you should never let anything stop you from contacting an agent in a professional manner. (Stalking or pestering isn't considered a professional manner.) Because agents are busy people, you should be aware that their work load changes during the year. After you're aware of the seasonal nature of show business, you can use that knowledge to your advantage.

For commercial agents, the busy season occurs in the fall when ad agencies start developing and filming commercials for the upcoming Thanksgiving, Christmas, and New Year's holidays. For television agents, the busy seasons occur at the beginning of the year and in the fall. In the fall, the major networks are busy developing and taping their new shows for the start of the upcoming season, which usually lasts from September to May. At the beginning of the year, the major networks are busy developing and taping new shows to replace the shows that got cancelled earlier in the season.

The slowest time for television agents is in the summer when most of the major network shows go on vacation and are simply shown as reruns. Another slow time for *all* types of agents is December when most projects are wrapping up for the holidays, and little new work is being developed. With less work to worry about, agents can spend more time seeking out new talent.

Although getting an agent to see you during the peak of the busy season (such as in the fall) is certainly possible, consider re-contacting agencies during a slower part of the year. An agent may tell you *no* if you contact her when she's busy, but may say *yes* if you contact her when she has more time available.

Why agents may turn you down

Ask those early agents why they rejected Kevin Costner, Angelina Jolie, and John Travolta, and they're likely to hide their faces and push you out of their offices without telling you anything. The truth is that everyone gets rejected by agents simply because no one knows who may hit it big tomorrow, next week, next month, or next year. So if you get rejected by an agent, don't take it personally. (Just consider yourself in good company with every major star since the history of acting.)

Sometimes, an agent may reject you because you may look too much like other actors that the agent currently represents. Other times, an agent doesn't believe that you currently have enough experience or training to justify taking on a new client at this time.

Take rejection professionally and get on with your acting career. The more agents you contact, the better your odds of finding at least one agent who agrees to represent you. If you're lucky, you may even find two agents interested in representing you. But remember, getting an agent to believe in you is just one step; the more important step is getting a casting director and producer to believe in you, too, by doing well at an audition.

You may very well wind up calling the same agent back four or five times over the course of several weeks, only to be turned away at the end. Don't despair! Just keep calling all the other agents until you've gone through the entire list and gotten some interviews.

If you've gone through the entire list of SAG or Equity franchised agents and they all told you no, don't give up! If your first package didn't grab an agent's attention, consider doing one or more of the following:

- Getting a new head shot
- Printing a new resume (hopefully, with some additional credits that you added since you printed your previous resume)
- Revising your cover letter to better promote your strengths as an actor

When you've updated your package, start with your list all over again and send out your new package once more. Most likely, agents won't remember your previous submission, so by sending them an updated package, you look like a new face to them.

Yes, it's still possible that after updating your package a second time, every agent on the list will turn you down again. (Nobody said that acting was going to be easy.) The key is persistence. If you really want to pursue acting, get more acting experience in theater or student films; update your resume, head shot, or cover letter; and try again until you find an agent who's willing to ask you in for an interview.

Interviewing with a Prospective Agent

If an agent wants to meet you in person, congratulations! You've just overcome one of the biggest hurdles in the acting business, so celebrate and then get ready for your appointment.

Preparing for your interview

Before the date of your appointment, make sure that you know exactly how to get to the agent's office and where you can park. That way, on the actual date of your appointment, you'll know how much time you should allocate for travel and parking, so you won't get lost or delayed. Nothing makes a worse impression on an agent than showing up late for (or completely missing) an appointment. If you can't keep an appointment with an agent, you may cause the agent to doubt your ability to keep an appointment to an audition.

Be sure to dress neatly for your appointment. If you want to promote a certain character or look, dress for the part. For example, if you look like a trustworthy business executive, emphasize that look in the way you dress. Just be careful not to go overboard or you may typecast yourself in the eyes of the agent who may think you can only play a Fortune 500 executive.

Although the agent will probably have a copy of your package in front of him during your interview, be sure to bring along copies of the following items just in case (The agent may want you to leave these materials with him, so make sure that you don't give an agent your only copies):

- Your head shot
- Your proof sheet that contains all the pictures taken during your head shot photography session (so the agent can tell you which pictures he likes best, which may not always be the picture you chose for your head shot)
- Your resume
- Favorable press clippings you may have about you
- A demo videotape (and DVD disc, if possible) that contains actual footage of you appearing in commercials, film, or television

The purpose of the appointment is to give the agent a chance to evaluate you as an actor, so be ready to perform for the agent. The agent may want you to perform one of your memorized monologues, so be sure to do a run-through before your interview. The agent may also ask you to do a *cold reading* from a script that the agent hands you on the spot.

To help you prepare for a cold reading, consider taking a cold reading workshop — discussed in Chapter 7. As an alternative, share scripts with fellow actors, get together, and practice acting from a script that you've never seen before.

Arriving for your interview

The most important thing to do is to arrive early. When you enter the office, tell the receptionist your name, who you want to see, and the time of your appointment. For example, "My name is John Doe, and I have a one o'clock appointment with Mr. Marvelous." The receptionist will likely check the schedule book to verify that you do indeed have an appointment and then will ask you to wait.

Even if your appointment is for a specific time, don't be surprised if you're still sitting in the agent's lobby half an hour later. Agents are busy people, and they may be on the phone, making a multimillion dollar deal while you're waiting. Don't take this personally. Just relax, be patient, and be assured that the agent isn't deliberately trying to make you suffer but is likely involved with something more important (translation: more lucrative) than interviewing an unknown actor.

Although waiting isn't fun, use that time productively. Now is a good time to rehearse your monologues in your head and to make sure that all the photographs, head shots, and resumes are neatly organized, so you can find and display them quickly. Relax and rehearse the highlights of your acting career that you want to talk about if the opportunity arises. In other words, use your waiting time to prepare for your interview because the way you conduct yourself at the interview may literally change your acting career (and your life) forever.

The receptionist may not consciously be watching you, but be aware that everything you do will be noticed by the receptionist. So if you're constantly pestering the receptionist for how much longer you have to wait, the receptionist will note these details and relay this information to the agent later after your interview. Based on the agent's assessment of you, along with any feedback from the receptionist, the agent may or may not decide to represent you.

Don't smoke, chew gum, or eat a sandwich while waiting. Above all, don't complain, whine, or moan to the receptionist, either. If you're serious about acting, you can afford to act like you don't mind waiting a little longer than you expected.

What agents want in an actor

Agents make money when actors make money, so it's in their best interest to find actors who can earn them lots of money while being easy to work with at the same time. An agent isn't just evaluating you as a potential client and an actor. He or she is also evaluating how you may appear to casting directors, producers, and anyone else who's in a position to hire you for a role.

When you meet an agent for the first time, the first impression that agent gets of you is based on the way you look and conduct yourself. Your clothes and posture can immediately tell an agent that you're a professional. Dress sloppily and slouch as you stagger into the office, and the agent is likely to believe that you'll make this same impression on casting directors.

After considering the way you look and hold yourself, the agent next evaluates the way you talk and answer questions. If your answers reveal that you've studied the business of acting and realistically understand the obstacles, the agent can see that you're prepared and knowledgeable. If your answers show you have no idea how the business of acting works, the agent will likely find a way to end the interview right away because agents don't have time to waste.

When the agent asks questions to start a conversation, what you say is just as important as how you say it. If you're an interesting person who shows a genuine enthusiasm for life in general and acting in particular, the agent will likely be impressed. If you give boring answers, you come across as a boring actor, and no one (probably not even your own mother) wants to pay money to see that.

The most important thing you can do is just be yourself. You can be reserved and shy yet still be interesting to talk to. Likewise, you can jump up and down and be totally enthusiastic yet still be a bore. Be yourself and let the agent evaluate your true personality.

Finally, the agent may evaluate your acting experience and training. But even previous experience and training can't make up for a sloppily dressed, unprepared, boring actor. This truth explains why newcomers can break into the ranks of acting every day — because they're more interesting than the current batch of veteran actors with more years of acting experience and training.

If you show tons of charisma, demonstrate knowledge about the business, and come off as an interesting person, you make an agent's job of promoting you to casting directors much easier. If you don't, the agent won't have much incentive to even bother promoting you. Agents only want to work with professionals, so the more professional you can appear to an agent, the greater the chances that the agent will want to represent you.

Conducting yourself during your interview

Eventually, the receptionist will inform you that the agent is ready to see you. Thank the receptionist and walk into the agent's office, maintaining your poise and appearance. Often times, when you arrive into the agent's office, the agent won't be waiting for you. Rather, the agent will be busy talking on the phone and may either ignore you altogether or usher you into a chair with a quick hand motion. Again, sit down and wait patiently until the agent is ready to talk to you. (In case you haven't noticed by now, part of acting is being able to handle the endless amounts of waiting.)

Starting off on the right foot

When an agent is ready to talk with you, he or she may start out with some preliminary chitchat just to help make both of you comfortable. Because the point of this interview is to evaluate how you come across to others, don't give short *Yes* or *No* answers. Instead, try to give the impression that you're darn happy to be there (you should be) and that nothing short of a space invasion can stop you from pursuing a career in acting.

Being nervous during an interview is only natural, and your prospective agent knows that, so just do your best to relax. Your goal is to promote yourself as an actor and prove to the agent that you can make that agent money through your acting skills. Because agents only make money when you work, an ideal client for an agent is someone who behaves professionally and appears to be skilled and talented enough to start earning money as an actor as soon as possible.

After the initial greetings and conversation, the agent will likely ask you a simple question like, "So, tell me about yourself." When this type of question arises, the agent wants to know about your acting career, not about your cat, how much you hate driving through traffic, or who your favorite movie stars may be. Instead, start out with your most impressive credits, such as, "I just finished performing the lead role in *The Wizard of Oz* in Dallas, which helped me earn my membership into Equity," or "I'm currently taking an improv workshop taught by the Second City improv group." The point is to show the agent that you're eager to learn and have some credible acting experience and training already.

Never insult or belittle anyone, such as a director, a star, or a producer. That agent just may be best friends with the particular person you're verbally attacking, which will just make you look like an idiot. If you're going to mention anyone's name, say something nice about them. Like your mom used to say: If you don't have anything nice to say, don't say anything at all.

During the course of the interview, the agent may ask to see your head shot and proof sheet. While studying your photographs, the agent may comment on what he or she feels are good pictures of you and which ones may be less than flattering. Don't be offended. The agent is simply giving you a professional opinion (and keep in mind that it's only one person's opinion) so rather than get defensive, ask what the agent liked or disliked about that particular picture. (***Note:*** If you meet with several agents and they all comment about how your head shot doesn't capture your true personality, take that consensus as a big clue that you need new head shots.)

Performing a monologue

If an agent is interested in you, he or she may ask you to perform a monologue or give you a script to see how well you can act, using a script you've never seen before. If the agent doesn't ask you to perform a monologue or cold reading, don't ask to do one. The agent may not be interested in you and doesn't want to bother seeing you perform a monologue. Or, perhaps the agent is interested in you but doesn't have time to see you perform a monologue. Either way, don't break out into one unless the agent requests it; you'll only look desperate.

If you get a chance to perform a monologue or read a script that the agent gives you, the agent may critique your performance. Don't be defensive! Just listen carefully and note any problems that the agent noticed so you can fix them the next time you perform. Remember, one agent may love how you act and another one may give you a long list of valid (or useless) suggestions, so don't take any criticism too seriously.

When performing a monologue, standing or sitting are both okay, depending on your particular monologue. But never touch the agent or anything in the agent's office! When performing a monologue or cold reading, don't worry about the physical layout of the room. If the script calls for you to throw a telephone across the room or slam a door, just act out the emotions of someone performing that particular action. Don't hurl the agent's phone against the wall or otherwise damage anything in the office (or else the agent may hurl you out the door). Just perform given the space limitations at the time and do your best. You want to appear as a professional actor, not a psychotic maniac who just escaped from an asylum.

While an agent is evaluating you, don't forget that this interview is also a chance for you to evaluate the agent. Look at the agent's office. If it's messy, disorganized, filthy, or located in a dangerous neighborhood in a building that looks like it should've been condemned a long time ago, that could mean that this agent isn't too successful.

During your interview, the agent may need to take an important phone call or two. Eavesdrop and try to figure out how this particular agent works. If the agent is constantly getting phone calls from Steven Spielberg or Russell Crowe, you'll get a general idea of how powerful this agent may be. Of course, if the agent is constantly getting calls from bill collectors, lawyers, or clients wondering why they haven't been paid yet, you may want to work on finding another agent.

Turing the tables: Interview the agent

Don't be afraid to ask questions during your interview. Here are some common types of questions to ask:

- **Who will represent me from your agency?** This is perhaps the most important question to ask a prospective agent. In small agencies that consist of a handful of people (sometimes even just one person), the person interviewing you will actually be your agent. In a larger agency, the person interviewing you may accept you as a client but pass you off to another agent within that same agency — often a junior agent. Getting a junior agent isn't always a bad thing. Such an agent may not have the influence, reputation, or clout of an older, more established agent, but a junior agent may be just as hungry to succeed as you are (or should be), in which case the junior agent may actually work harder to find you work.
- **How many clients do you represent?** By knowing how many clients an agent represents, you can get a general idea about how much individual attention you may receive. Remember, the lack of individual attention doesn't necessarily mean that the agent isn't any good — as long as he or she gets you work.
- **What category (businessman, sexy, the guy next door, sporty, and so on) of actor do you see me as?** Because agents are likely to represent a multitude of actors, they often lump them into different categories. That way, when a part comes up for a sexy, glamorous femme fatale, they immediately send off all the actors who fit that image. If you see yourself as a sexy, centerfold type but the agent sees you as an ordinary housewife and mother, you may not be happy with this agent because he'll likely send you out on roles for detergent or diaper commercials instead of the more glamorous roles that you want.

  Just because an agent sees you as a particular type of character doesn't mean that he or she is necessarily right. But if you get enough agents who see you as a certain type, chances are that you're probably that type of character — whether you want to accept this fact or not. Ideally, as an actor, you should be able to play any type of role possible, but if a certain look gets you more work, you shouldn't be shy about taking those roles, either.
- **How many other clients do you have in the category that you see me in?** The agent's answer will let you know how many actors you'll be competing against within the agency. If the agent has three dozen actors who look like housewives, the agent will likely send out all three dozen actors for the same roles. You'll not only be competing against the agent's other actors for a role, but you'll also be competing with these same actors for your agent's attention as well.
- **If you were to represent me, how would you direct my career?** By asking an agent how he or she would direct your career, you can get insights into how the agent thinks and what he thinks your strengths are. If your agent sees your career in commercials but you'd rather pursue film, you may not be happy with this agent if he rarely sends you out for film auditions.

- **What kind of work have you gotten your current clients?** Knowing this can give you a general idea what type of work you're likely to get. If the agent's biggest accomplishment for his actors was getting them to appear as giant quacking ducks in a local TV commercial, advertising the annual duck races in Deming, New Mexico, you can safely assume that this agent doesn't have much clout in the show business world. Maybe the agent will grow and expand, and you'll be able to grow and expand with him. Or maybe the agent simply can't do much for his clients, in which case you may want to reconsider this particular agent.
- **What do you expect from your clients?** By asking what the agent expects from his or her clients, you can determine the way the agent conducts business.
- **How do you prefer your clients stay in touch with you?** Some agents don't mind if their clients call to keep in touch, but other agents don't want a client to call unless that client has something important to say. If you don't like the way this particular agent works, you probably won't be comfortable having this agent represent you.

Finally, try to find out something about the agent's background. If the agent used to work as a casting director, he or she may have valuable contacts with currently working casting directors. If the agent used to work for a major studio, the agent may still have friends at that studio who can give information about upcoming projects before other agents get a chance to hear of them.

No agent is right for everyone. You have to decide what type of agent you'd feel most comfortable working with and who you'd trust to represent you. Ultimately, the right agent is the one who can get you the most work and the most money for your work.

Ending the interview

Let the agent end the interview. The interview may last a few minutes or an hour. The length of time spent doesn't necessarily tell you one way or the other whether the agent wants to represent you, but the longer an agent talks to you, the more likely you've piqued that agent's interest (otherwise the agent wouldn't be wasting valuable time talking with you). At the end of the interview, the agent may tell you one of three things:

- The agent can't use you.
- The agent needs time to evaluate your potential, so call back.
- The agent wants to represent you.

What agents don't want in an actor

Agents essentially promote actors, so, naturally, agents want to promote the actors whom they believe have the greatest chance of success. To get an agent to represent you, you need to give the agent reasons why you can and will succeed and eliminate any possible reasons for why you might fail.

One of the biggest warning flags for agents is an actor who's arrogant, egotistical, and overbearing — despite any past credits that actor may have. Nobody wants to work with an arrogant person, and agents know that they'll just be wasting their time representing an arrogant actor who's likely to turn off casting directors with an overly inflated ego.

Another big warning flag for agents is any actor who lies either on his resume or during the interview. Telling an agent that you played the lead role in a film that the agent absolutely knows someone else played simply labels you as a liar who can't be trusted, and nobody wants to work with people whom they can't trust, either. Rather than make up credits, be proud of the credits you legitimately accomplished, whether those credits include playing a bit role in a small film or simply completing an eight-week acting workshop.

Agents also steer clear of actors who don't have a realistic understanding of how the business of acting works. Many actors believe that as soon as they get an agent, their agent should do all the work for them. Wrong. An agent is your partner, not your mother. Work with your agent, and your agent will work with you. Sit on your butt and wait for your agent to work for you, and you'll be sitting on your butt for a long time.

If an actor understands how the business of acting works, he or she will also have a better understanding of the agent-client relationship. Expecting your agent to work exclusively for your benefit is unrealistic and will likely make an agent refuse to represent you at all or drop you from the agency as soon as possible.

Ultimately, your job as an actor is to make the agent's job easier, and that means being prepared, showing up on time, and doing your absolute best at every audition. Threaten to make an agent's job harder, and you probably won't ever get a chance to work with that agent (or maybe even any agent) at all.

You can get a general idea of the agent's mood by being a careful listener to both the words that the agent is saying and the tone he or she uses. An agent may tell you, "Good luck!" (Translation: "Get out of my office now!") Or that same agent may say "Good luck," and mean, "I sincerely believe that you're talented, and I hope that you succeed."

Agents never come right out and reject an actor (because they know that the actor they turn down today may become the superstar of tomorrow). Instead, agents may say that you're not right for that particular agency or that you're too similar to an actor that the agent already represents. This may or may not be the truth, but don't badger the agent and ask, "Why?" Simply thank the agent for the interview and leave on professional terms. (If you're lucky, you'll have other agents who are interested in you. Otherwise, you can always start the process of contacting different agents all over again.)

If an agent says that you're not right for that particular agency (because they specialize in glamorous types, ethnic types, or whatever else), don't be afraid to ask the agent to suggest other agencies where you may be more suitable. If the agent doesn't give you any specific names, don't push the issue. If the agent gives you some names, ask whether it would be appropriate to contact these other agencies and mention that that agent recommended that you contact them. Sometimes, agents genuinely believe that you may not be right for their agency, and sometimes, telling you that is just another way to get you out of the office right away.

Sometimes, the agent may want some time to think about your potential and will ask that you call back at a later date. Make a note of that date and call back on that date. When you call back, you'll likely reach the receptionist again (who may or may not be the same receptionist you met the first time). Explain why you're calling by saying something like:

> "Hi, my name is John Doe, and I met with Mr. Agent on June 4. He asked me to call back on this date to discuss representation."

At this time, the receptionist or the agent may tell you that the agent wants to represent you, or that the agent can't use you. If the agent passes on you, thank the agent for his or her time, hang up, and get busy contacting other agents. If the agent agrees to represent you, you'll have to schedule another meeting to show up at the office and sign a contract.

Sometimes, after a first interview, the agent may agree to represent you. If this happens to you after the first interview or after you've called back at a later date, get ready to sign a contract! (See the upcoming section, "Signing On with an Agent.") If an agent wants to represent you and you still have several other interviews with other agents, let the agent know that you'll be talking with other agents and that you'll give an answer by a specific date (and then do so).

Signing On with an Agent

Working with an agent is a business partnership, so before you sign on the dotted line, consider whether you think that you'll enjoy working with that particular agent. If only one agent agrees to represent you, you may not have much choice — any agent may be better than no agent at all. Then again, some agents can be worse than no agent at all. Choose carefully.

After you've made the decision to go with a particular agent, you have to sign a contract with that agent before he or she will actively represent you. When you sign a contract with an agent, you're agreeing that this particular agent will exclusively represent you. (See the "Working with multiple agents" sidebar in this chapter for more info on when signing with more than one agent is acceptable.) The typical initial contract is for one year, which gives both you and the agent time to evaluate one another. Presumably, after a year, both of you will know whether your business relationship is working. If both you and your agent are happy when the initial contract ends one year later, your agent may ask that you renew the contract for three additional years.

Never sign any contract without reading and understanding it as completely as possible. (For additional help, consider hiring a lawyer to help you understand the contract.) Be especially careful if you're signing a contract with a non-union franchised agency because if you have a problem, you won't have the union to protect you. A union-franchised agent will likely use a standard contract that the agency's used before, but you still need to read and understand any contract before signing it. If any parts of the contract aren't clear, ask the agent for clarification.

Two important clauses that any beginning actor should be aware of are

- **The "out" clause:** This clause states the conditions under which an actor may legally get out of a contract. The clause allows an actor to get out of a contract if the agent hasn't gotten him or her a certain amount of work within a given time frame. For example, an "out" clause may state that if your agent doesn't get you at least 15 days of work within any 91-day period, you can exercise your "out" clause and leave your agent. Of course, your agent can exercise this same "out" clause to rid himself of a particularly useless or annoying actor, too. (See the section, "Leaving Your Agent," later in this chapter.)
- **The clause authorizing the agent to cash your checks for you:** It's normal for your agent to cash your check for you because when you get paid, the production company writes a check out in your name but sends it to your agent to cash. Your agent cashes your check, keeps 10 percent for his commission, and writes you a new check for the remaining 90 percent. Because agents get paid when they get their clients work, an agent's not likely going to rip-off her clients and take more than she should. If an agent tried this, the union would no longer franchise that agent, effectively killing that agent's career. So let your agent have check cashing authorization. This clause simply guarantees that your agent will get his 10-percent cut as soon as the check arrives.

If you happen to sign with a non-franchised agency (something you try to avoid at all costs), be very careful about giving them check cashing privileges since they could take more than their share and you won't have a union to help you out.

Working with multiple agents

Some actors prefer working with just one agent, but others prefer working with two or more agents who specialize in particular fields. For example, if you sign a contract with an agent who specializes in theater, you can also sign with another agent who specializes in commercials or film. That way, you essentially have two or more agents looking for work for you simultaneously.

Agents typically specialize in one of the following fields:

- Theatrical and television (includes film)
- Commercials
- Young performers
- Adults

If you're lucky enough to find multiple agents who want to represent you, make sure that you don't sign with two different agents who specialize in the same field. For example, if you sign with an agent exclusively for getting you auditions for commercials, don't sign with a second commercial agent. Agents work hard to promote their clients, and if they find out that they're competing with another agent for you, they'll both get angry. Then you may wind up with no agent at all.

After you sign a contract, congratulations! You can now officially say that you have an agent. Now comes the harder part of actually getting work as an actor.

Working with Your Agent

Because your agent is your partner who shares in your success, you need to do the following when working with any agent:

- Stay in touch
- Follow the agent's advice for getting new head shots, taking additional classes, and so on
- Share information about auditions

Staying in touch

As soon as you sign with an agent, immediately ask how often you should contact your agent. Typically, agents expect all their clients to call (not drop in, but call) once a week or once every two weeks. By staying in periodic contact with your agent, you can demonstrate that you're still interested in acting and can keep your agent informed about any new developments in your acting career, such as any new classes you've taken. For example, if you just finished taking an improv class, call and let your agent know. If you just got back from filming a commercial, let your agent know that, too, to remind him that you're a working professional.

Be selective when calling your agent. If you call too often with irrelevant information (or just to say hi), you're simply wasting your agent's time. You want to be useful to your agent, not a pest.

Make sure that your agent has your up-to-date contact information (including your home number, your cell phone number, and any beeper or answering service numbers). If your agent can't reach you by phone right away, you may miss out on a lot of auditions. If you become too hard to reach, your agent may assume that you're not serious and stop sending you out on auditions altogether.

If your agent leaves a message about an audition, it's a good idea (unless your agent tells you otherwise) to call back to let your agent know that you'll be attending the audition. That way, the agent won't be left wondering whether all the actors he called will or won't show up at the audition.

If you're ever going be unavailable for any reason (taking a vacation, filming on location in Mexico, or whatever) call and let your agent know the exact dates you'll be gone and when you'll return. That way, your agent won't waste time trying to get you an audition during a time when you won't be around.

Following your agent's advice

An agent might see you and your promotional materials (head shot and resume) as absolutely perfect and ready to send out to casting directors. However, more likely, an agent may see the potential in you as an actor but ask that you modify your promotional materials in a way that the agent thinks will be best for you.

An agent may want you to take new head shots, may help you rewrite and format your resume, and may suggest certain classes you should take to improve your acting skills. Essentially, agents want to help you correct any deficiencies as an actor, so you can increase your chances of landing a role as quickly as possible.

Agents can be wrong sometimes, so if you strongly disagree with your agent's advice, say so. Don't be obstinate and stubborn about any disagreements but resolve them diplomatically and to everyone's satisfaction.

Sharing audition information with your agent

To an agent, nothing is more impressive than an actor who actively works to advance his own career instead of expecting the agent to do all the hard work.

Because agents are busy trying to look for auditions for all their clients, an agent possibly may overlook auditions or opportunities for someone like you. If you hear of an audition for a role that you think you can play, don't be afraid to call your agent and ask him or her to get you into that audition. For example, if you read in *Variety* or the *Hollywood Reporter* that a certain television series is looking for a 25-year old black actor (and you happen to be black and around 25 years old), let your agent know this news right away to see if your agent could get you an interview with that TV show's casting director.

By keeping your eyes open for acting opportunities, you can uncover possible audition opportunities that your agent may have overlooked. In the meantime, your agent is also looking for auditions for you to attend, too, so if you work with your agent, you can essentially double the number of possible auditions you would've found on your own.

Leaving Your Agent

An agent can give your career a boost by finding acting opportunities for you that you may never have known about on your own and relieve you from the burden of negotiating your own contracts. But eventually, the time may come when your relationship with your agent is stagnating or falling apart. When this happens, you'll need to consider the possibility that you may need to dump your current agent and find a new one.

Before you leave an agent, make sure that another agent has agreed to represent you. Agents are more apt to consider an actor who already has an agent than someone who doesn't. ***Note:*** When looking for a new agent, never insult or belittle your current agent. Simply explain to new prospective agents that you feel that you can no longer work with your current agent.

Also, if you're under contract, be sure that you have the legal right to dump your agent. Consult a lawyer if necessary.

Reasons to leave your agent

You may eventually consider leaving your agent for many reasons. Here are some possible ones:

- You don't trust your agent anymore.
- Your agent isn't getting much (if any) work for you.
- You've outgrown your agent.
- You disagree with the roles your agent picks for you.

Perhaps the biggest reason to leave an agent is if you don't trust your agent. You absolutely must trust that your agent is working for you. If you ask an agent to call a casting director and the agent says he'll do it but doesn't, and then lies about it afterwards, you may start to wonder what other areas your agent may be lying about. If an agent makes promises that he never keeps, you may not want to trust that agent either.

A second reason to reconsider your relationship with your current agent is if she hasn't sent you out on an audition in a long time (such as a month or two). Remind your agent with a phone call or a visit that you're still interested in acting. Keep in mind, you and your agent may encounter slow periods when there simply aren't that many opportunities for you, so don't blame your agent for the lack of auditions. Also, keep in mind that if you're a novice actor, your agent probably won't be calling you every day to give you new auditions. But, if your agent doesn't send you out on *any* auditions, your agent may have lost interest in you for one reason or another, and it may be time to move on to a new agent.

Eventually, you may feel that you've outgrown your agent. You may be getting along fine with your agent, but your agent is still submitting you for bit roles when you feel that you should be auditioning for larger, more lucrative, and higher profile roles. No matter how well you may like your agent, you may have simply outgrown your agent's capabilities, and it may be time to find an agent who can get you into the roles you feel that you deserve.

As a novice, you may be happy just landing any role, but as you get more experience, you may want to be more selective in choosing the roles that will help advance your acting career. Because agents make money when you make money, an agent won't necessarily have your best interests at heart. If your agent wants you to take as many roles as possible so that you can keep making him money (regardless of whether or not the roles will actually help your acting career), consider cutting ties. Appearing in the 32nd sequel of a film that most people forgot about long ago may bring you and your agent money right away, but performing in those types of roles won't necessarily help your career. If you spend all your time making money in meaningless roles, you'll never have time to appear in the more prestigious and, ultimately, more profitable roles.

If you think that you've outgrown your current agent, discuss this matter with your agent. Agents don't want to lose a working client, and if you start landing larger roles and earning larger paychecks, your agent would love nothing better than to help you reach this goal (and take 10 percent of your earnings, too).

While you as the actor can always choose to leave your agent, don't forget that your agent can always turn around and dump you first. Some of the reasons why an agent may want to dump an actor are

- You're hard to reach and don't return phone calls. See the "Staying in touch" section earlier in this chapter.
- You're embarrassing the agent and damaging the agent's reputation at auditions. Show up late, and both you and your agent look bad in the eyes of the casting director. Act like an arrogant, overbearing moron, and the casting director will start to question your agent's decision to represent you in the first place.
- You appear bored and disinterested in acting. If you decide that acting isn't for you, notify your agent and ask to break out of the contract. Agents are only too happy to let a disinterested actor go because that'll free up the agent's time to focus on finding work for actors who want to work.
- You aren't trying to help yourself. As an actor, you need to keep looking for work on your own and keep improving your craft by actually performing or taking workshops or classes. If you haven't gotten a role or taken a class in months, you probably won't be very good at acting. So it's only natural that an agent would want to drop you in favor of another actor.

How to leave your agent

Before you leave your agent, ask for an appointment to discuss your concerns. Often, a one-on-one meeting can clear up any misunderstandings and concerns that the both of you may have, so you can work together to rebuild your relationship. Still, no matter how much you may try to work with your agent, the time may come when you and your agent can no longer work effectively as a team. That's when you both need to go your separate ways.

Even if you absolutely hate and despise your agent, be polite and courteous. Your agent may still know some powerful people in show business, and if you really irritate your ex-agent, you never know what your ex-agent may say about you to people who have the power to hire you in the future.

The commonly accepted manner for leaving an agent is to write a letter, stating that you want to leave your agent. When writing this letter, keep it short, to the point, and free from any accusations or insults as shown in Figure 8-2.

Type your letter so that it's legible and save a signed and dated copy for your own records.

Dear Mr. Jones,

This letter is to inform you that your services as a theater agent for me are no longer required as of February 19, 2003.

Sincerely,

Your Name Here

Figure 8-2: The professional way to write a letter, stating that you want to leave your agent.

After you've written your letter, sign and date it, and then mail a copy to the following people:

- Your old agent.
- Your new agent (optional).
- The appropriate actors' unions.

To insure that everyone receives a copy of your notification letter, consider mailing your letter by using registered mail, which provides you with a receipt proving that your agent received your letter of departure.

You want your new agent to get a copy of the letter to let him or her know that you've officially severed ties with your old agent. (Of course, you want your old agent to get your letter to let him or her know that you're officially leaving.) You also need to send a copy of your letter to the actors' unions (whether you're a member of that union or not). That way, the union can keep track of which actors are being represented by which agencies.

After you get a new agent, make sure that your new agent understands what you expect and that you understand what your new agent expects from you. Although agents can greatly aid an acting career, even the best agent can't substitute for talent, personality, and professionalism on your part.

Even the best agent in the world can't promote a problem actor. If you keep having problems with different agents, the problem *might* be the types of agents you keep getting, more likely, the problem may simply be you. Ask yourself if you were an agent, would you want yourself as a client? If the answer is no, then consider correcting your problem behavior so an agent will want to work with you.

Chapter 9
Auditioning

In This Chapter

- Familiarizing yourself with types of auditions
- Getting ready for your audition
- Recognizing what casting directors look for in an auditioning actor
- Knowing what to expect from your audition
- Following up after your audition
- Handling rejection

Getting an audition for any role is a big step toward moving your acting career forward, and doing well at an audition gets you closer toward actually working (and getting paid) as an actor. Although auditioning may seem intimidating or frightening, relax. The next time you see a movie, a television show, a commercial, or a stage play, remember that everyone you see probably had to go through an audition. If those people can do it, certainly, you can do it, too.

This chapter discusses two common types of auditions you're likely to go through, how to prepare for each to maximize your chances of success, how to impress the casting director when it's your turn to perform, and how to evaluate your performance after the audition. Finally, we tell you what happens when you get a callback (and what the heck a callback is) and give you some tips for dealing with rejection.

Looking at Types of Auditions

In general, you could face two types of auditions: open casting calls (also known as *general auditions* or the more affectionate term *cattle calls*) and casting auditions (also called *casting interviews*).

Going to open casting calls (cattle calls)

Open casting calls get their name because they're auditions open to anyone, so don't be surprised to be standing next to a 300-pound man, a 4-foot-tall teenager, and a 69-year-old grandfather who are all vying for the same role to play the handsome, young basketball-playing college student who lives in a fraternity house.

Some of the advantages of open casting calls are that anyone can try out, even if the person doesn't have an agent. Open casting calls try to attract as many potential candidates as possible, so you'll often find advertisements for them in newspapers and magazines or on Web sites. Another advantage is that your chances of getting through the open casting call is actually pretty good, considering that 90 percent of the people attending an open casting call have no idea what they're doing and get weeded out almost immediately.

Of course, open casting calls also have their disadvantages. With so many people trying out for a role, the casting director can spend only a short amount of time evaluating each potential actor. That nugget of time means that you have about five seconds to make a good first impression on the casting director before you'll hear those four words that every actor dreads, "Thank you. Next, please!" (Sometimes, casting directors skip the pleasantries and just say, "Next!")

Another disadvantage is that casting directors often use open casting calls to fill relatively minor acting roles. Chances are good that Steven Spielberg isn't going to hold an open casting call to find the actor to appear in the lead role of his newest movie. So, if you want a more lucrative acting role, you need to attend more casting auditions. (See the "Casting auditions" section later in this chapter for more information.)

Sometimes, casting directors use open casting calls simply to meet new talent and re-evaluate veteran actors to see how much they may have (hopefully) improved. In these situations, the open casting call won't directly lead to a role, but if you impress the casting director enough, she may remember you the next time she's casting a project in the future and specifically call you in for a casting interview.

Even worse is that open casting calls can gobble up a lot of time that you could be spending at your day job, making money. Wasting hours of time just for the chance to audition for two minutes isn't most people's idea of fun, no matter how many "positive thinking" books they may have read.

The line for an open casting call usually starts at the door of the building and spills out on to the sidewalk. Because you may be standing for several hours in line, wear comfortable clothes (take an umbrella if it threatens to rain) and comfortable shoes (or bring a chair or pillow to sit or lay on), bring food and water, and bring a book or other item to keep yourself amused while waiting.

Despite the disadvantages, open casting calls can introduce you to casting directors and give you plenty of practice auditioning within a limited time frame in often less than ideal environments. Don't hesitate to get out there and attend an open casting call because you never know what may happen.

When conducting open casting calls, the casting director may specify that the audition will last a certain time, such as from 10 a.m. to 5 p.m. Get there early! If you show up at 10 a.m., you'll be lucky if you're seen by 5 p.m. If you show up 8 a.m., you'll probably audition around 2 p.m. If you show up later than 10 a.m., the casting director may not have time to see you at all.

Attending casting auditions

Most actors try to focus the majority of their time on attending casting auditions. A *casting audition* occurs when a casting director puts out the news that he needs to fill a certain role that requires an approximate age range and appearance, such as a certain ethnicity, height, build, or look.

Your agent sets up your casting auditions, assuming that you have an agent to represent you. (For information on how to find and work with an agent, flip back to Chapter 8.) When agents receive word of a casting audition, they immediately send out all the actors they represent whom they think may have a shot at winning that role. So, if you show up at a casting audition, don't be surprised to find that all the competing actors look almost exactly like you.

If you don't have an agent yet, don't despair! If you impressed a casting director during an open casting call, he may possibly invite you to a casting audition whether you have an agent or not. Sometimes (but not always), news of a casting audition leaks out through the trade publications or word of mouth. (Refer to Chapter 7 for more information about hunting out roles by reading trade publications.) If you hear of a casting audition, send the casting director your head shot and resume. If the casting director is impressed with your looks and credentials, he may invite you to the casting audition. (If you have an agent, contact your agent the moment that you hear of a casting audition and ask your agent to get you into the casting audition.)

Because casting auditions generally cast the more lucrative and higher profile roles, many actors (with or without an agent) try to "crash" the audition by showing up unannounced. In general, casting directors discourage this practice because it disrupts their schedules. Still, show business has no set rules, so if you do plan to crash an audition, keep in mind that you may have a small chance of making a good impression on an important casting director. However, you have a much greater chance of making a negative impression on that casting director. Make your choice and be prepared to deal with whatever consequences may happen to you afterwards.

Casting auditions offer several advantages over open casting calls. First, a casting audition is usually for a major (and, thus, more lucrative) role in a film, television show, commercial, or play. Second, you have fewer actors to compete with because the agents have weeded out the actors who are obviously inappropriate for the role.

Of course, casting auditions have slight disadvantages as well. Unlike open casting calls, casting auditions are often limited to clients of a select group of talent agencies. Because some agencies are considered more prestigious and reliable than others, casting directors may not always contact every available talent agency. That selectivity means that if the agency that represents you has a poor reputation, your agent may never hear of casting auditions for certain roles.

Another problem with casting auditions is that although the number of actors competing for the part is usually small, the competition can be very tough because nearly everybody has an equal chance (more or less) at landing the role. Still, if your agent thinks enough of you to send you out on a casting audition, that means that you have as much chance of winning the role as anyone else — so don't be intimidated by the other people in the room and do the best you can.

If you pique a casting director's interest, you could get a second audition, known as a *callback.* (For more details about callbacks, see the section titled, "Hoping for the Best that Can Happen: The Callback," later in this chapter.)

Some actors don't have to audition to get a starring role. When an actor achieves a certain amount of *star power* (which virtually guarantees that a certain number of viewers will see whatever the actor happens to appear in), directors and producers will design projects around that particular actor. A custom-designed project for such a star is called a *vehicle,* as in, "This latest movie is a vehicle to highlight Tom Cruise's sex appeal with the public." Obviously, an actor never has to audition for a role in a vehicle designed to showcase his talents, which is one sure sign that you've "made it" (at least temporarily) in the world of show business.

Preparing for an Audition

An audition is a job interview. On one side, you have the casting director, producer, writer, or director desperately hoping that the next person who walks through the door will be "perfect for the part," so that the auditioning can stop and the fun part of actually making a film, TV show, commercial, or stage play can begin.

On the other side of the audition process, you have aspiring actors and actresses hoping to get a role that will make them rich and famous (or at least rich). So, knowing the goals of each side of the audition process, how can you maximize your chances of getting cast from an audition? That's easy, you prepare for the part and then go out and do your absolute best. The only part of the auditioning process you can control is you, so focus on making yourself the best actor you can be and don't worry about what the producer may be thinking or what the casting director may be feeling when they see you walk into the room.

If you feel uncomfortable with any questions or direction the casting director gives you during your audition, don't be afraid to speak up. Casting directors may legitimately ask you to remove parts of your clothes to examine the way your body looks, or they may just be sleazy individuals who deserve to be eliminated from the face of the Earth as quickly as possible. So be careful and use your best judgment.

Planning for the audition

Whether you're attending an open casting call or being sent by your agent to a casting audition, be sure to do the following before every audition:

- **Find out the time, date, and location where the audition will be held.** If possible, visit the location of the audition the day before, so you'll know how long the commute is (via car or public transportation), where the best parking spaces may be, and what type of neighborhood the audition will be held in. Try to visit the audition site at about the same time of the day when you'll actually be arriving. If you don't have time to visit, then try to map out your route to the audition. If you're driving, make sure that you know what roads you need to take. If you're using public transportation, make sure that you figure out exactly which buses or trains to take.

  Auditions are often held in slightly dangerous to outright frightening locations (due to cheaper rent and availability), so you may want to make sure that you arrive (and leave) during daylight hours or bring a friend or fellow actor along for protection. If an audition is being held late at night or is in a really dangerous part of town, don't be afraid to leave and ask if you can audition at another time.

- **Gather several copies of your headshot and resume.** Usually, you need to hand out only one copy of your headshot and resume to the casting director, but being prepared never hurts. Take along extra copies just in case other people want a copy or in case they misplace your headshot before your audition. You're always better off having too many than not enough. (For more on headshots and resumes, see Chapters 4 and 5.)

- **If you have any appointments before your audition, cancel or reschedule them to give yourself plenty of time to get to the audition.** Don't schedule anything before your audition, such as a dental or salon visit, and make sure that you set aside plenty of time to deal with unexpected road construction, car accidents, subway delays, or (especially in big

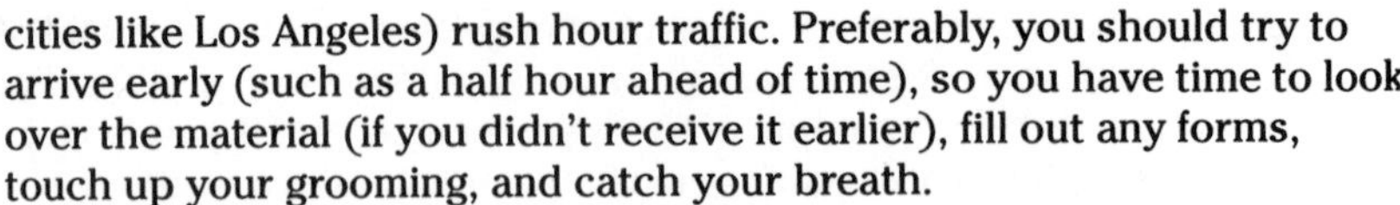

cities like Los Angeles) rush hour traffic. Preferably, you should try to arrive early (such as a half hour ahead of time), so you have time to look over the material (if you didn't receive it earlier), fill out any forms, touch up your grooming, and catch your breath.

- **If possible, ask for a copy of the script from the casting director, so you can study the part (or parts) that you hope to get.** If a complete script isn't available, try to get the pages or *sides* of the script that contain the dialogue that you'll present during your audition.

When you only have a few pages of a script that you'll be reading during an audition, those pages are called the *sides*.

- **Practice the night before your audition.** For many theater auditions, actors need to have at least two different *monologues* (a long speech presenting the words or thoughts of a single character) memorized and ready to perform. Be sure to brush up on your monologue delivery and performance the night before your audition while also rehearsing the role you hope to get. (See Chapter 6 for more information on preparing monologues.)

Deciding what to wear

Depending on the role you're trying out for, consider wearing appropriate clothes for that role. For example, if you're trying out for a role as a nurse or a firefighter, it helps to dress like a nurse or a firefighter (preferably in that order). But make sure you have additional clothes besides any uniform or costume you may need. Just because a casting director is looking for someone to play a police officer doesn't mean that she won't also want to see what you look like in ordinary clothes (in case the role is for an undercover cop).

Rather than dress in obvious clothes for a certain role, try dressing in less obvious ways. For example, anyone can look like a cowboy in a cowboy hat, but not many people can still look like a cowboy by wearing just jeans and a shirt. If you can dress up for a role without looking like you're going to a Halloween costume party, your subtlety could help distinguish you from the amateurs who think that renting a costume alone will help them win an audition.

For auditions that don't have specific clothing requirements, try to wear clothes that reflect who you are, and that you think make you look good. Most importantly, you want to be comfortable. Although you do want to look professional and well groomed, you may have to sit and wait for a long time (especially for open call auditions), and you want to be at ease. If you're singing, make sure that the clothing allows enough room to breathe; avoid clothes that are tight or constricting. Try to have a few nice outfits for all different kinds of weather that you can wear to various auditions.

Check out the following tips for additional advice on what to wear and what not to wear to your next audition:

- Avoid white clothes because they tend to absorb light when you appear on-camera.
- Avoid dark clothes and excessive (or noisy) jewelry that may distract from your face.
- Avoid heavily patterned clothes because the pattern can appear to jiggle and move on its own on-camera and can simply be distracting in person, too.
- If you have any tattoos or body piercings, now is the time to cover them up (unless your role calls for someone who may wear a tattoo or body piercing).
- If you need to wear a bathing suit, wear a modest one (not a thong bikini) and consider wearing it to the audition in case you can't find a safe place to change.

Bring a grooming kit to straighten up your hair or apply any last-second makeup. You want to look fresh, well rested, and energetic for your audition. Buy a small carry-on bag that's large enough to hold one change of clothes, all your grooming supplies, and your headshots and resumes. Your goal is to be — and look — organized. Dropping stuff on the floor as you walk doesn't help you one bit.

Arriving at the Audition

You may be auditioning for the part before you even arrive at the audition! So remember to act like a professional the moment you step out of your house and into the public eye. If someone cuts you off on the road and you verbally attack and threaten that driver, you may be unpleasantly surprised to find that the driver you nearly attacked is the casting director for your audition. Treat everyone with respect. Be nice to everyone before, during, and after your audition. Being polite overall isn't only the nice thing to do; it could also prevent embarrassing mistakes later on.

When you arrive at the audition location, collect any headshots and resumes you brought with you (you did remember to bring some, didn't you?) along with any change of clothes and grooming kits you may need. If you drive to your audition, find a safe place to park that's reasonably close to the location where the audition is being held. (See the section titled, "Planning for the audition," earlier in this chapter.)

The most important step to arriving at an audition is to check in with whomever may be in charge (usually someone other than the casting director). Checking in lets the casting director know that you are present and ready to audition.

When you check in, ask for the following:

- A copy of the *sides* (the part of the script that you'll be reading from during your audition).

  When you arrive, ask for the latest copy of the sides or script that the casting director is using, even if you already have a copy of the script. Often times, the script changes, so the part of the script that you have may be completely different from the one the casting director is now using.

- The particular role in the script that you should be studying.
- When and how the casting director will ask to see you. Sometimes, you just stand in line in front of a closed door, and you'll know when it's your turn to audition. Other times, you may be crammed into a tiny room, and the casting director seems to be calling out names at random (and if you miss hearing your name called, you could miss your chance to audition). So make sure you know how you will be called in for your audition because you don't want to have traveled all that way for nothing.

You may also want to ask the receptionist for an address where you can mail a thank-you card to the casting director after the audition. See the section titled, "Sending out thank-you cards," later in this chapter.

Rather than reading a script silently to yourself, find a place (such as outside or in a rest room) where you can actually speak the words and get into the physicality of the character, and analyze the script without any distractions. Sometimes, actors team up in pairs and help each other read a part. Just make sure that you don't roam too far away and miss your turn to audition.

Some malicious actors try to intimidate the competition by name-dropping ("Oh, I just got a callback from Steven Spielberg to star in his next movie"). These actors may also try to discourage you by boasting of their acting credits; if you believe them and bail out of the audition, they increase their chances of winning the role over of you. Remember, you have as much chance as anyone, no matter what your experience may be, so do your best and forget about what other actors may do or say.

Impressing a Casting Director

Casting directors want to find the best person for the role, which actually means selecting the best person out of the group of actors who happened to show up for that particular audition. Essentially, a casting director wants an actor who's easy to work with, takes direction well, and possesses enough talent to deliver what the casting director wants.

Beyond looking for an acting professional who looks neat, knows how to follow directions, and can act, casting directors also look for certain intangible qualities that may separate you from everyone else. Think of an audition as a date, and your job is to get a second date.

Casting directors are your allies, not your enemies. They are (for the most part) normal people, and most normal people want to be around other normal, energetic, sincerely happy people. If you fit that bill, you can endear yourself to almost any casting director.

What won't work in your favor when auditioning are anger, hostility, bitterness, cynicism, desperation, rudeness, and arrogance. Think of the type of qualities that repel you from certain people (such as your co-workers, in-laws, neighbors) and avoid exhibiting those qualities during an audition. You want the casting director to like you as a human being. Because show business is actually a small business, people tend to run into each other over and over again, which means you may meet the same casting director on several different projects throughout your acting career. The more likeable you are, the more likely you'll eventually get a role.

Sometimes, a casting director may be looking for a particular type of person to fill a role but after spotting someone during the audition process, suddenly decides to use that person instead. (Ripley, the lead character in the original *Alien* movie, was supposed to be a male character but got changed into a female at the last moment to accommodate Sigourney Weaver.) Casting directors are also looking for actors to fill other roles, so it's entirely possible that you could audition for one role but get another one instead.

Auditioning: What to Expect

When you're called in to audition, the only people present will include you, the casting director, and maybe a handful of other complete strangers staring at you. Some of these other people may be the producer, a camera operator (in case they're taping the auditions), the casting director's bored friend or relative, (in the case of a commercial audition) a representative from the advertiser, or (in the case of a musical) a dance choreographer or musical director. No matter who is in the room, treat everyone in the room with respect. If someone looks like a sloppily dressed janitor, that person could actually be the producer, so play it safe and treat everyone with courtesy.

By the time it's your turn to audition, the casting director has probably seen hundreds of other people ahead of you, which means the casting director and anyone else in the room is likely to be tired, bored, and irritable. Make the director's job easy and you increase your chances of having a successful audition. Make the job harder (by not being ready, talking too much, and so on) and you may seriously kill any chances of getting any role.

After brief introductions (and make sure you keep them brief), someone may ask for your headshot and resume if you haven't already handed one in. (Don't be afraid to pass out multiple copies of your headshot or resume.) At some auditions, someone may take your picture with a digital camera, so the casting director can review all the people who auditioned that day. Be sure to smile and look your very best. If your picture doesn't look anything like your headshot, you need to get a new headshot.

In the world of commercials, the way you look is extremely important because you'll be considered a salesperson for a product. To get a good look at you, the casting director may ask you to pose for a look at your front and side profile.

Next, someone tells you where to stand, which is usually a mark on the floor so the casting director and everyone else in the room can see you clearly.

If you're auditioning for a TV commercial, the casting director may start by asking you to *slate,* which simply means to state your full name clearly. When you slate, you may just say your name or your name followed by the agency that represents you.

The casting director then tells you to start. (Sometimes they say, "Action!" and other times they'll just say, "Go," "Start," or some other monosyllabic grunt of exasperation.) At this point, you're supposed to start acting the role.

If you're auditioning for role in a movie, TV show, or theatrical play, your audition may require you to sit in a chair, walk around, or stand still, depending on the part of the script the casting director asks you to read from. Whenever you audition, expect the unexpected, and be ready to work with unusual situations at a moment's notice. To help prepare for the unexpected, many actors take improvisation classes. With these lessons, actors learn to quickly improvise their way out of any acting situation and still remain in character.

Speaking your lines

When auditioning for a role in a TV commercial, you read from *cue cards*. Cue cards are like large flash cards that have an actor's script printed on them in big letters. If a TV performer forgets the lines, she ever-so-subtly looks at the cue cards and reads from them. The viewing audience doesn't see cue cards because the person holding them is standing next to (not in front of) the camera.

When auditioning for a role in a movie, TV show, or theatrical play, you read from a script. Keep the following script etiquette in mind when auditioning:

- If you just received your copy of the script moments before your audition, it's okay to ask for a little time to study the role (just don't take too much time and inconvenience the casting director).
- Don't be afraid to read directly from the script while acting. The important part is to see how well you can interpret the part, not how well you can memorize a script on short notice.
- Try to say the words of the script correctly, but don't be too worried if you mispronounce a word or two. If you completely mess up your lines, it's okay to ask if you can start from the beginning again.

During an open casting call or casting audition, another person may read lines with you. This person could be anyone from the casting director to another actor to the man who just delivered a pizza to the casting director for lunch. Many times, the person reading with you is not a professional actor and, therefore, may not give you much to work with. Don't let any acting inadequacies bother you; stay focused, and give your best audition. During a callback, however, you may be asked to audition and read lines with an actor who already has been cast. The casting director wants to see how you look and sound next to an actor who has already been assigned a role.

To avoid confusion and a messy audition, find out where you should focus your attention when you're reading the script. Requesting this information is a good idea if you're not reading with someone or if you have no camera to look at. In general, you want to look near the casting director (so he can see your face) but not directly into the casting director's eyes (so he can evaluate your performance without feeling the need to acknowledge or react to your acting).

You may be asked to read the same script several times with the casting director giving you suggestions to be angrier, more forceful, softer, and so on. This direction is a good thing! You want the casting director's attention because it means he (or she) is interested in you.

Minding your auditioning manners

A lack of courtesy shows disrespect, no matter where you are in life. If directed toward the folks running the audition, however, acting like a spoiled brat can kill an acting opportunity faster than you can say, "Exit stage left." Keep the following pointers in mind whenever you try out for a role:

- Never touch the casting director or any of his or her possessions, such as the notepad, laptop computer, food, and such. Doing so is rude and definitely works against you.
- Never smoke or chew gum during your audition. If you must smoke, do it outside where no one can see you and where your smoke won't interfere with others.
- If you bring a small tape recorder to record and then later evaluate your performance in the comfort of your home, hide the device so that it doesn't distract from your performance. Otherwise, the casting director may be looking at your tape recorder rather than watching you. Don't ask for permission to tape record because it will take time and distract the casting director. Just hide it in your pocket or purse and let it run.

Some casting directors frown on actor's tape recording their auditions while others don't care. So if you're going to bring a tape recorder, be aware that its discovery could work against you.

Making your exit

After you complete your audition, thank everyone (the casting director, the camera operator eating a sandwich in the back, the receptionist who helped you check in, and anyone else who may be sitting in the room). If you read from a script, be sure to hand that script back to the casting director or his assistant. In general, you want to leave the room exactly the way it appeared when you arrived.

Before leaving the audition, you may have to sign out and record the time you left. Union rules stipulate that actors can be held for only a certain amount of time at an audition, so the sign-out sheet verifies that you weren't kept for an abnormally long period of time. (See Chapter 3 for more on unions.) Even if you don't yet belong to an actors union, signing out shows that you are no longer on the premises. After you sign out, leave as quickly as possible, and congratulate yourself for what you've accomplished.

Preparing for the Next Audition

Like everyone, you have some days when all goes right for you and other days when all goes wrong. Sometimes, when everything goes right, you don't get the part, and sometimes when everything goes wrong, you do. Despite the outcome of any audition, preparing for the next one is important to do.

Auditioning, like acting, takes practice. The more you audition, the more familiar and comfortable you become with auditioning. Auditioning is a skill in itself, and as long as you keep showing up, continue learning from your mistakes, and keep improving, you increase your chances of one day getting the part.

Go to as many auditions as possible, even for roles that you think you won't get. You may surprise yourself and actually land a role, or the casting director may like you and decide to cast you for an entirely different role instead. Auditioning gives you a chance to land a job. Sitting on your butt at home doesn't.

Sending out thank-you cards

Many actors like to send out thank-you cards to their agents (if their agents set them up on the audition) and the casting directors. The purpose of thank-you cards is twofold:

- They make people feel appreciated.
- More importantly, they get your name back into the memories of the people who can help you, such as your agent or casting director.

The simple fact is that most actors don't send out thank-you cards because they don't want to take the time or bother with the expense of buying and mailing thank-you notes. That's exactly why you should send out thank-you cards — agents and casting directors get so few of these cards that doing so helps separate you from the teeming masses of actors trying to hit it big in show business.

Many actors have special post cards made up with their name, head shot, and one or two additional photographs printed on the front. Then they use these post cards for all occasions, such as writing out thank-you notes or notifying people of their latest accomplishments. (See Chapter 4 for more information about choosing a head shot to create a post card.)

In case the cost of postage and printed thank-you cards is too much for you, consider making up your own thank-you cards by using a computer or even by writing a neatly handwritten note. Deliver the thank-you note in person, to your agent or the casting director's office. Not only will this personal delivery save you money, but it gives you another chance to put your face and name in front of your agent and casting director, which further demonstrates your commitment and sincerity in working as an actor. (Then again, if you make a nuisance of yourself, you'll simply imprint in the agent or casting director's mind that you're a pest who should be ignored at every conceivable moment. So be professional, respect other people's time, and just drop off your cards without trying to see or talk to anyone as an ulterior motive.)

Evaluating yourself

After you're done auditioning, try to evaluate yourself as objectively as possible. Was there anything you're proud you did that you could do again at another audition? Did you do something really stupid that you should never ever do again in public? Everyone makes mistakes, and nobody will consider you a loser — unless you fail to learn from your mistakes and keep making them over and over again.

Consider the following post-audition pointers:

- **Evaluate your acting itself.** Ask yourself what you can improve upon and then decide right away what you can do to improve that particular skill. For example, if you stuttered too much, spend more time studying the script ahead of time. If you felt like your acting was wooden and artificial, maybe you need help in analyzing a script to understand the type of emotions the role required.
- **Evaluate the other aspects of your audition.** Were you tired and restless because you stayed up too late the night before? Did you look your absolute best or did it look like you just rushed in off the street and read the script without putting any thought into the character or material?
- **If you brought a tape recorder with you to the audition, listen to your audition as well as any comments that the casting director may have made.** During your nervousness at your audition, you may not have clearly heard what the casting director said. Playing back your tape gives you another chance to listen to see if you followed the casting director's directions or if he made a comment or remark that you missed, forgot about, or overlooked.

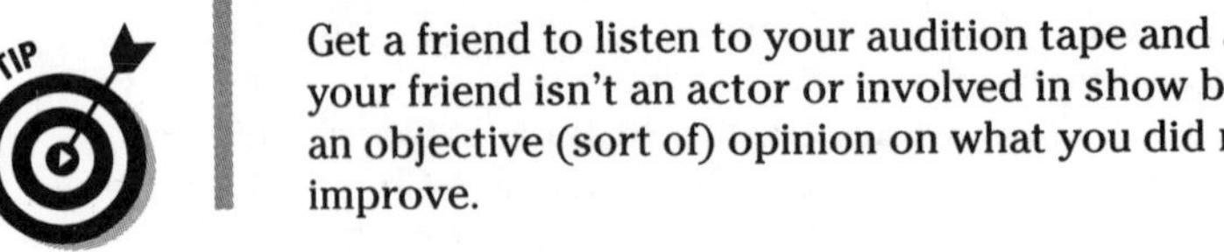

Get a friend to listen to your audition tape and ask for feedback. Even if your friend isn't an actor or involved in show business, he can give you an objective (sort of) opinion on what you did right and what you could improve.

Getting on with your life

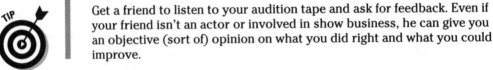

Nobody (and that includes all the big name celebrities and stars) gets every part that she auditions for every time. Despite the numerous auditions you attend, you probably won't get a large majority of them, but all it takes sometimes is getting that one good part. That one part could be either your big break or a huge steppingstone to giving you the confidence, experience, and money to continue your pursuit of acting.

After you complete an audition, you can't do anything more to change your performance, so get busy with finding out where the next audition may be (refer to Chapter 7), taking classes to improve your acting skills (flip back to Chapter 6), and otherwise getting on with the daily routine of your life as an aspiring actor. When you get that one *yes* that lets you know you aced an audition, you'll quickly forget all the *no's* that you got on the way to becoming a working actor.

Casting directors aren't always right. Although they do their best to find the best actors for each role, they sometimes pick the wrong people and completely overlook actors who are more talented and better suited for the role.

Hoping for the Best that Can Happen: The Callback

The best that can happen during your audition is that the casting director absolutely loves you and thinks you'll be perfect for the part — just as long as you come back again so he can compare you with the half a dozen other actors whom he also loves and thinks is perfect for the part.

An audition simply gets you a second chance, known as a *callback,* to get a role. (In some rare cases, you may even get the role after going through just a single audition.) After a casting director weeds out the initial hundred or so actors vying for a role, just five or six actors could remain whom he wants to look at a second time. Thus, the casting director calls back (hence the name) those promising actors to get a second look at them.

A callback is like an audition, except this time you're facing fewer (but tougher) competition, and you'll probably be treated less like a herd of cattle and more like a human being. Sometimes, you may have to go through several callbacks until the casting director is finally satisfied that he chose the right actor (which is not always the case, but that's out of your control).

Getting a callback is even more important than the initial audition because that means the casting director liked you for some reason (even if your relatives don't). Treat every callback seriously! Find out the time, location, and date for each callback and arrive early to give yourself plenty of time to look over the script (which may be entirely different from the one you read during your initial audition).

If you receive a copy of the entire script, read the whole thing so you can better understand the character you're supposed to play. That way, when you audition again, you'll have a better understanding what your character is supposed to be thinking and feeling at each particular point of the story.

When going on a callback, many actors wear the exact same clothes they wore during their initial audition, and they even wear their hair the exact same way. The reason for this is that casting directors see lots of people, and if you look exactly like you did during your first audition, chances are good they'll remember who you are. If you show up wearing completely different clothes with different colored hair, the first reaction of the casting director may be, "Who the heck are you and what happened to that aspiring actor I was about to hire?" Although many casting directors say it doesn't matter what clothes an actor wears during a callback, wearing the same clothes you wore during your first audition doesn't hurt your chances.

If you're being called back for a different role, you may want to wear different clothes that may be more appropriate for the new role. So, if your first audition was for a cowboy but your callback is for the role of an astronaut, you probably wouldn't want to wear the same clothes that made you look like a cowboy. Ultimately, the clothes you wear should help you look appropriate for a role.

You may get a role after the first audition, after a single callback, or after two or three additional callbacks. You may never know for sure if you've won a role until your agent calls and gives you the good news — and that's when you can start celebrating. After you're done celebrating, you can start looking forward to attending your next audition all over again in pursuit of your next acting job.

Dealing with Rejection

A producer or casting director may not choose a particular actor for a number of reasons, and most of those reasons rarely reflect on that actor's talent. If you don't get called back for a second look, don't sweat it! Producers and casting directors often reject actors for obscure and irrational reasons. The most common reason is that they're looking for a certain type of person to fit a role. For example, the casting director may want an actress who is 5 feet 3 three inches tall with red hair and freckles. If they find someone who matches that description, they'll hire that person instead of you.

You may be a great actor that the public absolutely loves, yet you still won't be right for every possible role. An actor like Michael J. Fox has a loyal following, yet no one would have thought of casting him in Arnold Schwarzenegger's role as the cyborg in the Terminator movies. So although some roles will always be inappropriate for you, other roles will always come along that are absolutely perfect for you. How do you find those perfect roles? You have to keep auditioning long enough, and, eventually, you'll find them.

Similarly, the casting director already may have cast the roles for the other actors, and now, she needs someone who would fit in with the looks of those other actors. If you don't look like you could be the teenage daughter of the actors playing the roles of the mother and father, the casting director will hire someone else and pass on you.

Don't fool yourself, though. Sometimes, you won't get a role because someone else really is better qualified or more experienced than you. Then again, sometimes you may beat someone else for a role just because of the way you look, regardless of either one of your abilities. Just keep in mind that rejection at an audition doesn't necessarily mean the casting director hates you or that you're worthless as an actor. Just think — the casting director may hate her ex-husband and you happen to remind her of him, so she'll wind up hating you, as well. Sometimes, casting directors may be in a bad mood and hate everyone they see who happens to audition that particular day. Because there can be so many reasons why you didn't get the part — from how you look with the other actor they have cast, to having the wrong hair color — don't get too upset because you thought you aced that audition but didn't get the part.

Don't take rejection personally. Every actor (yes, every one of them) has been rejected at one time or another while pursuing an acting career. Although failing to get a part never feels good, never give up if you really want to become an actor. The more you can remain upbeat and positive, the more likely you eventually will land a role sometime soon.

Part IV
Scoping Out the Markets

"Excuse me! Witch number three, your line is also 'Hail,' not 'Whatever'."

In this part . . .

You can work as an actor in many different ways. The traditional route is through the theater, with the ultimate goal being to appear on Broadway. Another more modern route is through appearing in films and television shows in Hollywood.

But this part of the book also discusses other forms of acting that can be even easier and, sometimes, more lucrative, such as commercials and voice-overs. Still another market for actors is working as extras in film and television. As the name implies, extras get paid to fill out the background of a scene, but they also get a sneak peek at the workings of an actual film or television set. If you have children, this part of the book also explains how you can get your child into show business.

The acting market is big enough for all types of actors, no matter what their appearances, backgrounds, or talents may be. So browse through this part of the book and find all the available acting markets in your area and start working as an actor right away!

Chapter 10

Acting in Film and Television

In This Chapter

- Comparing film and television acting to theater acting
- Knowing what happens on a set
- Exploring the film and television markets

Film and television actors come from all sorts of different backgrounds, and none of them followed the same route to success. Some actors started as models (Brooke Shields), some as stand-up comedians (Tim Allen), some as musicians (Will Smith), and some as classically-trained Shakespearean actors (Patrick Stewart, the captain of *Star Trek: The Next Generation*).

Although you can rarely predict a career in film or television, you can prepare for one. And this chapter helps you do just that by telling you about the differences between theater acting and film and television acting, what occurs on a typical film and television set, and what kind of work you may be able to find as a film and television actor. (One of the more lucrative markets for television actors is commercial acting, so take a peek at Chapter 11 if you're interested in the commercial market.)

Landing a Job

Film and television are unpredictable, so what launched an actor's career in film or TV today probably won't work tomorrow. Sometimes, actors who couldn't buy a role on television suddenly skyrocket to success as film actors. And sometimes, television actors, no matter how popular they may be, can't seem to break through as big movie stars.

Although dreaming of acting in soap operas, situation comedies, or feature films is certainly okay, make sure that you audition for anything and everything that becomes available to you. You never know what strange quirk of luck may spin your career in a completely different direction that you never thought was possible. The secret to success is to keep honing your acting skills through actual work experience and training classes, keep looking for and attending auditions, and keep focusing on improving yourself as an actor and a person. Just rely on a little bit of luck, a little bit of timing, and a lot of persistence to get your first big break into film or television acting. You just may become the next big star that everyone's talking about.

Film and Television Acting Versus Theater Acting

Although theater acting is often considered to be more prestigious, film and television acting is generally considered to be much more lucrative. A stage actor may have to wait for years before he or she can perform the lead role in a hit Broadway play. But literally overnight, you can appear in a hit film or TV show and start earning more money than most theater actors ever make during an entire lifetime.

Besides being lucrative, film and television acting offers a much greater chance of becoming a star overnight. Because film and television shows can be broadcast over and over again throughout the world, appearing in a film or television show puts your face in front of millions of people on a daily basis for several years. More people know the names of actors who appear in soap operas and sitcoms than they do the names of their own political representatives or next-door neighbors.

In film and television, acting occurs in segments unlike theater where actors tell an entire story from start to finish every night. As a film or television actor, you may spend an entire day shooting a handful of scenes, and then there's a good chance that some of your best scenes may wind up getting edited out of the final version. As a theater actor, talent is everything because costumes, makeup, and special effects can't hide bad acting. As a film or television actor, looks are everything with talent being of secondary (or sometimes nonexistent) importance.

Not all actors in theater can make the transition to film and television, and vice versa. Theater actors may find that performing for a camera lacks the intensity of performing for a live audience, and film and television actors often fail to project their voices and gestures for a large audience to see. If you're not having much success auditioning for theatrical roles, perhaps you may be better suited for film and television, and if film and television auditions never call you back, perhaps theatrical acting may be more your style. (Then again, you may just need to take more classes to become a better actor no matter what medium you choose.)

Another big difference between theater acting and film and television acting is that theater allows you to perform for a live audience night after night. The reaction the actors get from their audience helps them to know what works and what doesn't and to tweak their performances accordingly. Because film and TV actors perform for a camera, they often don't have the opportunity to see what works for audiences and what falls flat. For example, if you're shooting a funny film, you don't have any idea how funny (or awful) something may be until that film is actually released. Many TV sitcoms try to overcome this problem by taping in front of a live studio audience — not only so they can use the recorded laughter for that show's laugh track, but also so the actors (and sometimes the writers) can get the audience's reaction as to what's funny and what isn't.

To compensate for the lack of an audience, film and television actors often perform the same scene over and over again with minor (or sometimes major) changes in acting, movement, or attitude. Then the director chooses the best scene to use. As a result, film and television acting often gives actors a chance to experiment more freely with their acting.

Fine-Tuning Your Performance on Film

Because film and television can show anything from two people eating dinner at a restaurant to spaceships blowing entire planets to pieces to microscopic people swimming through a vein filled with white blood cells, acting in film and television requires an additional set of skills. Some of these skills are:

- Knowing how to play towards the camera
- Acting consistently with each take
- Acting scenes out of order
- Dealing with the technical aspects of filmmaking

Playing to the camera

In film and television acting, you often don't have the luxury of a live audience giving you feedback of any kind. Instead of a theater full of people, your audience is just a camera, the camera operator, the director, and any sound, light, and makeup technicians who happen to be standing around at the time. This means that you need to use your imagination and pretend that the cameraman staring at you is actually your long-lost lover, or that the stern look on the director's face is actually the friendly face of your best friend. When you play to the camera, you have to project emotions to the unblinking eye of the camera.

The magic of test audiences

A new film or television pilot represents millions of dollars at stake, so studios try to reduce their risks by using *test audiences* to provide early feedback on how well a particular film may be received by the public. Test audiences are usually made up of people who are randomly recruited from movie theater lines and asked to watch a version of a film that hasn't been released yet. In exchange for seeing a film for free (and getting a chance to see the film before the rest of the general public gets to see it), test audience members have to fill out a fairly detailed survey stating what they thought of the film in general, what five things they liked best, what five things they disliked, which scenes they liked the most, and which characters they felt that they could identify with.

The idea is that if test audiences don't like a particular character or scene in a film, the studio can go back, reshoot new scenes (or edit out existing ones), and release a (theoretically) stronger film that will please more people and, ultimately, make more money as a result.

Test audiences made a difference in the endings of *E.T.* and *Pretty Woman.* Initially, test audiences hated *E.T.* because E.T. died in the original version of the film, so Steven Spielberg filmed an ending where E.T. lives. In *Pretty Woman,* Julia Robert's character was supposed to reject Richard Gere's character in the end until test audiences encouraged the studio to change the film in favor of the happier ending.

Of course, test audiences can also be glaringly wrong, too. Test audiences of 1939 thought that having Judy Garland sing "Somewhere Over the Rainbow" slowed down the pace of *The Wizard of Oz.* Despite this negative feedback, the studio kept the song in and, now, most people can't imagine how the film could've worked without that song being included.

So, if you ever land a role in a film or television pilot and think that you did a decent job acting in front of the camera, you may be surprised (or dismayed) at how test audiences may really perceive how you performed in front of the camera.

To help you "play to the camera," keep these ideas in mind:

- **Know where the camera (or cameras) are at all times.** You can give the best performance of your life, but it will be worthless if the camera can't see your face.
- **Know what the camera is trying to capture.** If the camera is capturing a long shot of you off in the distance, concentrating on arching your eyebrow to convey emotion will just be a waste of time since the camera won't be able to see it.
- **Know where the other actors and props are located in relation to the camera.** If you step too far forward or back, it's possible that your body or a simple gesture such as waving your hand could block the camera's view of another actor.

Watch a television show or movie on video with the sound turned off. Without any dialogue to guide you, can you guess what the actors are trying to say to each other? Body and facial gestures can convey more information to an audience than you may think. By studying films or television shows with the sound off, you can study how gestures can help (or hinder) an actor's performance on-camera.

The old saying, "The camera never lies," means that acting in front of the camera captures every gesture, motion, glance, breath, and posture. In the theater, you can get away with talking to another actor while shifting your glance from the actor to someone in the audience, but try that in front of a camera and your eyes will look like they're shifting from side to side for no apparent reason. Unless you're going for a certain look that you want your character to portray, inappropriate movements and gestures, such as shifting eyes, can destroy your acting performance in film and TV productions.

Videotape yourself performing a monologue and look for inconsistent actions that detract from your character. For example, if you're portraying a tough, confident business-person, twirling your hair around your finger and biting your lower lip probably isn't going to support your character portrayal. Ask your acting coach or instructor to watch your videotape and comment on the type of character that he or she thinks you're portraying. If you think that you're portraying a tough guy but your acting coach thinks that your portrayal represents a timid character, you may need to work on your acting skills so that you can portray different types of characters consistently and accurately.

Acting consistently with different takes

Because everything you do in front of the camera is captured on film or videotape, you just have to deliver the best possible performance once and that's it, right? Wrong. In the world of film and television, you don't just perform a scene once. You perform the same scene over and over again, so the director can capture that scene from different angles, or so the actors can try different variations on their acting. The same scene may be shot three or four or ten different times.

If a director wants to shoot the same scene over and over, don't take it personally as if you're doing something wrong. Sometimes, the director just wants to capture several different versions of the same scene, so he can choose the best one to use later. Actor John Ritter once did a commercial where he had to kiss a woman on the beach, and the director made him do it over and over and over again. John Ritter couldn't understand what he was doing wrong, so he asked the director. The director told him that he wasn't doing anything wrong. The director just wanted to capture the different appearances of the sunset in the background.

To maintain consistency from take to take (a *take* is a short scene that is captured on film or videotape), you have to be aware of continuity each time you perform a scene on camera. (*Continuity* means making sure your body movements and appearance are identical in every take.)

From an actor's point of view, the problem with shooting the same scene over and over again is that the actors never know which scene (or parts of each scene) will ultimately be used, so they need to be consistent in appearance, movement, and acting in every scene. Part of the first scene that they filmed may possibly be used followed by part of the last take of that same scene and ending with part of the fourth take of that same scene. When viewed one after another, the different mish-mash of scene takes need to blend together seamlessly as if the camera recorded the whole scene at once from start to finish.

To achieve this illusionary blend of reality, film and television actors must know how to act consistently each time they perform a scene, no matter how many times they need to perform it. For example, if an actor is filming a dinner scene and picks up a glass with his right hand, he needs to remember to keep picking up that same glass with his right hand and not suddenly do a retake of the same scene and pick up the glass with his left hand.

The script supervisor is supposed to make sure that the actors perform, dress, and act as closely as possible with each retake of a scene. That way, when the director chooses which scene takes to use, the film or television show gives the illusion that every part of the scene was captured at the same time (even if part of the scene was captured in the morning, another part captured in the afternoon, and the beginning part of the scene captured last).

When doing multiple takes, you need to know the difference between acting and action. *Acting* deals with how you portray a character, while *action* is what you do with your body and any props. When shooting another take, subtly altering your acting is okay, but make sure that your actions remain exactly the same.

To see how well you can maintain consistency in front of the camera, videotape yourself and a fellow actor performing a short scene. Shoot the scene three or four times, and if you have a video editing program for your personal computer (such as *iMovie* found on the iMac), you can mix and match different parts of each take together. Does the entire scene appear to have been filmed at the same time, or can you notice any glaring differences between parts of the scene (such as your hand resting in your lap in one scene but not in another)? If you notice glaring differences, you may need to work on being more consistent when performing in front of the camera, whether it's the first take or the twenty-third take.

Continuity mix-ups

Nearly every film sports continuity flaws that a whole host of fans enjoy pointing out. Common types of flaws include modern items being seen in a historical film (in *Titanic,* one of the passengers boarding a lifeboat can be seen wearing a digital watch), camera operators and other filmmaking equipment being caught on film (in *Jurassic Park,* you can see a hand holding the raptor's tail as the raptor opens the kitchen door), actors or props suddenly disappearing or changing positions between camera angles of the same scene (in *Ghost,* Patrick Swayze's killer gets hit by a car and tumbles into the gutter, but in the next shot, the killer is sprawled across the hood of the car), or illogical or inconsistent scenes (in *The Matrix,* when Keanu Reeves arrives at work, the name of the company is Metacortex, but once he gets inside, a banner on the wall says that the company's name is really Meta Cortechs).

To find out more about continuity problems in your favorite movies, visit Movie Bloopers (`www.moviebloopers.com`) or Movie Mistakes (`www.movie-mistakes.com`), two of many Web sites dedicated to spotting continuity problems. So the next time you appear in a film or television show, try to remember to keep your clothes, body position, and gestures exactly the same for every take. You can't single-handedly prevent a film from having continuity problems, but at least you can help minimize the chance that *you'll* wind up looking stupid on film.

Successfully acting scenes out of order

Besides maintaining continuity throughout multiple takes of the same scene, you also have to worry about continuity between different scenes. For financial reasons, film and TV shows are often shot out of order. For example, if a film opens and ends with a scene on the Golden Gate Bridge in San Francisco, the director has two choices:

- He can shoot the beginning scene on the Golden Gate Bridge and then move on to shoot the rest of the film until the end when the film crew and actors will need to travel back to the Golden Gate Bridge to film the ending.
- Or, he can save travel and lodging expenses by shooting both the beginning and ending of the film on the Golden Gate Bridge at the same time (while the actors and film crew are already set up).

Not surprisingly, most directors opt to save money and shoot scenes out of order.

As a result, on your first day on the set, you may possibly shoot the last scene of the film. Then on the final day on the set, you may shoot the first scene. If your character is supposed to be timid and shy at the beginning of the film but aggressive and domineering by the end, your acting must reflect these characteristics. If you fail to act appropriately in a scene, your character won't make any sense when someone views the scenes in their correct order.

(Many actors mark up their scripts with notes for how their character should be acting and feeling in every scene. That way, when director shoots a scene out of order, the notes in the actors' scripts can remind them how to portray their characters accurately.)

Videotape yourself and your fellow actors performing three consecutive scenes from a play. Now perform and record the last scene, take a 10-minute break, record the first scene, take another break, and, finally, record the middle scene. Rearrange these recorded scenes (by using a video editing program on your personal computer, such as *iMovie* on an iMac) and play them in order. Do the three scenes appear to flow as if they really did occur one after another? Or does the acting appear jumpy and inconsistent from one scene to the other? If your acting is inconsistent between the different scenes, you may need more work acting in front of the camera.

Hitting your mark

In film and television acting, *blocking* (which means choreographing each actor's movements in a scene) must be absolutely precise so that the camera can capture every actor and anything else of importance in the scene such as a gun laying on a table. Moving to your exact position on a set is known as *hitting your mark*. If you can't consistently hit your mark exactly, the lighting or camera focus may be messed up, and the director won't be able to use that particular take in the final film or television show.

The following list includes three tricks actors use to help themselves hit the mark. Give each one a try to see which is more comfortable for you.

- Put a chalk mark on the floor where you're supposed to stand, so when you walk on to the set, you can know exactly where you're supposed to stop. That way, you'll be perfectly in focus of all the cameras.
- Count the number of steps needed to reach the mark.
- Look for the mark out of the corner of your eye while acting at the same time.

Recognizing different shots

When browsing through a film or television script, you may see different camera directions, such as *long shot, medium shot, close-up,* and *two shot.*

By knowing the type of shot you'll be appearing in, you can concentrate on giving your best performance in front of the camera for that particular type of shot. Here's a list that describes each type of shot:

- A *long shot* films an actor from a distance, which can mean that the actor may appear as an unrecognizable speck on the horizon or as a barely recognized face. Long shots typically are used to establish a setting (such as a long shot of a man on horseback riding through the desert), which, in turn, quickly establishes the time, place, and genre of the film.
- A *medium shot* reveals more details of an actor, such as showing the actor sitting in a chair in the middle of a crowded living room that's filled with empty beer bottles, old cardboard pizza boxes, and half-empty bags of potato chips. Medium shots typically show most or all of an actor's body along with any additional scenery around him.
- *Close-ups* focus on a specific feature, such as an actor's face or hands, or on a prop, such as a gun or key lying on the sidewalk.
- A *two shot* simply includes two actors in a scene, such as two actors sitting at a table, eating dinner.

Dealing with close-ups

One unique aspect of film and television acting is the *close-up*, where the camera zooms in so that a single actor's face fills the screen. (In the early days of film, many audiences got confused when films used close-ups because it appeared that the actor's head was suddenly decapitated from his or her body.)

Because a close-up usually involves one actor only, you may have to act out intense emotions all by yourself in front of the camera. Sometimes, a fellow actor may read his lines to you off-camera, so you can react. But other times, you may be forced to pour out your heart and your soul to the camera, the camera operator, the director, and anyone else who happens to be wandering through the set at the time.

A close-up can be the most intense type of acting you'll ever experience because your face is all that the audience sees. On the plus side, you're the star for that particular scene. But on the negative side, you may always have the fear that you'll make the biggest fool out of yourself, and the close-up will only highlight your embarrassment for everyone to see. When acting in a close-up, just do your best and realize that no matter how well (or poorly) you may act, you'll always have someone who likes you and others who criticize what you do. Because you can never hope to please everybody, do your best to please yourself (and the director as well).

Perform a scene with another actor, but only record yourself on videotape. (For added effect, edit out the sound of the other actor's voice, so you can concentrate solely on your own performance.) Now, videotape that same scene all by yourself without performing with another actor. For an added challenge, have your fellow actors work the camera, stare at you, or otherwise populate the scene behind the camera without helping you act one bit. View the two different scenes and see whether you can tell which scene was recorded with the aid of another actor reading lines to you and which scene was recorded by yourself.

Two unique close-ups that you may encounter while acting in film and television are:

- *Chroma Key* (which involves acting in front of a big blue screen that blocks out the background, so the director can later add another image on to that blue screen, such as special effects of asteroids flying towards you)

  When performing in front of a blue screen, you have to muster up your imagination and pretend that you really do see those asteroids heading your way when you're really looking at nothing but a blue screen. If you're in a scene with other actors, the group can collectively stare at the blue screen and support each other's acting, but sometimes, you may be alone, which makes acting very difficult.

- Intimate love scenes (when you may appear half naked in a close-up, either by yourself or with your fellow actor)

  Besides the uncomfortable feeling of being half-naked with another actor (whom you may or may not like), you also have the added problem of pretending to talk to someone on an intimate basis while a sound technician hovers a microphone over your head, the director watches the action like a Peeping Tom, and the camera operator aims and focuses the camera in your direction. To help you deal with intimate love scenes (especially with someone you really don't like), pretend that the other actor is really someone you do like. Hey, nobody said that acting was going to be easy.

The film crew is on your side and wants to do everything possible to help you succeed. So even though the sound and lighting technicians may be staring at you with blank looks on their faces, they want you to do the best job possible. After all, the sooner you get the scene done right, the sooner they can be done for the day and go home. If you feel uncomfortable, ask the director for help, and he'll often try to accommodate you as best he can, such as kicking out everyone from the set who isn't absolutely essential at the moment.

Performing on a Set

Film and television sets can be noisy, chaotic, and busy places. If you're inside a studio, the set (which always looks smaller in person than it does on TV) may be crammed with a multitude of lights dangling from the ceiling, cameras mounted on huge stands that roll back and forth, and cables snaking their way across the floor. And the actual set itself, which consists of wooden walls (some of which may move), may be crowded with furniture and decorations to make different parts of the set look like an actual interior of a house or office.

If you're *on location* (which means you're filming outside of the studio buildings and lot), the set may be even more hectic. You may be outside in a public area, such as a park, beach, or sidewalk or inside a house or office building. When you arrive on a location set, you may see police cars redirecting traffic, barricades closing off the streets around the set, a virtual convoy of trucks (containing dressing rooms, makeup and costumes, and sound, lighting, and camera equipment with cables of different sizes and colors neatly wound in coils and hung on the inside walls of the trailer), and the all-important catering truck that dispenses hot meals and provides a constant stream of snacks through the day. If filming takes place outdoors, you may also see generators parked on the street along with lights and cameras mounted on mobile cranes, making the entire set look like a military invasion.

To give yourself an idea of what being on a working set is like, attend a live taping of your favorite late-night talk show or situation comedy the next time you're in New York or Los Angeles. Studios freely invite people to watch a taping, so the actors and talk show hosts can play their jokes off the audience and see what works (and what doesn't work) based on the audience's laughter. The taping for a half-hour sitcom typically takes three or more hours, so be prepared to spend most of your time watching the technicians prepare the next scene. Getting tickets to some of the more popular shows can be extremely difficult and may require contacting the network directly. For less popular shows, visit one of the many Web sites that offer free tickets to show tapings. Here are a few of these sites:

- Studio Audiences (`www.studioaudiences.com`)
- Television Ticket Co. (`www.freetvshows.com`)
- Free TV Tickets (`www.tvtix.com`)

A typical day on the set

Actually, there is no typical day on the set. Every day is different because a different problem occurs every day. On the set, the weather may start to rain (and kill any chance of filming a sunny beach scene), or the equipment may break down, lights may burn out, and film may jam. Actors can also pose different problems, from being late to getting hurt on the set to being too unprofessional (such as being drunk) to show up and perform that day.

Expect the unexpected (such as tempers among the film crew heating up, people treating you rudely, or having to film an intimate love scene with an actor you can't stand). If you're ready to act under the most adverse conditions imaginable, you'll do fine on a film or television set.

Arriving on the set

Usually a day or two before you're supposed to be on the set, your agent (or one of the many assistants, such as the second assistant director) will call and give you directions to the set and the time you're supposed to be there. Be sure to get plenty of rest and arrive early. (The stars, of course, get someone to pick them up and drive them to the set.)

The following list helps organize the early part of your day on the set:

1. **Upon arrival, check in with one of the assistant directors, so they know that you're on the set and available.**

   When you arrive on the set, stay on the set. If you must leave the set for any reason, be sure to let one of the assistant directors know where you'll be at all times. The time you decide to go to the restroom may be the time that they suddenly need you in a scene, and if you keep the director or stars waiting, you may find yourself out of a job.

2. **Grab something to eat from the caterer if you're hungry.**

   Try to eat before you head to the makeup and costume department. After you're in costume and makeup, the simple act of eating and drinking suddenly takes on much more significance because you have to be careful that you don't wipe egg off your face (and mess up your makeup) or spill orange juice on your sleeve (and mess up your costume).

3. **Go to the makeup and costume department.**

   Sometimes, you may visit the costume department first and then visit the makeup artist depending on whether the costume department may be too crowded at the moment or if the makeup artist needs additional time to apply your makeup.

   Makeup: Depending on the type of scene you'll be filming, applying the appropriate makeup can take a few minutes to several hours. (Actors in *The Planet of the Apes* had to arrive several hours ahead of time — around five o'clock in the morning — so that the makeup artists could spend the next few hours applying the ape makeup to their faces.) After the makeup artist has applied your makeup, don't do anything to alter, modify, or "improve" it in any way. Sometimes, your makeup may look odd or less than flattering on you, but makeup artists know what looks good on camera, so you need to not change their work. If you feel that your makeup isn't right, ask the makeup artist to correct it. Fixing and applying makeup is the makeup artist's job, not yours.

Costume: After you're in costume, check to make sure that it's comfortable because you may be wearing it for the next ten hours or so. If you're in a particularly bizarre outfit, such as a hoop dress from the Victorian times or a Klingon battle outfit, make sure that you know how to remove part of your costume so that you can use the restroom. In case you're unable to remove part of your costume easily for using the restroom, don't be afraid to ask one of the many assistants on the set to help you or to find someone else who can help you.

Going through the process of makeup and costume can take up the better part of the morning. So if you arrived at six o'clock that morning, you may be ready by eight or nine o'clock. Unfortunately, the rest of the actors may still be getting makeup applied or fitted into costumes, and the technicians on the set may still be checking the lighting and readying the set, so be prepared to wait some more. Because you'll be spending most of your time on the set waiting, you may as well take some time to study the script so that you know your lines.

At long last: Filming a scene

When all the props are in position on a particular set, that set is known as a *hot set*, which basically tells everyone (including the director) not to touch anything on that set.

When the set is hot and the time's finally come to shoot a scene, an assistant will round up the necessary actors, and you may go through some rehearsals. The purpose of these rehearsals is partly so that the actors can rehearse their lines and partly for the technicians to check that nobody's movement blocks another actor from the camera or puts a shadow on another actor's face. (To capture as much of a scene as possible, multiple cameras usually will be recording the scene. One camera may be focused on two actors, a second camera may just be focusing a close-up on one actor, and a third camera may just be focusing on the second actor.)

When the director is ready to start filming, the following process takes place:

1. **Someone yells, "Quiet on the set!"**

   If the set is outdoors, you may hear these words relayed from one person to another, so that everyone is aware that filming has begun. Someone is stationed at every possible entrance leading towards the set to keep everyone away and to remind everyone to keep quiet. If the set is in a studio, a loud bell rings to alert everyone that filming is about to occur. Someone shuts all the doors leading to the set and stations himself outside the door. To alert anyone outside, a red light above the door outside starts flashing and will only stop when the filming is done for the moment.

Quiet on the set! means exactly that. Microphones are more sensitive than you may think, and any conversation or extraneous noise will be picked up and could possibly ruin a scene. When you hear, "Quiet on the set!" stop all talking — even whispering — unless absolutely necessary.

2. **Various technicians and directors shout out seemingly bizarre phrases in the following order:**

   Assistant director shouts, "We're going for a take. Roll sound."

   Sound technician shouts, "Sound rolling." (Translation: "We're recording every noise, so everybody had better shut up now.")

   Assistant director shouts, "Roll camera."

   Camera operator shouts, "Camera rolling." (Translation: "We're starting to film now, so nobody better get in the way of the camera, and the actors had better be ready to start acting.")

   Sound technician shouts, "Speed," (Translation: "The movement of the film or tape is now synchronized with the movement of the tape recording the sound.").

   Assistant director shouts, "Mark it," (Translation: "Put the clapboard in front of the camera, so we know what scene and number take of that scene we're filming.")

   Slate person shouts, "Scene 12, take three."

   After stating the scene number and take number, the slate person holds a clapboard in front of the camera with the scene and take number printed or scribbled in chalk across its front, slaps the top part of the clapboard down, and quickly darts away. (In case you're wondering, the clapboard allows the director to synchronize the sound with the film. As soon as the sound of the clapboard snapping shut matches the visual image of the clapboard snapping shut, the director knows that the rest of the sound and visual images of that particular take will match up, too.)

3. **The director yells out, "Action!"**

The time to get into character is *before* the director says, "Action!" Before you hear "Action!" make sure that you're in position and then remain perfectly still. The moment you hear "Action!" you should already be in character, ready to start acting.

Now's the time to put all those acting classes and workshops to good use and act the best you can while making sure that you hit your marks, perform your blocking correctly, and ignore all the distractions (such as having a microphone dangling back and forth over your head while hot floodlights blind you and make you sweat).

Depending on how long the scene may be, the actual filming may be as short as a few seconds or as long as several minutes. No matter how long or short the scene may be, remain in character! If you have to sneeze, do so in character. If you or another actor flubs a line, remain in character! Sometimes, the director may find that a foul-up is actually better than any of the rehearsed scenes and use a scene where you accidentally coughed and spilled your drink in the final film.

After you hear the director say, "Cut!" you can relax, but not too much. Stay in position because the director may want you to move your head an inch to one side and film the scene starting with the last line. If the actors immediately walk away, sit down, or otherwise drastically disrupt their positions after hearing, "Cut!" the director won't be able to recapture part of the scene with the actors in the exact same positions.

No matter how brilliantly you thought you performed in the scene, you'll probably have to do it again (and again, and again). In the world of television, where looming deadlines (the show must be done by Friday, so it can air three weeks from now) force taping to go much quicker, you may only need to perform the same scene a handful of times. In the world of film where the financial stakes are much higher and getting the scene filmed right is more important without the pressure of a fixed deadline, a director may film the same scene a dozen or more times.

Sometimes, the director will only want to reshoot part of a scene, such as the middle or the first three lines of dialogue. Out of these multiple takes, the director may only choose to keep, or *print*, a handful. At the end of the day, the director (and anyone else really important) may view these selected prints to review how the film is progressing. Viewing these prints is known as *watching the dailies*.

Obviously, the director won't use all printed scenes. But having as many printed scenes as possible gives the director a choice to use only the best scenes or the best parts of different takes, which are then smashed together to give the illusion that each scene was shot in one take.

Filming a single scene can take an hour or more. Although performing the same scene may be tedious, it's certainly not as bad as what your fellow actors are going through because they have to just sit around and wait while you're busy filming your scene. If you think that performing the same scene over and over again is tedious, think about working as a waiter for the next ten years. Waiting for your big break (or any break, for that matter) is much more tedious in comparison.

In the world of film, the director may be lucky to get one or two scenes shot before lunchtime and another one or two scenes shot before the end of the day. In the world of television, the director may simply plow through the taping from start to finish with only a few short breaks in between.

What to do when your scene's done

When you're done shooting a scene, stay on the set, stay in costume, and don't mess with your makeup. Even if you aren't supposed to appear in any scenes scheduled to be shot that day, stay on the set. The director may need you to say a line or walk around in a later scene. Never leave the set until the assistant director or production assistant tells you that you can leave the set and go home.

If you're scheduled to appear in scenes to be shot the following day, the assistant will let you know what time to show up, and you get the fun of starting the whole "typical" day on the set all over again.

Before the crew breaks down a set, the director may ask for everyone to be quiet one final time, so the microphones can record the silence on that particular set. Silence in film is never the same because the silence you hear outside in a forest is different from the silence you hear in an abandoned subway station. If the director needs actors to dub in new dialogue into the scene later, the actors can use the recorded silence for the background noise.

Participating in Post-production: Looping

Even after the filming or taping is done, you won't be quite done just yet. When reviewing a rough cut of a film, the director may notice that the microphone didn't pick up an actor's voice or that some outside noise is interfering with the actor's dialogue. That's when the director may ask the actors to return to dub in their own dialogue — a process known as *looping*. Scenes showing an actor in a long or medium shot usually require looping because the microphones may not have been able to get close enough to the actor's mouth to record his or her dialogue.

In looping, you have to go to a recording studio, which contains one or more sound-proof rooms with a microphone and a screen. The idea is that you get to watch yourself on the screen and try to dub in your dialogue, one or two lines at a time, to match the movement of your lips exactly.

You may be looping in an intense love or anger scene or responding to another actor, but you're the only one in the room, and you recorded that scene months ago. To help you out, the sound technician can play back the dialogue that they recorded during the original shoot, so you can try to repeat the rhythm, tone, and cadence of your original dialogue. Then you have to act your heart out in front of a microphone while watching yourself on a screen. Each scene may require different ways of speaking. For example, looping an intimate love scene will force you to speak differently from how you would if looping a high-speed, car chase scene.

For most actors, looping is the most boring, tedious, and difficult part of acting, but it's also completely necessary, too. Think of looping as a challenge, not a burden. Have fun with lip-synching yourself and look at looping as one final way for you to improve your performance before the general public sees it.

To give yourself an idea of what looping can be like, videotape yourself doing a scene without recording any sound. Then try to speak your dialogue to match the movement of your lips as you watch your video. Doing this exercise probably won't be that easy — or very exciting, either. But at least you can be prepared for the task when the time comes to do it for real.

Gaining Experience and Exposure by Working in Different Markets

Although the goal of most actors is to star in a multimillion-dollar feature film, the careers of most actors usually don't start there. Instead, most actors work in a multitude of different film and television markets to earn money, gain valuable working acting experience, and gain valuable additional exposure for further promoting themselves as actors.

Options in the film market

In the unofficial hierarchy of show business, feature films are the most prestigious and lucrative, but starring in a feature film is nearly impossible unless you're already a known name. Acting in smaller productions first can help you jumpstart a career that may lead to feature films in the future. Here are some of your film options:

- **Independent films (usually films produced by a small studio or sometimes just one person):** These films offer actors a chance to star in a film and showcase their talents. Positive reaction to an independent film can boost an actor's career to the larger feature films, starting out as supporting characters and gradually evolving to co-stars and, finally, principal players.
- **Cable and network TV films:** Many production companies produce films designed specifically for cable or network television broadcast. Films designed for cable viewing often use big-name movie stars, while TV films (usually a two-hour film that airs as a *movie of the week* or a three- or more-hour film that's broadcast over a span of a few days as a *mini-series*) tend to use both major film and television stars. But both types of films offer another way for aspiring actors to break into film acting in supporting roles.

- **Straight-to-video film market:** These types of films are usually *low-budget films,* (which are films shot with a minimal amount of money with few props and special effects). Unlike appearing in an independent film, acting in a low-budget slasher-type horror flick or a sci-fi film probably isn't going to attract too much attention to you because the acting and storyline are usually simplistic and laughable. But you can pay your bills with your earnings and get great acting experience and a credit for your acting resume.
- **Student film market:** Not to be overlooked, student films can give you experience acting in front of the camera and put you in contact with the writers and directors of tomorrow. Student films won't pay you anything, but they give you a chance to peek behind the way films are made, so you can better understand the technicalities involved. Because student films require plenty of volunteers, you may find yourself starring in a student film while also helping move props around, sew costumes, apply your own makeup, and work the cameras at the same time. Because filming can be so expensive, student films rarely have the luxury of shooting multiple takes on a scene.
- **Industrial films:** These films are created by corporations to teach their employees safety procedures, to provide a short orientation on their new workplace, or to offer tips for improving productivity and increasing harmony in the office. Industrial films are also produced for use in the classroom, such as a short film teaching kids the dangers of taking candy from strangers or how to cross the street safely. Basically, when a corporation or organization produces a film, the films are called industrial films.

  Although an industrial film is meant for a corporation or organization's own use and is rarely shown to the general public (and industrial films aren't likely to make anyone rich or famous), they can help actors pay their bills and get valuable acting experience working on a film set. After appearing in an industrial film, you can use your best scenes to create a demo reel to show casting directors and agents how you look and act in front of the camera.

Options in the TV market

The television market in the United States includes the three major networks (ABC, CBS, and NBC), the smaller, but still growing Fox, Warner Brothers (WB), and United Paramount Network (UPN), and cable networks (such as HBO and Comedy Central). The types of shows on these networks include hour-long dramas (such as *The Sopranos* on HBO), half-hour situation comedies (such as *Will and Grace* on NBC), and soap operas (such as *General Hospital* on ABC).

- Hour-long dramas are similar to films because they may rely on special effects (such as exotic sets made to look like a spaceship) and may require acting on a set inside a studio for a few scenes and then traveling to a different location for another scene. To give a drama a more realistic look, many dramas are shot on film, making them more expensive to produce as well. (Unlike videotape, film cannot be erased and reused. In the future, many directors like George Lucas have been shooting movies using digital video technology, which offers the sharpness of film but with the ease of editing like videotape.)
- Half-hour situation comedies (sitcoms) are almost always shot inside a studio and shot on videotape to save money. Taping a sitcom usually takes a week, where the first part of the week is spent rewriting the script, the middle part of the week is spent rehearsing, and the final day of the week is spent taping one show as a dress rehearsal and a second show in front of a live audience.
- Soap operas, like situation comedies, shoot the majority of the time on a set inside a studio. Because soap operas are broadcast daily, production is always frantic and fast-moving. One or more complete episodes may be shot in a single day, and actors often have little time to rehearse and memorize their lines before they have to perform. Of all the different types of acting, soap opera actors tend to work the longest hours — ten or twelve hour days, five days a week is common. Although grueling, soap opera acting provides steady work year-round (unless, of course, the writers kill off your character).

Anyone appearing in a drama, situation comedy, or soap opera has accomplished an important goal, even if the show gets canceled three episodes later.

Create your own *Wayne's World*

Even in a large city, such as Los Angeles or New York, appearing on a public access cable channel to gain experience in front of the camera is often an easy thing to do. Public access channels allow anyone to put on a show of any kind (with the exception of pornography). Contact your local cable company, and you can either try to get on an existing public access show or start your own show.

Public access talk shows are the easiest to produce because they essentially consist of just a host and invited guests chatting on a set with chairs and a desk. Trying to produce your own public access situation comedy or drama can be difficult because you need to create a set (or shoot on location) and write scripts. Still, if you want to exercise your writing abilities, give it a try and see what happens. You just may find yourself earning more money as a writer than an actor, or you may be able to sell a script with you attached as a star.

Chapter 11

Acting in Commercials

In This Chapter

- Getting yourself in a commercial
- Identifying different types of commercials
- Getting paid in various ways
- Understanding the markets for commercials

In the world of commercials, the product is the star. Acting in commercials won't necessarily make you a celebrity (unless you appear in a particularly popular commercial, such as Mr. Whipple for Charmin bathroom tissue). But commercial acting can be extremely lucrative, requires little time, and puts your face in front of the movers and shakers of show business who can help you break into the larger film and television markets.

Best of all, commercial acting is also more open to accepting newcomers than any other type of acting. This chapter discusses the wonderfully weird and wacky world of acting in commercials and how you can get started right away.

Understanding How a Commercial Gets Made

A commercial gets made because a corporation or business wants to advertise a product or service. In the world of commercials, this corporation or business is known as the *client*. And because the client is paying the bills, the client has the final word about what goes into a commercial, how it looks, and who performs in it.

Here's the typical process that a company or organization goes through to get a commercial on the air:

1. **The company contacts an *advertising agency*.**

   The advertising agency helps the client decide what they want their commercial to promote.

2. **The advertising agency comes up with several possible ideas for the client to choose from.**

   Most commercial ideas include humor, sex appeal, a miniature story, a celebrity spokesperson, popular music, special effects, stunts, or a combination of these themes to hook the viewer's attention.

3. **After the client chooses one of the ideas proposed by the advertising agency, the advertising agency hires a production company to produce the commercial.**

4. **This production company hires a casting director, who, in turn, contacts different agents to search for actors to play specific roles.**

5. **During a commercial audition, a representative from the advertising agency and the client may be present to choose the actors they want to callback and ultimately hire for the role.**

6. **After the client and the advertising agency agree on the actors to hire, the production company begins filming the commercial, which can take a day or more to complete.**

   Once again, a representative of the client and the advertising agency may be present on the set to ensure that the commercial properly promotes the client's product or service.

7. **When the commercial is done filming, the client and advertising agency representatives may be in the editing room along with the director to decide which scenes to keep and which to throw out.**

8. **When the commercial is completed, the client takes one last look at the finished product and often releases the commercial to test audiences to gauge their reaction.**

At any time, the client can decide to kill the commercial. Even after a commercial has been finished, the client may decide never to air the commercial for various reasons. As an actor, you still get paid whether or not the commercial ever airs, but if it doesn't air, you'll miss out on a potential source of income known as *residuals* (or *royalties*), which is an additional payment each time the commercial appears on television (discussed in more detail later in this chapter).

Preparing for a Career in Commercials

Although nearly everyone loves looking at young and beautiful people, commercials need actors of different ages, looks, and ethnic backgrounds to target different audiences. Having a toddler advertise denture cream wouldn't make any sense, and neither would having a centerfold market a children's toy. Because commercials need a wide range of actors, eventually, you'll be able to find a role that's just perfect for you.

After you decide to pursue work as a commercial actor, you may need to take additional classes to prepare you for the slightly different world of commercial auditions.

Taking a class or workshop

Because the more lucrative and numerous acting jobs come from commercials, many classes focus strictly on teaching actors how to audition for commercials and how to act during a commercial in order to best emphasize a specific product.

These workshops can teach you seemingly trivial but crucial information that can make the difference between getting a role in a commercial or being rejected. These workshops teach skills like how to hold a can of pork and beans in your hands properly (don't cover up the label), ways to improve your odds of landing a role in a commercial audition (dressing the part and acting cheerful), and how to play towards the camera, even while moving.

A commercial workshop can also guide you through the mechanics of a typical commercial audition where you stand in front of a camera, *slate* (state your name and agent), and *profile* (turn from side to side to allow the camera to capture you from different angles). In addition, you can practice auditioning in front of the camera while reading off cue cards. At some commercial auditions, the advertising agency may have a storyboard available, which contains sketches of what the advertising agency envisions the commercial will look like. By studying this storyboard, you can find out what the advertising agency may be looking for in an actor. (More on commercial auditions later in this chapter.)

Studying working actors

The best way to learn about commercial acting is to actually work on a dozen or more commercials. Until you manage this feat, the next best way to learn about acting in commercials is a lot easier — just watch television. Study the faces that appear in commercials because these people's faces are obviously what attracted a casting director to hire them for their particular roles. What kinds of people tend to play business executives? Kids just out for a good time? Housewives, mothers, and fathers? Bosses, doctors, and police officers? Casting directors need faces that instantly project a certain role, so by studying the faces of working commercial actors, you can get a general idea of what types of faces casting directors have used in the past and what types of faces they may likely use in the future. This kind of evaluation can also give you an idea what types of commercial roles you may be best suited for based on your appearance.

As much as you may want to believe that you can play any role, your physical characteristics can instantly typecast you in certain roles more so than other roles. For example, an actor with a thin face, glasses, and long hair tied in a pony tail may not be cast to play the part of a business executive in a suit, flying in first class, no matter how good that actor's acting abilities may be. Yet that same look may help that actor fit into a role calling for a computer hacker. An agent can help you decide which types of roles you may be best suited for, but remember that agents can always be wrong. So consider their advice carefully before radically changing your appearance.

Besides studying the faces of working commercial actors and noting what types of roles similar faces get cast in, also study the way actors speak, gesture, and hold their body posture. For example, if you have an upcoming audition for a role as a business executive in a cellular phone commercial, study how other actors portray business executives in car, computer, or even antacid commercials. By seeing how business executives look and act in all types of commercials, you can get a better idea of how to modify your behavior and appearance to more closely model what commercial casting directors look for in actors portraying business executives (or any other type of character for that matter).

Unlike film and, to a certain extent, television and theater, casting directors rarely cast an actor in a commercial that challenges the stereotype. In a film, you may see an articulate, clean-shaven, well-dressed actor portraying a cab driver. But in the world of commercials, you're more likely to see an older, overweight, grubby, fast-talking, chain-smoking actor portraying a cab driver — which is how most people picture cab drivers.

Hiring a commercial agent

Although commercial auditions occasionally hold open casting calls, the best way to get an audition for a commercial is through an agent. (Refer to Chapter 8 for more info on finding and hiring an agent.)

Many actors have two or more agents, one for film and television and another just for commercials. To find a commercial agent, ask your fellow actors for references, get a list of approved agencies from the SAG or AFTRA union offices, or browse through a current edition of *The Ross Reports.*

Of course, having a commercial agent can get you into an audition, but actually getting the job is still up to you. To increase the odds of landing a commercial acting role, you need to focus on your appearance and your acting.

Auditioning for a Commercial Role

In the world of commercials, people are always happy, streets are always clean, and children are always well-behaved. No tragedies occur in the world of commercials that the right product can't clear up, nobody ever gets seriously hurt, and nothing offensive or insulting ever appears (except inadvertently).

The key to acting in this artificial world of commercials is to be likeable at all times. If viewers like and sympathize with your character, they'll likely have positive feelings towards the product being advertised as well. And if you come across as likeable during your audition, the casting director will likely have positive feelings towards you, too (and will then hire you to do the commercial). The following sections give you more advice on auditioning for a commercial role.

The commercial's client is likely to be on the set during your audition, so you don't want to ruin your chances before you start by saying something negative about the client's product or service. If you don't know who the client is, don't insult any type of product at all. If you're auditioning for a soda commercial, you probably won't help yourself if you inadvertently insult the company's products by saying that you prefer a different soda.

Fitting the part

As an actor in a commercial, you're selling a product by presenting the virtues of a given product or service by acting out a story. But because actors only appear in a commercial for a brief amount of time, the viewers don't have time to get to know their characters like they can for actors in a television series, nor do actors have time to gradually develop their roles like they can do in film and theater. So when you audition for a commercial, the first thing casting directors will notice about you is whether you project the "right" look for a specific role based on the way you dress, wear your hair, and walk or sit.

Because commercials emphasize the visual aspects of an actor, you need to find out ahead of time from your agent (or from a copy of the script) what type of role you may be playing, so you can dress, act, and look the part at the audition. You may be the greatest actor in the world for a particular role, but if you dress like a motorcycle gang member for a role as a clean-cut business executive, even your best acting skills aren't likely to overcome the handicap of your inappropriate appearance.

If you need a copy of a script in a hurry, visit the Showfax, Inc. Web site (`www.showfax.com`) where you can order and download a copy of any commercial auditioning script.

Many producers and casting directors for film and television productions study commercials to spot actors with a unique and interesting "look." Often times, actors appearing in commercials can go on to film and television roles because casting directors may be impressed by the way they act and appear in commercials.

Preparing your part

When actors audition for a play, they often read the play ahead of time to understand their role and their relationship to the other characters. When actors audition for a commercial, they may have time to review the script or study the storyboard, which is an artist's depiction for what the commercial should look like.

A *storyboard* consists of a frame-by-frame artist's drawing of key scenes with the dialogue printed underneath. The purpose of the storyboard is to create a rough plan for the way the commercial should appear and what camera angles the director should use. The details may all change later, but the storyboard shows you what the advertising agency and the client have seen and approved.

Study the storyboard carefully because it can show you how the advertising agency pictures how an actor should hold the product or how the actor should stand in a particular scene. The more closely you can resemble the depiction of the actors in the storyboard, the more likely the advertising agency and casting director will say, "That's exactly what we're looking for!"

Handling yourself during the audition

During a commercial audition, you'll likely stand on a mark in front of the camera, and the casting director will say to you, "Slate." *Slate* means state your name and your agent's name with a smile (of course). The casting director may also ask that you turn to show your profile to the camera (or the casting director may just say, "Profiles").

After you've slated and shown your profile to the camera, you get to audition. To keep your hands free, most commercial auditions display giant cue cards underneath the camera, so you can read the script and act at the same time. Read the words on the cue cards exactly as they're written, but don't worry if you make a mistake or two. The casting director may ask you to read the script in a slightly different way, or he may simply say, "Thank you," and call in the next actor.

How actors eat food over and over again while filming a commercial

If you've involved in a commercial where you need to drink or eat food, don't worry. No matter how wonderful the food may be, the director knows that few actors can maintain the same level of enthusiasm for a product after they've already eaten it seventeen times in a row and are feeling stuffed. So if you're involved in a commercial where you need to eat something, you'll be supplied with the unceremoniously named "spit bucket."

As the name implies, the spit bucket (which is hidden off-camera, of course) is used to catch the food that actors spit out after takes. After taking a mouthful of a sandwich and relishing the taste in your mouth, wait until you hear the director say, "Cut!" At this time, you may lean over and spit the entire mouthful of food into the spit bucket. Then it's time for a fresh chunk of food and another take, with another mouthful of food destined for the spit bucket. By using the spit bucket, actors can perform several takes without getting bloated and full, neither of which would aid in the actor's performance.

To help yourself get used to reading off cue cards, place some cue cards near a camera (or have a friend hold them up) and practice reading your lines while acting and looking towards the camera at the same time.

Here are a few tips to keep in mind as you audition in front of a camera:

- Face the camera at all times (unless the casting director or someone else in authority tells you otherwise). In a commercial, the camera is your audience.

  Although a casting director and the representatives from the client and the advertising agency may evaluate your audition in person, they may also videotape your audition, so they can see how you look on camera.

- Stay within focus. During an audition, a mark should be on the floor, which not only tells you where to stand or sit but also where the camera can capture you in focus. Move too close to or too far away from the camera, and the videotape of your audition may appear blurry.

- Keep your voice and body gestures natural, yet still interesting. Project the illusion of reality by speaking to the camera with variations in your voice, such as speaking certain words with different intonations or emotions behind each word.

  Although the commercial script (known as *copy*) may require that you be frustrated or upset, by the end of the commercial, you'll inevitably be happy, cheerful, and satisfied.

Bringing your energy level down is usually easier than bringing it up, so you may want to start with a higher energy level than normal. That way, if the casting director wants you to modify your delivery down a little bit, you'll be able to do so easily and make yourself look more polished and professional as a result.

No matter how horrible you may think that you did at your audition, don't criticize yourself in front of the casting director. He may have loved what you just did, so just thank the casting director and leave immediately.

Recognizing Commercial Patterns to Improve Your Performance

Although every commercial is different, most commercials tend to follow the same patterns. After you understand and recognize these patterns, you can better prepare yourself for the types of roles and acting that the casting director wants to see.

Some common types of commercials include the following:

- Slice-of-life
- Spokesperson
- Dialogue-less

The slice-of-life commercial

The *slice-of-life commercial* performs a miniature play that quickly identifies a problem, offers a solution (which is the product or service being advertised) and displays the final (always) happy result.

Slice-of-life commercials generally consist of a small cast of characters, such as two or three, where characters tend to represent stereotypes (such as a busy house wife or a consumer who's frustrated with the inadequacies of their current brand of trash bags), which allow viewers to quickly identify and sympathize with the characters and their problems. Sometimes, commercials mix things up a bit by using stereotypes to surprise the viewer. For example, a character may appear to be a stereotypical motorcycle gang member who elbows his way through a bar full of thugs, hops on his motorcycle, and squeals to a stop in front of his house. Then to surprise us, the character may rush inside to drink a new brand of pink lemonade that, as the off-screen announcer reminds us, "Can satisfy even the toughest taste buds."

Slice-of-life commercials often emphasize the emotional aspects of a product or service where one character represents the product (the seller), and a second character represents a potential customer (the buyer). The seller demonstrates or discusses the virtues of the product while the buyer often appears skeptical or frustrated at the beginning, but that buyer inevitably becomes a believer of the product by the end of the commercial.

Some of the key points of slice-of-life commercials are:

- The seller and the buyer must quickly establish the type of relationship that they have with one another, even if they may be complete strangers.
- Both the seller and buyer play easily identifiable stereotypes (husband and wife, best friends, parent and child, boss and worker, and so on).
- The seller believes in the product and works to change the buyer's mind.
- The buyer has a problem, but with the seller's help, he or she discovers a solution.

When auditioning for a slice-of-life commercial, you need to know whether your role is the buyer or the seller. As the seller, your character must be enthusiastic and persistent throughout the dialogue, despite any pessimism from the buyer. As the buyer, you may be at odds with the seller at first, but your skepticism stems from your doubt about the advertised product and not from any distrust of the seller. (The seller must always project an air of trust, respectability, and truth. After all, the seller does represent the advertised product.)

The relationship between characters in slice-of-life commercials can vary from loving and friendly to competitive.

- Examples of loving and friendly characters may be husband and wife, parents and children, or best friends. In these types of relationships, both characters must come across as likeable, so the audience sympathizes with the problems of the buyer but believes and trusts the message presented by the seller.
- Examples of competitive relationships may be boss and worker, feuding neighbors, or an average person versus any authority figure, such as a police officer, teacher, or father. In these types of relationships, the seller is often the underdog and either proves the buyer wrong by making him or her look foolish or, in a milder version, simply proves in a good-natured way that the authority figure isn't so smart after all.

In these adversarial slice-of-life commercials, the seller must be likeable and trustworthy, and the buyer must be the object of ridicule and mild scorn. Viewers should root for the seller and laugh or smile at the defeat of the buyer for not having the intelligence to accept the clear superiority of the product represented by the buyer. Here's an example of a typical slice-of-life commercial for phony Phony Punch.

(A young couple, wearing tennis outfits, enter a living room that has a bar.)

WOMAN: Great game!

MAN: *(Tries to put his arm around the woman)* I know a better one.

WOMAN: *(Brushes the man's hand away)* Ooooh, don't touch me. I'm hot enough already.

MAN: *(Goes behind the bar)* Want to cool off? I've got some fruit punch in the refrigerator.

WOMAN: *(Smiles, then frowns)* Oh no. I'll just have a glass of water instead. I know how expensive fruit punch drinks are these days.

MAN: Then you haven't tried Phony Punch. *(Teasingly)* It's loaded with artificial colors and preservatives.

WOMAN: *(Innocently)* What does that mean?

MAN: That means it's inexpensive, so you shouldn't feel guilty about drinking some. Here, have a glass.

WOMAN: Mmmm, it really does cool you off, and it tastes great, too!

MAN: *(Snuggles closer to woman but doesn't touch her)* That's because it took over ten years for a polymer chemist to develop the formula for Phony Punch. Phony Punch doesn't just taste good, but it's made entirely from petroleum waste-by-products. That makes Phony Punch the only artificially flavored fruit punch drink that solidifies at room temperature.

WOMAN: *(Snuggles closer to the man)* The next time I'm thirsty for something inorganic, I'm going to buy a gallon of Phony Punch.

MAN: Cool enough now?

WOMAN: No, I'm just warming up.

The spokesperson commercial

A *spokesperson commercial* uses an authority figure (such as a doctor or a celebrity) to lend credibility to a product right away.

In the spokesperson commercial, the actor either directly addresses the camera, as if giving a formal presentation, or speaks to the camera, as if sharing advice with a friend. Sometimes, the spokesperson may be the only actor visible while, other times, other actors may appear but play minor roles.

Here are some of the key points of spokesperson commercials:

- The spokesperson is an expert either by appearing to be a respected authority (such as dressing up to look like a doctor) or through experience (such as a housewife who's tried dozens of detergents only to finally find the one detergent that works every time).
- *How* the spokesperson speaks is nearly as important as the words the spokesperson uses. The spokesperson needs to speak from a position of authority and confidence but still remain likeable and friendly.
- The spokesperson is indirectly selling a product by his or her appearance and presentation in addition to directly selling the product by emphasizing the benefits and superior features of that product.

Two types of spokesperson commercials are formal-presentation and friendly-presentation commercials.

Formal-presentation commercials

An actor in a formal-presentation commercial rarely laughs and may smile only occasionally, acting primarily through his voice and inflection because hand and body gestures will be limited and terse. Typically, the spokesperson appears in a business suit or a doctor's laboratory coat. The attitude of this type of spokesperson is, "I'm the expert, and I have something important to tell you." Formal-presentation commercials tend to include a generous sprinkling of the word "you" because the spokesperson speaks directly to the audience. Here's an example of a formal-presentation commercial for Paranoia Insurance:

> **ANNOUNCER:** Your home is insured, your car is insured, and your life is insured. But what about your fears?
>
> *(Actor holds up an elaborate insurance policy.)*
>
> **ANNOUNCER:** Introducing new Paranoia Insurance. Paranoia Insurance protects you from all forms of delusions, madness, and hallucinations you may be suffering from right this moment. When it comes to your sanity, why take chances? Now, you can insure your home, your car, your life, *and* your fears with Paranoia Insurance. Get some today before those voices in your head tell you that you're too late.

Friendly-presentation commercial

Another variation of the spokesperson commercial is the friendly, "I'm sharing a secret with you" type of commercial (also known as the friendly-presentation commercial). This type of commercial is much more conversational than a formal-presentation commercial. The actor's clothes are usually informal and represent the typical clothes that the audience may likely wear. The actor can be animated, smiling, laughing, and gesturing more freely than in a formal-presentation commercial.

In a friendly-presentation commercial, the spokesperson asserts his or her authority as the expert but also treats the audience as a guest or friend by appearing in a scene that viewers are familiar with, such as unloading groceries from a car or watering the lawn as if the camera just caught them in the act. These types of spokesperson commercials tend to emphasize the word "I," which lets the audience know what the product has done for the spokesperson.

Here's an example of a friendly-presentation commercial:

> *(A business executive walks through a busy office, handing out pink slips to workers.)*
>
> **ANNOUNCER:** As the CEO of a Fortune 500 company, I can't afford to let a headache interfere with my self-serving interests. That's why I take Extra-Strength Dextrinol. Unlike other headache remedies, Extra-Strength Dextrinol stops both the physical and mental causes of headaches by deadening the brain cells responsible for developing a conscience. Without a conscience, I never have to risk getting another headache again from stress, anxiety, or guilt, so I can continue to enjoy my self-destructive life-style without any physical or psychological pain. So the next time that you get a headache from worrying about the consequences of your actions, try Extra-Strength Dextrinol. Tough enough for the Fortune 500. Gentle enough for you.

The dialogue-less commercial

Dialogue-less commercials (also known as *minus optical track* or MOS commercials) are often filmed without recording any sound. The point of an MOS commercial is to emphasize a visual image with the spoken words of an announcer, such as a young couple driving in their new luxury car while someone sings a love song in the background.

Another version of MOS comes from a story told of a German director who couldn't say "with" and, instead, would say "mit." So when he asked the crew to film a scene without sound, he would say, "mit out sound," hence the acronym MOS.

Not speaking a single word of dialogue can paradoxically make the acting role both easy and difficult. Without any dialogue to memorize (and mess up), you can focus your attention on your acting. But without the aid of dialogue to assist you, you may have to respond to situations and dialogue from an unseen announcer (which will later be dubbed into the commercial). Acting without the benefit of visible or audible cues can make acting seem disconnected and uncomfortable, much like trying to hold a telephone conversation by yourself.

May the actor beware

You can earn a comfortable living from commercials without the general public ever knowing your name. Commercial acting can be extremely lucrative. But if you've got your sights set on bigger and better acting roles, you should know that commercial acting can also hurt your acting career in the long-run, if you're not careful.

The most common career killer is getting stereotyped with a particular product. If you become the spokesperson for a particular product, such as the Maytag repairman, Mr. Whipple squeezing Charmin bathroom tissue, or the computer guy promoting Dell Computers, you'll make plenty of money, but casting directors will be extremely reluctant to hire you for any other types of commercials any time in the near future. (Sometimes, advertising agencies will hire a former rival's spokesperson after the rival's commercial has been off the air for several years. By using a rival's former spokesperson, a company can imply that the spokesperson used to use Brand X but now uses Brand Y because it's superior.)

Getting stereotyped for a particular company can also keep you from landing roles in film and television because casting directors want the public to watch a film or television show and see actors, not a product spokesperson. If everyone sees your face as that "Hamburger Chain Guy," any appearance you make in a film or television show will cause the audience to stop and say, "Hey, that's that Hamburger Chain Guy," which essentially destroys the suspension of belief necessary for an audience to enjoy watching a film or television show.

Although appearing in a commercial isn't very likely to hurt your acting career, be aware of the potential problems. If you need money, commercial acting can be the fastest and most reliable type of acting to get it. But if you're serious about pursuing acting for artistic reasons, you may want to make sure that you don't kill your career by acting in *too* many commercials — despite the large sums of money you could earn as a result.

To help yourself act, study the storyboard for the commercial. The storyboard will show what the actors should be doing and how they should appear in the camera at different key points of the commercial. (Taking an improv class can also help you adapt and perform in unusual situations like this, too.)

In one type of MOS commercial, the actors perform a scene while being completely oblivious to anything the off-screen announcer says. By studying the script, actors can learn what types of feelings they need to express at every part of the commercial, using nothing but body language and facial gestures. As in most commercials, there's usually an initial problem that a product or service can suddenly solve within seconds. Here's an example of an MOS commercial for Mr. Ed's Cat Food:

> *(A woman bends down and puts a bowl of cat food on the floor. A cat walks up to the bowl, sniffs it, and walks away.)*
>
> **ANNOUNCER** (from off screen)**:** Cats are finicky eaters, so why not give your cat only the best?
>
> *(Close-up of a can of cat food with the Mr. Ed's Cat Food logo.)*

ANNOUNCER: Introducing Mr. Ed's Cat Food. Unlike ordinary cat foods that contain fillers, meat by-products, and chemical preservatives, Mr. Ed's Cat Food contains 100 percent pure ground horsemeat. But not just any horsemeat goes into Mr. Ed's Cat Food. . .

(Snapshots of race horses flash across the screen)

ANNOUNCER: . . .only the finest Kentucky Derby winners. Names like Comet Chaser, Lucky Charm, and Catch Me If You Can!

(Woman bends down and puts a bowl of Mr. Ed's Cat food on the floor next to a can of Mr. Ed's Cat Food. The cat runs up to the bowl and starts eating like mad.)

ANNOUNCER: So why not give your cat only the best? Mr. Ed's Cat Food. It's the cat food that makes every cat feel like a Triple Crown winner!

Understanding the Market for Commercials

Although acting in film and television offers more prestige, commercials are more numerous and, thus, offer more opportunities for actors to work and get paid. Given a particularly popular commercial, you can earn a six-figure (or more) income just from one commercial alone. However, actors more commonly earn a sizable income from several commercials running at any given time.

The commercial pay scale is divided up as follows:

- **Test commercials:** As the name implies, test commercials are produced to give a client an idea of what a particular advertising campaign may look like. Sometimes, test commercials are ultimately broadcast (in which case, you'll earn more money), but in many cases, the test commercial gets shelved and never seen by the general public. If you film a test commercial, you get paid for your time on the set and that's about it.
- **Dealer commercials:** One step above test commercials, dealer commercials usually broadcast locally and advertise the neighborhood used car dealer or the gun shop down the street. Dealer commercials pay a flat-fee for unlimited use of a commercial within a specified time period, such as six months.

  Unlike test commercials, dealer commercials actually get broadcast and seen by the general public. If a dealer commercial proves popular, it may run for an extended period of time, which means that you'll get another flat-fee for this extended run.

- **Wild spots:** These commercials aren't broadcast over a national network but through individual broadcast stations in different cities. A wild spot commercial can earn you a flat-fee for a specified period of time, such as thirteen weeks. If a wild spot commercial proves popular, you may get paid again for another period of time (such as another thirteen weeks).
- **Nationally broadcast commercials:** The most lucrative, these types of commercials pay each time the commercial airs, and your payment is called a *residual* (or *royalty*). The first time your commercial airs, you get a certain amount, and each succeeding time it airs, you get a slightly lower amount.

Generally, only the principal actors get the chance to earn residuals. If you worked as an extra or had a bit role, you may only get paid a flat-fee — no matter how many times a particular commercial airs.

Sometimes, you may land a role for a commercial that'll only be broadcast in an overseas market. Depending on your contract, you may get a chance to earn residuals from an overseas commercial, even though you (and probably most of your family) may never see it broadcast.

When you get paid for a commercial, you typically agree to *exclusivity,* which means that for a specific period of time (such as twenty-one months), you agree not to appear in a commercial for a rival product or company. For example, if you're currently appearing in a car commercial, even auditioning for a commercial for any rival auto makers would be considered a conflict.

How your favorite movie stars appear in commercials that you'll never get to see

Many movie stars won't appear in commercials for fear of tarnishing their acting reputation by associating themselves with a common household product. But because the commercial market can be so lucrative for a single day's shoot, movie stars often agree to appear in commercials that only appear in overseas markets instead.

Arnold Schwarzenegger once appeared in a Japanese commercial advertising DirecTV. Other major film stars who appeared in Japanese commercials include Leonardo DiCaprio (pitching credit cards), Meg Ryan (beauty cream), Harrison Ford (beer), Brad Pitt (Rolex), Keanu Reeves (whisky), Christian Slater (Toyota), Demi Moore (energy supplements), and Sean Connery (Mazda). (To see videos of these Japanese commercials, visit the Gaijin A Go-Go Café Web site at `www.gaijinagogo.com` or the Japander.com Web site at `www.japander.com`.)

By limiting their commercials to specific overseas markets, movie stars can capitalize on their worldwide appeal, make a lot of money, and still protect their reputation in the larger American market.

Chapter 12

Acting in Theater

In This Chapter

- Comparing theatrical acting to other acting
- Rehearsing for a play
- Preparing for a career in theater
- Looking at different markets for theater

Acting has its roots in theater. (Actually, acting has its roots in children's games of "Let's Pretend," but it sounds more important and academic to say that acting has its roots in theater.) So whether you plan to pursue a theatrical career or not, acting in theatrical productions can be an important learning experience for any type of actor. The more acting experience you can get, the stronger you'll become as an actor, and for many actors (such as Patrick Stewart from *Star Trek: The Next Generation*), the first place they start is in the theater.

In this chapter, you discover the differences between theater acting and film and television acting along with what to expect when performing in theater (including odd quirks like actors' superstitions).

Broadway stars are rarely household names, and few theatrical actors sign multimillion-dollar contracts like their film and television counterparts do with astonishing frequency (and, as theater purists like to point out, often with a lot less experience and talent, too). If you're interested in pursuing a career in theatrical acting, do it for the love of acting, not for the money or fame. (But where theater lacks in fame and fortune, it makes up for it in prestige. Still, you can't pay your bills on prestige, but it's nice to have anyway.)

Mastering Your Skills Onstage

Many actors consider theatrical acting to be the purest form of acting because you're forced to create and sustain a character for an hour or more, in front of a live (at least physically) audience, telling a story from start to finish. As soon as the play begins, there's no turning back. If an actor forgets a line, there's no stopping the play and starting over again. If the scenery falls down in the middle of a scene, the actors are forced to remain in character and improvise the best they can. With this type of pressure haunting the stage every second of the play, you're practically forced to learn and grow as an actor, whether you like it or not.

Unlike commercials, television, and, to a certain extent, film, actors in theater can't get by on their good looks alone. (If you're the type of actor looking to parlay your looks into an acting career, you may have better success in commercial acting instead.) To survive live performances night after night, on a consistent basis, you actually need talent — and not just acting talent but sometimes singing and dancing talent, too.

Because theatrical acting relies less on realism and more on the suspension of belief, theatrical acting offers actors more free rein to play different age ranges, from little children to senior citizens. With a little makeup and the proper costume, an actor can appear 18 years old in one scene and 65 the next (or even male in one scene and female in the next).

Theatrical acting also gives actors a chance to study and learn from their different roles. Because you play the same character over and over again, you can view each performance as another chance to experiment and fine-tune your acting until you learn what works best for you. (Plus, you can study and learn from your fellow actors and pick up tips from them.)

From an actor's point of view, theater is truly an actor's medium because the actor is in control of his performance, unlike film and television where the director can selectively choose which scenes to use (which may inadvertently make a particular actor look incompetent or just plain stupid). That's why many film and television actors often appear in theatrical productions from time to time, so that they can hone their acting skills in theater and control their performances themselves.

Gearing Up for a Theatrical Career

One of the most common ways to start a career in theater is to begin studying theater or drama in school — starting in high school, if possible, and continuing on through college. Another common way is to just jump right in and get started — usually in community or church plays — and build your credits and experience from there.

The academic route

If you're reading this book and you're still in high school, you should take a drama class or two to get a peek behind the chaotic and flamboyant world of theater. For some people, acting in a high school play can satisfy the "acting bug," but for others, it simply whets their appetite for more.

Outside high school, the next opportunity to study acting comes from the various college and universities all over the world. Many schools offer undergraduate Bachelor of Arts (B.A.) degrees in drama or theater. If you already have a college degree or simply wish for more experience, you can continue your studies to obtain a Master of Fine Arts degree (M.F.A.) in theater, which is considered the theatrical equivalent to a Ph.D.

The main advantage of studying theater in a university is that you get a chance to act, build sets, work the lighting, sell tickets, and perform a thousand other minor chores associated with putting on a theatrical production that you may never get to experience anywhere else in such a short amount of time.

You may also get a chance to read, study, and analyze different plays that you may later wind up auditioning for, so the more you know about a particular play and playwright, the better you can tailor your acting skills to fit that particular role.

Although you can study theater and get valuable theatrical experience at nearly any university, you may want to be selective in the schools you choose. Studying theater at a community college or in a small college isolated in a place like El Paso or Anchorage may offer less competition and give you greater access to theatrical roles. However, it won't look as impressive on your acting resume as a more prestigious university with a highly rated theatrical department. (For more on acting resumes, flip back to Chapter 5.)

For the truly serious and dedicated, certain high schools and colleges actually specialize in theater, such as the New York City High School for the Performing Arts (the school highlighted in the musical *Fame*). Getting into a famous and prestigious theatrical high school or college can be nearly as tough as landing an acting role because the competition can be fierce. Still, if you're serious about acting, you can get much better training in one of these schools instead of taking a drama or theater class from someplace more remote.

If you go to a more prestigious university, such as UCLA, you're more likely to run into casting directors who have gone to that same school. Given two actors of equal ability and the only difference is that one went to the same school as the casting director, guess which actor may get the job?

Even if you don't pursue acting full-time, a college degree — especially an M.F.A. — offers opportunities for teaching theater and drama. Although teaching won't get you worldwide fame and multimillion-dollar salaries, it will provide a steady income and allow you to live a decent, relatively stress-free life without worrying about your rent or where your next meal may be coming from — a lifestyle that many aspiring actors never get to see their entire lives.

The pounding-the-pavement route

No matter what school you go to, eventually, you'll have to leave and enter the "real world." And that's when you may find that someone who took one drama class from the University of North Dakota is now a star, while you're busy busing tables at a restaurant in Hollywood, despite going to the best theatrical schools and earning the top grades in your class.

Whether or not you go to a university, every actor needs to follow the "pounding the pavement" route, which simply means getting out in the world and trying out for every audition you can get. Actors vying for auditions need to pursue two goals simultaneously: training and experience.

Outside of the relatively cloistered confines of the university setting, actors can get training through private workshops and classes offered by (hopefully) reputable instructors. Some acting instructors have near legendary, cultlike status, but any instructor can be helpful if he or she helps you improve your acting abilities.

Although you should constantly work to sharpen your acting skills, you should also take classes in other types of performance, such as dancing, singing, improvisation, voice, mime, comedy, cold reading, and auditioning. Acting demands a healthy body, so you should also consider starting a regular exercise program and learning some of the more esoteric skills that could come in handy for acting one day, such as fencing (for performing in plays set during medieval times).

Training can certainly help you, but no amount of training can substitute for real-life working experience. For that reason, you need to get as much acting experience as possible doing anything and everything you can (that's legal and within your moral standards, that is).

Through the Equity Membership Candidate Program (EMC), anyone can work in select professional theaters as an apprentice, which usually means helping run all aspects of the theater, from making sets to cleaning up the theater after the show (with possibly a little bit of acting thrown in there, as well.) After 50 weeks of work, the actor is then eligible for membership in the Actors' Equity Association. (For more details about the Equity Membership Candidate Program, visit the Equity Web site at `www.actorsequity.org`.)

Getting into the EMC program can be nearly as tough as auditioning for a role, so be prepared for stiff competition. In addition to getting membership into Equity through the EMC program, you can also become eligible for Equity membership through membership in a related actor's union or by auditioning so well that an Equity production hires you for a role.

Read to succeed

One important activity that can aid theatrical actors is reading. In addition to reading any plays that you're planning to audition for, consider also reading one or more of the following as well:

- **Other plays by the same playwright:** You can get a better understanding of the themes and ideas that the playwright has emphasized in his or her other works.
- **Biographies and autobiographies of the playwright:** Reading about the playwright's past gives you a sense of the playwright's thoughts and background.
- **History books:** Many plays are set in the past (when was the last time you saw a science fiction play?), so it's important to understand the historical setting of the play. You can add credibility to your acting by knowing the mannerisms and customs of a specific time period. By probing deeper into the historical background of a play and understanding the customs that may have influenced the way your particular character could behave, you can add depth to your role that someone just putting on a period costume can never hope to portray.

Although every actor dreams of being a star, many professional actors make a fine living without ever becoming famous at all. If you never become a star, don't consider yourself a failure. The real failures are all those people working in jobs that they can't stand when they'd rather be pursuing a career in acting.

Auditioning for Theater

Members of Equity can find out about the latest theater auditions from their local union offices. Many times, theaters advertise auditions in local newspapers, so be sure to peruse those regularly. Finally, keep in touch with your fellow actors because they may hear of auditions that you're right for.

Theatrical auditions may be held in an office, an empty room, or in a theater (but not always the same theater where the play will be performed).

Many theatrical auditions are for popular and well-established plays, so take advantage of this fact by getting a copy of the play ahead of time and studying it thoroughly so that you understand the story, the locale, the time period, the relationships between the different characters, and the setting of the play. The more you know about a particular play before an audition, the more prepared you'll be during that audition.

Sometimes, directors may set a play in a different time period from normal. For example, many productions of Shakespearean plays are often given a modern setting, so try to find out this information from your agent or the casting director (if possible) before you appear at an audition. Your Elizabethan garb will look pretty weird if the play is going to be a gritty urban drama set in modern-day Harlem.

On any theatrical audition, be prepared to perform a monologue. When performing a monologue, don't look directly at the casting director or anyone else who may be evaluating you during your audition. Instead, look away, such as over their heads or to one side. If you look directly at them, they may feel obligated to acknowledge your eye contact and won't be able to relax and evaluate your performance as an actor. After seeing the hundredth actor staring at them in the eyes, you can imagine how tiring this can get to a casting director.

Preparing a monologue

In the world of film and television, actors are often chosen for their looks first and their talent second. But in theater, talent is much more important than looks because most of the audience isn't going to be able to clearly see your face (or even your body) onstage anyway. So when auditioning for theatrical roles, casting directors need to evaluate your acting abilities, and the best way to do that is to ask the actor to perform a monologue.

Essentially, a monologue is a miniature one-person show where you act out a scene so that the casting director can evaluate your acting ability. To better evaluate an actor's skills, casting directors often ask that actors perform two completely different types of monologues, such as one serious and one comical or one classical (such as a Shakespearean play) and one contemporary (such as a Neil Simon play). The goal is to see how an actor can perform in diverse types of roles.

Because you, the actor, can choose your monologues, take care to choose the best monologues that highlight your acting strengths (and minimize your acting weaknesses). An acting coach and even your fellow actors can give you feedback on how well (or poorly) you perform a particular monologue. The key is to memorize at least two monologues that are likely to be interesting to a casting director and that allow you to demonstrate your acting range and skill.

Ideally, you should memorize a handful of monologues, so you can choose a monologue that closely matches the type of role you may be auditioning for at the time. Also be wary of choosing monologues that other actors are currently doing, because you want to be unique and not bore the casting director with yet another scene that he's seen a hundred times before from everyone else.

In the world of theater, monologues give you a chance to act in front of a casting director, and this may be the only chance you'll get to demonstrate your acting talent. So practice and perfect your monologues.

Friends in high places

Running a theatrical production involves a lot more than just actors (which is something that most egotistical actors don't want to recognize).

- **The director:** She has the final say over the play, from the way costumes and sets look to how actors should say their lines to what lines stay in the play and which ones get thrown out.
- **The stage manager:** He's responsible for working with the actors, calling the actors to remind them of rehearsal times, scheduling breaks during rehearsals, herding the actors back to rehearsal, and making sure that the stage is properly set and ready for each performance. If you have a problem for any reason with another actor, with the way the stage is set up, or with the way your costume fits (or doesn't fit), the stage manager is the person to talk to. The stage manager is there to help ensure that the production runs smoothly, so respect the stage manager at all times.
- **The property master:** She's in charge of all the props used in the play, and she repairs or replaces them if necessary. The property master also makes sure that all props are set up for easy access when needed, so if your prop is broken or missing, the first person you should talk to is the property master.
- **The company master** (sometimes known as the business manager): In large productions, he is in charge of travel and lodging requirements for everyone involved in the production. He also works with the theater to handle the box office receipts and to make sure that the actors get paid on time. So if you have a question (or complaint) about your travel arrangements or your paycheck, talk to the company master.

Sometimes, you can't even see the casting director because the audition is held in a darkened theater. In that case, be sure to stand in the light illuminating the stage; if casting directors can't see you clearly, they won't be able to evaluate your audition. Don't worry if a spotlight is shining on your face — you're not going to be interrogated like a prisoner (although you may feel like one!). Your face is illuminated to allow the casting director to see you clearly.

If a role involves singing, be ready to sing a song or two at your audition so that the casting director can evaluate your singing range and voice. If a particular role requires an accomplished singer, the casting director may hold a separate audition just for singers. Then, those singers who pass that audition may need to go through an acting audition as well.

Just as you should memorize a monologue, you should also memorize a song, preferably one from a musical rather than a popular song. Unless your role requires a substantial amount of singing, you probably won't have to sing an entire song (you may just have to sing 16 bars so prepare the best 16 bars of a song that makes your voice sound great), but be ready to do so if necessary.

During a theatrical audition or performance, you may have the benefit of a wireless microphone to amplify your voice. But you should still know how to project your voice to be loud enough for everyone to hear in case you don't have a wireless microphone or if the microphone fails in the middle of a show. (See Chapter 13 to get more details about voice lessons and voice projection.)

Familiarizing Yourself with Stage Types

Plays take place on stages to ensure that everyone in the audience can see the actors and the scenery. The three most common types of stages include

- Proscenium stages
- Thrust stages
- Arena stages (also known as theater-in-the-round)

Proscenium stages

Proscenium *(pro SEE nee um)* stages are the most common types of stages. This type of stage is bounded by three walls and the audience views the action though the imaginary *fourth wall,* as shown in Figure 12-1. When performing on a proscenium stage, actors must take care that they don't stand in front of a fellow actor and risk blocking the audience's view.

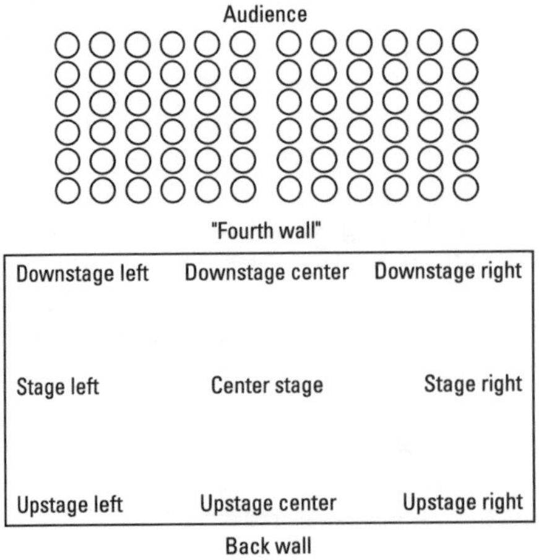

Figure 12-1: A proscenium stage where the audience peers through the fourth wall.

Upstage is the part of the stage farthest from the audience. *Downstage* is the part of the stage closest to the audience. In the old days, stages were sloped, so the back of the stage was slightly higher than the front, hence the terms upstage and downstage. *Stage right* is the actor's right when facing the audience, and *stage left* is the actor's left when facing the audience. Upstage right means the area of the stage to the right and behind the actor. (Downstage right means the area of the stage to the right and in front of the actor, and so on.) The *fourth wall* is the imaginary line where the stage ends and the audience begins.

You may also hear the term *upstaging* used when one actor steals the attention of the audience from another actor, either accidentally or accidentally on purpose. Upstaging can occur if an actor moves while another actor is speaking or stands in front of another actor, thereby blocking the audience's view of that other actor. The moving actor catches the audience's attention and pulls it away from the actor speaking his lines, thereby preventing most of the audience from hearing what the actor even said. Upstaging is considered rude and should never be done deliberately.

Working as an understudy

For the more lavish (expensive) productions, if an actor is too ill or hurt to appear on stage, the theater can't just cancel the show, especially if an actor just hurt himself ten minutes before show time and several hundred people have already paid, sat down, and filled up the theater. To prepare for emergencies like these, the theatrical world uses understudies.

Typically an understudy is an actor who has a bit role in a play but, throughout rehearsals, also memorizes and practices a major role at the same time. That way, if an actor gets into a car wreck on the way to the theater, the understudy can replace that actor quickly and allow the show to go on.

To a certain extent, working as an understudy is even more difficult than working a major role since you have to remain as practiced and prepared as the actor you're replacing, but you never know when you may be called upon to perform that other actor's role. In rare cases, an actor may hurt himself seriously in the middle of a play, and the understudy must be ready to rush in within minutes to replace that actor so the show can go on.

If you ever get a role as an understudy, consider it a crash course in acting under pressure. Although you may not necessarily see your name on the marquee as an understudy, rest assured that you'll still be paid to be an understudy whether you ever perform in a major role or not.

Thrust stages

A thrust stage has only a back wall, and the audience surrounds the stage on three sides, as shown in Figure 12-2. On a thrust stage, the positions and gestures of actors aren't quite as critical because any movement or position is likely to block part of the audience's view at any given time. On a thrust stage, actors must take care to perform toward all three sides of the audience at various times. If you spend too much time facing the left side of the stage, the people on the right side of the stage will see only your back and may miss any facial or hand gestures you make.

Audience
Downstage left
Downstage center
Downstage right
Stage left
Center stage
Stage right
Upstage left
Upstage center
Upstage right
Back wall

Figure 12-2: A thrust stage sticks out into the audience.

Arena stages

An audience surrounds an arena, or theater-in-the-round, stage on all four sides, as shown in Figure 12-3. When performing on an arena stage, actors must take care to play to all sides of the audience. Sets are often kept to a minimum to avoid blocking the view of certain audience members during the show, and actors often spend more time moving around so audience members on all sides of the stage will never be forced to stare at the back of an actor for a lengthy amount of time.

Even though the audience completely surrounds an arena stage, the director will often assign an arbitrary upstage and downstage direction to help the actors orientate their positions during rehearsals and the actual performance.

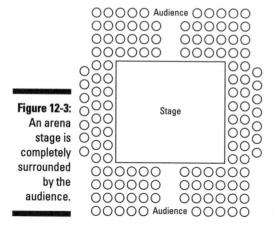

Audience

Stage

Audience

Figure 12-3: An arena stage is completely surrounded by the audience.

Rehearsing for a Play

In theater, rehearsals are extensive and exhaustive because a play must go from start to finish in front of a live audience without any mistakes. Typically, theatrical rehearsals go through one or more of the following steps:

- Read-through
- Blocking with stage directions
- Scene work
- Work-throughs
- Run-throughs
- Technical rehearsals
- Dress rehearsals

Treat every rehearsal as a performance that gives you a chance to act, if not with your body, then at least with your voice. That way you can correct any problems with your acting during rehearsal instead of suddenly discovering them in the middle of an actual performance.

Read-through

The *read-through* is a time when the director and the actors sit around a table and read through the entire script to get familiar with the story, their roles, and their fellow actors. During a read-through, directors are looking for ways to cut or modify the script to make it stronger. So if you find that certain lines are too clumsy to say, speak up. Also, if the director cuts some of your favorite lines, rather than protest and demand that you keep your lines, suggest alternate ways of improving the scene.

Mark up your script in pencil, not pen. You may be making many changes to your copy of the script, so erasing pencil is easier than scribbling and crossing out numerous pen markings.

Blocking with stage directions

After a few read-throughs, the rehearsal next progresses to the *blocking stage,* where you get to rehearse as if you were actually on a stage. Typically, these early rehearsals are held in warehouses, parking lots, or someone's living room. As a result, you won't be rehearsing with any actual props or sets, so you have to use your imagination. ("That pillow on the floor over there is the sofa, my tennis shoe over there is the front door, and this magazine in the corner is the bathtub.")

The show must go on!

The film and television industry can easily accommodate illness or emergencies, such as in cases when an actor may need to be absent for a period of time. The director can simply rearrange the shooting schedule to shoot scenes in which the actor doesn't have a part. Unfortunately, the theater doesn't offer that luxury. When the curtain goes up on the 8:00 p.m. show, every actor had better be ready to start the show at 8:00 p.m.

Therefore, in theater, actors often have to perform with headaches, colds, sprained ankles, or even broken bones. Unless you physically can't stand or speak, you're expected to perform to the best of your abilities, no matter what may be ailing you at the time.

The idea that the show must go on extends to emotional and psychological problems, too. If your spouse tells you just five minutes before showtime that he or she wants a divorce, you have to forget about your problems and focus totally on the show.

(In the world of theater, the cast is also called a *troupe,* so when an actor performs while ill, he's commended by saying he performed "like a trouper.")

Acting while under emotional or physical anguish isn't easy, but that's part of being a professional in the theater. Get used to that fact now and be ready to limp, sneeze, and stagger across the stage at some point in your theatrical career because everyone has done it before and, as a professional actor, you'll eventually have to do it, too.

The purpose of rehearsing with imaginary sets and props is to identify *blocking* (the various movements actors need to make on the stage), which can be as simple as walking onto the set or as complicated as staging a fake fight with another actor on the set. By learning the blocking for each scene, you can avoid having one actor stand in front of another actor (and thus hide that actor from the audience). Blocking can also help you discover problems in moving from one part of the set to another if you find that furniture (or even another actor) gets in the way. By discovering blocking problems as early as possible, you can spend most of your time rehearsing your lines instead.

Scene work

Because not all actors may be available to rehearse at certain times, the director often schedules rehearsals of individual scenes for those actors who can get together at a specific time. This means that it's possible to rehearse the last scene of the play first, and the first scene of the play last.

When rehearsing individual scenes, you may still be using pillows, books, or folding chairs to represent the parts of the set, but the emphasis is on learning your lines and saying them with the other actors in the scene. This is the time that actors should start memorizing their cues to speak and enter or exit the stage. (Yes, this may involve more marking up of your script.)

If your script has a large number of added or modified dialogue and stage directions scribbled on it, consider making a copy of your script and storing this copy in a safe place. That way, if you lose your original script, you won't also lose all your invaluable notes that you may have added since the rehearsal period began.

Work-throughs

A work-through rehearsal takes you through the entire play from the first scene to the last, in order and onstage. The main purpose of the work-through is to get used to performing the entire play and to iron out any technical and logistical problems that may crop up along the way.

For example, the work-through gives actors a chance to determine whether they have enough time between scenes to change into different costumes, if necessary. Actors also use the work-through to identify any problems entering or exiting the stage. If an actor needs to exit stage right on one scene but enter on stage left immediately afterwards, the director wants to identify and fix this problem now.

During the work-through rehearsal, the director may ask that the actors stop carrying their scripts and start memorizing their lines. If you forget a line during rehearsal, just say, "Line!" and someone will tell you your line.

Because a work-through runs through the entire play, seemingly stopping every five seconds to correct yet another problem, a work-through rehearsal often takes a long amount of time, usually an entire day. Even if you're only in a scene or two, you may still need to attend a work-through rehearsal because you never know what time you may actually be needed. Assume that a work-through rehearsal will go from morning to night and plan accordingly.

Run-throughs

As the name implies, a run-through means that the actors rehearse the entire play from start to finish, but without stopping this time. If you forget a line, improvise and keep going. If you miss your cue to enter or exit, remember the problem but keep performing.

The run-through gives you a chance to do a real performance, without the pressure of a paying audience watching you the whole time. Run-throughs usually take place on the actual stage and set that you will be performing on, but don't be surprised if all the props or scenery aren't done yet, in which case you'll still have to use your imagination. ("This banana that I'm holding is actually a gun. Bang, bang.")

The only time you should stop during a run-through and break out of character is when the director tells you to stop. Otherwise, keep going to the end. Consider any goof-ups as practice for handling any real goof-ups that may occur during an actual show.

Technical rehearsals

As the name implies, a technical rehearsal gives the director and actors a chance to practice the more technical aspects of a play, such as shooting a gun, pretending to drive away in a car, or just turning on a light.

During a technical rehearsal, the simplest items need to work. For example, doors must open properly, and shots must be heard when an actor pulls the trigger on a fake gun. Props may come in one of three varieties:

- **Working (also known as practical):** A working prop does just that — it works. A working prop can be as simple as an umbrella or closet door, or something more complex, such as a kitchen sink or fire escape ladder. When using a working prop, be prepared for when it doesn't work, usually in the middle of an important scene during a show where the theater critic from *The New York Times* is in the audience. When using any working prop during rehearsal, think of what you can do if the prop doesn't work (or isn't even on the set where it should be).
- **Non-working:** A non-working prop is an actual item, such as a lamp or television, that doesn't work even though the actors may pretend to use it. To use a non-working prop, such as a radio, the actor may pretend to turn it on while a technician offstage actually plays a recorded sound. Non-working props are always perfect; the technician offstage is the one that you have to worry about. If you twist the knob of a television set and the sound of a ball game is supposed to come out, be prepared for a time when the technician misses his cue and you get only silence (or even worse, a totally incorrect sound) instead.
- **False:** False props simply give the suggestion of their existence without actually being onstage. For example, a bathroom set may have a bathtub painted on the wall rather than a real one. This way, no one has to lug in a tub and put it on stage. A false prop merely exists as background scenery and usually plays no part in the play other than as decoration. Actors will never interact with a false prop because (obviously) it doesn't work and isn't really there.

Dress rehearsals

A dress rehearsal involves everyone wearing their costumes and roaming around the final set. During a dress rehearsal, you run through the entire play one or more times to iron out any last-minute problems. (Don't worry, even more last-minute problems will crop up during the performance, but do your best to identify and correct as many problems as possible now.) This is the time to see whether your costume allows you to make certain movements easily and whether any costume changes you need to make can occur within the amount of time you have.

Dress rehearsals are held on the stage and set where you'll be performing; you may need to walk through a door, wearing an elegant dress, only to find that the dress won't fit comfortably through the doorway without snagging on the doorknob.

Dress rehearsals are for the actor's benefit as much as for the costume designer's. Don't be surprised if your costume doesn't quite fit or is missing some pieces. This is the time to talk to the costume designer if certain parts of your costume are uncomfortable.

Break a leg! (Theater superstitions)

Theater is one of the oldest forms of entertainment around (after the oldest profession in the world, that is), so all sorts of weird superstitions have popped up in the world of theater. One of the more common superstitions is the belief that it's actually bad luck to wish an actor good luck. So rather than say, "Good luck," actors just say, "Break a leg," to each other instead.

Another strange bad-luck-is-really-good-luck superstition involves black cats, whose presence is actually considered good luck in a theater. The Haymarket Theatre Royal in London once had a black cat as a permanent resident to ensure good luck for all its productions.

Don't ever whistle in a theater because this is considered bad luck. In the old days of theater, sailors worked the ropes that raised and lowered the curtain and any scenery, and sailors communicated to each other by whistling. So if you happened to whistle back then, a sailor would possibly mistake your whistling for a command and drop the curtain or scenery at the wrong time.

For some odd reason, peacock feathers are considered extremely bad luck, which many people believe has to do with the "eye" on the feather. Wearing the color green is also considered taboo. This superstition may have come about when early plays were performed on lawns and, thus, wearing green would make you hard to see. Some early theaters also illuminated the stage with a green light (hence the term *limelight*), so a green light illuminating a green costume also made the actor hard to see.

Perhaps the most peculiar superstition involves the play *Macbeth,* which is considered an unlucky play, with horror stories of actors dying onstage and scenery collapsing. Many actors won't even mention *Macbeth* by name (unless they're actually *in* the play, of course), instead referring to it as "The Scottish Play."

So when you get your first theatrical acting role, be aware of these and many other superstitions that actors may force you to follow. (Many actors have personal superstitions, such as carrying a "lucky" coin or always stepping onto the stage with their right foot first.) Maybe these superstitions help and maybe they don't, but it won't hurt to go along with them. Then, if the play bombs, you can blame the failure on all these superstitious actors and not on anything you did instead.

If you'll be using your own clothes as your costume, treat those clothes with care! If something happens to your clothes, such as getting lost or getting mangled in a dryer, you suddenly may find yourself without the crucial costume you need for the play.

If you need to wear makeup for your role, put it on exactly as you would during a real performance. The director needs to know how every actor looks and moves in costume and in full makeup. When the dress rehearsals are done, you're (hopefully) ready for opening night!

Always arrive early for all your performances. Doing so gives you time to make sure that your costume is ready and in good shape and that all your props are in place and working.

Working in Different Markets

Broadway may be your ultimate goal as a theatrical actor, but don't overlook the myriad acting opportunities where you can earn valuable experience and a little bit of cash, besides. Most larger cities support a variety of niche theaters that target specific audiences, such as children or specific religions; specific types of people, such as gays and lesbians, blacks, Hispanics, or Asians; or experimental plays by different playwrights or directors.

Many actors tour public schools and present plays or stories in school auditoriums around the country. Much like industrial work, touring through schools won't make you famous, but it does give you additional experience working in front of diverse crowds. You even receive a steady and dependable paycheck at the same time.

Then there are the industrial shows where a large corporation may hire actors to perform at a company meeting or act as a spokesperson at their demonstration booth during a national convention.

Don't overlook putting on your own show. Rent out a theater, get a bunch of fellow actors together, and you can be the star in your own production (and with a little luck, actually sell enough tickets to make money doing it, too).

If you're going to put on your own show, consider showcasing your talents completely and putting together a one-man (or one-woman) show instead. These types of shows typically run an hour or more and feature a single actor telling a story by portraying different characters. A one-person show is an excellent show to invite agents and casting directors to watch, because you'll be the only actor they see.

Chapter 13

Performing Without Being Seen: Voice-Over Acting

In This Chapter

- Gearing up for a career in voice-over acting
- Recording a demo tape
- Auditioning your voice
- Getting paid

When most people think of acting, they think of the theater, film, or television, all situations in which actors dress up in costume, walk around a set, and speak memorized lines of dialogue. Although these three forms of acting are certainly the most traditional ones for an aspiring actor to choose from, you can also choose from a less well-known form of acting involving just your voice (called *voice-overs*).

Using only your voice may not be as glamorous as starring in a blockbuster film or hit Broadway play, but voice-over work can be another way for you to gain acting experience. It can also provide an alternative or main source of income for your acting career.

Voice-over can be another way for actors with disabilities to work in show business. Although someone on crutches or in a wheelchair isn't likely to get a role in film, television, or theater (unless a part specifically calls for someone on crutches or in a wheelchair), that person's disabilities are irrelevant when it comes to voice-over work. The way you look is unimportant compared to your voice and vocal acting abilities.

As a beginner, your first step in becoming a voice-over actor is to learn your craft by taking classes and training. Next, get work on your own and then record a demo tape. After you have a professional-quality demo tape, you need to look for an agent. This chapter explains each step in the lucrative, but often overlooked, world of voice-over acting.

What You Need to Succeed in Voice-Over Acting

Voice-over work is classified as anything in which you hear the person's voice but don't actually see the person's face. (Think of the voice of Darth Vader in *Star Wars,* which was really the voice of James Earl Jones.)

Just like ordinary acting, anyone with enough persistence and training can pursue voice-over acting. You don't necessarily need a distinctive voice (although that can help) because you can always find roles for all types of voices. Here's what you *do* need to succeed in voice-over:

- Articulation
- Versatility
- Ability to play to the microphone

What's that you say? Speaking clearly

A distinctive voice can be like a pretty face. You may grab an audience's attention right away, but if you don't have any other skills to back up your distinctive voice or pretty face, casting directors ultimately won't be able to use you very often, if at all. More important than a distinctive voice is the ability to speak clearly under a variety of circumstances without sounding robotic or artificial. (See the "Training for a Voice-Over Career" section, later in this chapter, for more advice on preparing for a career in this area of acting.)

Unlike television commercials where the name of the advertiser or product name may be seen, radio commercials rely entirely on your voice to promote the advertiser's name or product, so you never want to mispronounce that name or product.

Polly want a cracker? Voice versatility

Versatility means the ability to do different voices well while still maintaining the ability to speak clearly.

Versatility can be as simple as knowing how to vary your own natural voice in a multitude of ways. And it can be as advanced as knowing how to do celebrity impersonations, regional and foreign accents, or different characters, such as a sexy woman or a 5-year-old kid.

Taking care of your voice

In traditional acting, your body and your voice are your instruments for expressing your character. In voice acting, your voice is your only tool, so you'd better take care of it. Without a healthy voice, you can't work — no matter how talented, experienced, or in demand you may be.

One of the first steps in taking care of your voice is learning to speak properly, which includes correcting any speech deficiencies you may have (such as not pronouncing certain words or letters correctly) and learning to speak from your diaphragm and not from your throat. Speaking from your throat produces a raspy sound while also irritating your throat and vocal cords at the same time.

Another key to speaking well is knowing how to breathe properly through the diaphragm, not the chest. Breathing from the chest only partially fills your lungs with air, which means that your breath will be shallow and will prevent you from speaking long sentences without running out of breath.

Just as singers use vocal exercises to warm up their voices, voice actors should practice exercises to loosen up their vocal cords. Finally, voice actors should stay away from drugs, alcohol, cigarettes, coffee, and soft drinks. Drugs and alcohol can impair your ability to perform, and cigarettes, coffee, and soft drinks can dry up your throat, making speech more difficult.

The more you take care of your voice, the more your voice can earn you money and ultimately start taking care of you.

If you can do only one voice well, you may have to audition for dozens of voice-over roles until you find a role that needs your particular voice. But if you can do a variety of different voices, you can offer the casting director a choice of which particular voice of *yours* to use, instead of which particular voice actor to use.

A lucrative and challenging voice-over job is dubbing in foreign films and television shows. *Dubbing* forces you to match the actor's lip movements with your spoken dialogue while you're still acting in character. If you can speak a foreign language, you may also find work dubbing in English language films for overseas markets, too.

Testing . . . testing: Playing to the microphone

Having a versatile voice can open up many opportunities for you, but you must also be able to understand how to work with a microphone as well. Microphone technique, like camera technique, simply involves knowing how to use the equipment to your best advantage.

Here are some basic rules to follow when using a microphone:

- **Eliminate all unnecessary sounds.**
  - Don't touch the microphone while speaking because even the slightest touch can come across as a loud thump through the microphone.
  - Remove any jewelry that may rattle or clank together.
  - Make sure that your clothes don't rustle or rub loudly together when you move.
  - If you're sitting down, don't swivel in your chair while you speak because the chair may make a creaking sound.
  - If standing, be sure that you don't wear squeaky shoes or shoes with hard heels that make a clicking sound every time you adjust your footing.
- **Don't move the microphone.** In a sound studio, a recording engineer will help you adjust the microphone to where it's comfortable for you. Once adjusted, leave it in place because even a subtle movement can alter the recorded sound of your voice.
- **Don't tap the microphone or blow into the microphone to test it.** The noise that it makes is just plain annoying to the recording engineer. The best way to test a microphone is to speak into it in the exact same way that you'll be reading your script.

Most microphones have a *wind screen* (a piece of foam that protects the microphone) that's designed to help prevent the popping noise from an actor's voice, such as the popping that may occur from saying any word that begins with the letter *p,* like *p*lastic or *p*opcorn. ***Note:*** Even if a microphone has a wind screen, you need to be aware of every word you speak because the wind screen may not stop all popping sounds, which can ruin an otherwise excellent recording.

Many voice actors stand while talking and even use their bodies to act out their performances to help them better express their emotions. Some voice actors even dress the part to help them mentally feel like the character that they're portraying. Although the recording of your voice is all that's necessary, you should still dress professionally in whatever makes you comfortable and enables you to deliver a superb voice performance.

Training for a Voice-Over Career

The first step to finding voice-over work is to get good at it, which means taking training classes and practicing constantly. (Even the professionals take classes or hire voice coaches to help them refine their existing talents, develop new talents, or correct any flaws that they may currently have.) Unlike the world of commercial acting, where a certain look can get you a job, you won't be able to get any work as a voice-over actor until you demonstrate that you have a voice worth listening to in the first place.

Take voice and singing lessons along with classes or workshops from dialect coaches who can help you eliminate any existing dialects you may have or help you develop new ones. In addition to any type of voice training, take acting and improv classes. When you feel that your voice is better than the average person, you're ready to start working. (If your voice isn't any better than the average person, the casting director will have no reason to hire you.)

To get experience exercising your voice, contact the Braille Institute or the public broadcasting station in your area. Blind people need volunteers who can read books, newspapers, and magazines to them, which can give you experience reading long amounts of text (while still making it interesting and not monotone and drab). In addition to the Braille Institute, many public broadcasting stations use volunteers to read printed material to the blind as well.

Finding Voice-Over Work

Two of the major sources of work for voice-over talent are radio and television commercials, so target the commercial market. Watch TV and listen to the radio and note which local advertisers use voice-over talent. Some local advertisers may just have the radio DJ read the copy instead of hiring a voice-over actor. Depending on the interest of the radio DJ at the time, this choice can either be useful or awful. If the DJ verbally slaughters the advertiser's message, that may be your open door to convincing the local advertiser to use your talents as a voice-over actor instead. (Find a problem that you can solve for a client, and you increase the odds that the client will listen to you and possibly even hire you.)

Contact the local advertising agencies in your area. Many of them may go through agents to find voice-over talent, but if you contact them directly, you may be able to get work. Also, try contacting your local chamber of commerce to find out the larger companies in your area. Big companies often need voice-over talent for commercials or industrial films.

The more voice-over work you can do, the more you learn, and the better you get (hopefully). At a certain stage, you'll need to take the next step in your voice-over career and create a demo tape to showcase your voice acting to potential clients and agents. We discuss the ins and outs of making an impressive demo tape in the next section.

Preparing Your Demo Tape

In traditional acting, your head shot is your calling card because it gives people an idea of what you look like. In voice-over acting, a head shot is irrelevant because nobody really cares what you look like. Instead of a head shot, voice-over actors need a *demo tape* or a recording used to showcase their voice acting abilities so that someone will hire them. (The term demo tape can mean an audiocassette or an audio CD.)

Don't be anxious to create a demo tape too soon. If you create and distribute a mediocre demo tape, your tarnished reputation may take months or even years to recover. Wait until you're capable of doing and recording at least one unique voice well. Then as you add new voices to your repertoire, you can make a new demo tape to include your new abilities.

Including all the right stuff

The demo tape needs to demonstrate your vocal range and accurately represent your capabilities — essentially providing a sample of what you can do.

When you show up to do a voice-over job, you must sound exactly like your voice on the demo tape. Any voice you record on a demo tape must be a voice that you can do well and consistently. If you can't repeat a particular voice on a consistent basis, don't put it on your demo tape because, inevitably, that will be the voice you'll be asked to do while reading multiple lines of dialogue.

In order to sell you as a voice actor, your demo tape has to keep a potential client listening. Here are some ways to make your demo tape easy and interesting to listen to:

- **Put your best voice first.** If potential clients don't like what they hear within the first five to ten seconds, they may turn off the tape and never hear anything else you've done.
- **Keep each audio clip short.** You want to provide potential clients with a taste of your abilities. You'll rarely record an entire script for your demo tape because it takes up too much time.
- **Offer variety.** Put different styles of your voice acting on your demo tape to make it more interesting. Record parts from several different scripts (commercials, narratives, or cartoons) and then choose bits and pieces of your best speaking parts to paste together for your demo tape.

You can get a copy of old commercials from an advertising agency or radio station, or you can record commercials off the radio or television and transcribe the words into your own script, or make up your own voice-over spots. Never misrepresent yourself. If you record an existing commercial, using your voice, never give the impression that your recording was actually aired or broadcast. Even seasoned voice-over actors may want to record different types of commercials just to showcase their versatility and the variety of voices they can offer a client.

- **Include only your very best voices.** You want your demo tape to showcase the best you can do, so quality is more important than quantity.

As you get more experienced in voice acting, your demo tape can contain actual voice-over work you've done as well as voice samples that are different from your previous work. That way, potential clients will be able to hear what types of voices you've done for previous jobs as well as the different kinds of voices you're capable of doing.

In addition to your demo tape, you should also include a voice-over acting resume that lists the different types of work you've done and the different types of voices you can do.

Laying down the tracks

Your demo tape must represent professional-quality voice acting because you'll be competing against seasoned voice acting professionals. So when you're ready to record a demo tape, you need to rent out time in a sound studio.

Use a sound studio that specializes in voice-over work. (Call different sound studios and ask for references from any past voice-over actors who have worked with them. Also ask for any sample copies of demo tapes the sound studio may have made for others.) If you use a sound studio that specializes in music, they may not have the proper equipment or expertise to record your demo tape properly.

Unless you own or have access to the type of equipment normally found in a professional sound studio, don't try to record a demo tape by yourself. A home-recorded demo tape will sound amateurish, despite your best vocal acting abilities. Voice-over work requires professional sound quality, and your demo tape must present your voice as it would sound in a professional sound studio.

Renting out time in a sound studio isn't cheap. Expect to spend a few hundred to a thousand dollars for all expenses involved to create a demo tape. Some of the expenses in addition to renting time in a sound studio include

- Post-production expenses for editing and arranging your vocal tracks.
- Labor costs for the recording engineer.
- Music licensing fees. If the sound studio provides any music to use for your demo tape, you must pay a licensing fee. Be careful about using music from your own music collection because you won't have the legal right to duplicate that music unless you get permission from the artist. For more information about music licensing fees, contact the National Academy of Recording Arts & Sciences (`http://nationalacademyofrecordingartssciences1.visualnet.com`).
- Material costs for creating a master audiocassette or CD and any duplicates.

When making duplicates of your demo tape, make sure you have your name and contact information printed both on the tape (or CD) and the case that holds your demo tape. That way, if your demo tape gets separated from its case, a potential client can still reach you. In many cases, you can get your demo tape (or CD) duplicated at the recording studio itself or at a special tape or CD duplicating business (which may charge much less for duplication costs than a recording studio would). When you're just starting out, don't make too many demo tapes or CDs. If you find yourself constantly making duplicates, that's a sign that you need to order more duplicates in bulk (which may also mean that you're auditioning and hopefully getting more voice-over roles as well).

Recording subsequent demo tapes

As a beginner, your demo tape will simply highlight the best voices you can do consistently well. As you gain more experience, you may want to create several different demo tapes that target different types of voice-over work, such as the following:

- **Commercials:** Commercial demo tapes are geared for radio and television commercials, so this type of demo tape exhibits your range of voices while reading real or made-up commercials.
- **Narratives:** Narrative demo tapes are geared towards corporate work, such as training films designed to teach employees of a large company how to practice safety in the workplace or how to become a more effective salesperson. Besides voice-over work for industrial films, narratives may include voice-over for documentaries.

- **Characters:** Character demo tapes are meant to showcase the more unique skills of a voice-over actor, such as celebrity impersonations or cartoon-like characters.

Getting an Agent

As in all forms of acting, an agent can be useful in helping you find voice-over work, but he or she is often more important in negotiating your fees. You don't necessarily need an agent to do voice-over work, but without an agent, you may never hear of the numerous voice-over jobs available every day.

To get an agent, contact the local Screen Actors Guild (SAG) or the American Federation of Television and Radio Artists (AFTRA) union offices and ask for their lists of union-franchised agencies. As another alternative, grab a copy of *The Ross Reports* and check its listings of agents. Go through these lists and contact each agency to find out whether they represent voice-over talent. As soon as you have a list of talent agencies who represent voice-over actors, contact each one and find out to whom you should send your demo tape, resume, and cover letter.

If an agent is interested in you, he or she will contact you right away. However, making a follow-up call a week or two after mailing out your demo tape isn't a bad idea.

Auditioning for Voice-Over Work

Of course, taking voice lessons, making a demo tape, and finding an agent is pointless unless you actually get out of the house and start auditioning for voice-over work. Auditions for voice-over work are similar to traditional acting auditions, except that casting directors are interested in your voice rather than your appearance.

Your audition will be recorded, so you'll need to stand or sit near the microphone. During this time, you may be asked to speak so that the recording engineer can adjust the recording level. When the recording level is set, the casting director will ask you to read from a script two or three times, either giving you directions to modify your reading each time or leaving it up to you to decide how to alter each reading by emphasizing different words or phrases, or by changing the tone, pitch, or volume of your voice. After a few readings, you'll be done.

After auditioning various voice-over actors, the casting director and anyone else involved with the voice-over spot (such as an advertising agency representative) may listen to the tapes of the actors to determine which one they want, or which group of actors they want to re-evaluate for a callback.

During your audition, you may have the aid (or hindrance) of a scratch track or music track. A *scratch track* is a rough version of a commercial, developed as a demo for the client. By reading along with a scratch track, you can get a sense of the timing and rhythm you'll need for the final version. Many commercials have background music, so the music track can help you adjust your voice to match the tempo and rhythm of the music.

Getting Paid as a Voice-Over Actor

You can make a little or a lot of money from voice-over acting, just like from any form of acting, depending on the type of work you do. Different types of payments include

- **Flat-fee or buy-out:** This type of payment offers a single fee for unlimited use of your voice. Payment may vary, depending on how much time you spend in the studio. But after you're paid, you get no additional money — no matter how many times your voice may be used.

  Buy-outs are common in narratives for industrial films and information kiosks, books on tape, character voices for computer video games in arcade machines or personal computers, and radio or television commercials for local advertisers.

- **Wild spot fees:** This type of payment is common for work in regional and national commercials. It pays you for the right to use your voice for a fixed period of time, such as 13 weeks. After the initial 13-week time period is up, you may get paid an additional fee if the commercial is run for another 13 weeks. So the more popular your commercial, the more money you make.

- **Residuals:** The most lucrative types of voice-over work are the ones that involve residuals (also known as *royalties*), which are typically paid for nationally broadcast commercials or voice-overs in film, television shows, and animated features. With residuals, you get paid for your time plus an additional payment every time the commercial, film, television show, or animated feature is broadcast again. Think how much money actors make for doing the voices of a hit film like *Shrek* or a hit animated series like *The Simpsons.* (Sometimes, for commercials, you won't get paid each time the commercial airs. Instead, you may receive a residual payment from the advertiser, so the advertiser has the right to air your commercial any number of times for a certain period of time, such as for the next 13 weeks.)

Voice-over acting can be another way you can pursue acting either in addition to more traditional theater, film, and television acting, or as a separate career on its own. Because voice-over acting doesn't rely on looks or appearance like film or television acting does, you can look any way you like and be any age without fear of discrimination of any form. If you have a distinctive voice, you just may find that voice-over acting can give you the chance to be a star while still maintaining your privacy.

Chapter 14

Working as an Extra

In This Chapter

- Exploring a silent and unsung aspect of acting
- Making the most out of being an extra
- Knowing the disadvantages of taking on roles as an extra

Watch any movie or television show and you see people standing, walking, or moving around in the background. Often, you don't even see these people's faces or recognize them as anything other than a blur as the camera moves past them. In the world of show business, people who appear as nondescript characters without speaking lines or without performing any important action are called background actors, or *extras.*

The goal of having an extra is to fill up a background with a real live body to give the scene an illusion of reality. Extra work is easy, plentiful, and (at first) relatively interesting. If you want to get an idea of what working in movies or TV is like, occasional extra work may be the perfect opportunity for you to experience show business without having to quit your day job to do it.

Delving into the Glamorous World of an Extra

Anyone can be an extra, regardless of age, sex, or looks, because most people watching the movie, TV show, or commercial won't even know you're there anyway. Extras add a touch of realism by populating a scene and making it look natural. While nobody may remember the faces of the extras who charged the Normandy beaches in the film *Saving Private Ryan,* viewers would have noticed the absence of such extras if they saw only Tom Hanks charging the beach by himself.

An iceberg by any other name . . .

To show you how unimportant looks, age, nationality, and even language can be for an extra, consider the story behind James Cameron's *Titanic,* filmed in Rosarito Beach, Mexico — about a one-hour drive south of San Diego. Because the faces of most extras would never be seen and none of the extras needed to speak, Cameron simply dressed up the local population of Mexicans in the appropriate period costumes and had them stroll around the deck of the ship to masquerade as wealthy, first-class passengers from England. So the next time you watch this film, just remember that unlike history, most of the passengers who sank with Cameron's *Titanic* spoke Spanish.

Essentially, an extra is a living piece of scenery that can walk and move under his own power, given the guidance of the director. As an extra, your job is to sit down (so the director can find you whenever she needs you), be quiet (so your excessive talking doesn't interfere with the more important people on the set), and be ready. In return for eight hours or more of work each day, you get a (tiny) check and a trivial credit you can but may not want to put on your resume. (See the section "Advancing Your Career Beyond an Extra," later in this chapter.) You also get a peek behind the scenes of show business that most people never get to see, and you have a lot of interesting stories you can tell to your family and friends when you finish.

Recognizing types of extras

In show business (and in the world in general), a pecking order is standard, and extra work is no exception. Generally, the three types of extras you may catch wandering around aimlessly on a television or movie set are

- Day extras
- Special extras
- Silent bit extras

A *day extra* is lowest on the status hierarchy of extras. Essentially, a day extra fills the background with a live body. Day extras may need to act as if they're talking on the phone or to another extra, or as if they're just standing or walking around. Sometimes, mannequins or computer-generated images fill the roles of day extras, as in the large-scale battle scenes in *Gone with the Wind* and *The Patriot.* These inanimate "actors" won't take over all the roles that extras play — directors will always need real people to help fill in a scene.

Special extras perform a specialty skill in the background, such as juggling, skateboarding, diving, fencing, playing a musical instrument, or horseback riding. None of the actions required from a special extra are dangerous or particularly complicated, but they do require enough familiarity with a particular skill so that the action looks authentic. (If you find that being a special extra is too boring, consider becoming a stuntperson, instead.)

Silent bit extras often interact with the principal actors in some way, such as serving them a drink in the middle of a conversation or opening a door for them as they walk through. A silent bit extra appears in the same scene as one of the bigger stars, so the chances are excellent for a silent bit extra to be seen in the final movie, commercial, or television show. As a silent bit extra, you don't make any more money than any other type of extra, but at least you may actually get your face on the big screen for a split second or two.

Risking your life for anonymity: The life of a stuntperson

If the idea of standing around to fill up a crowd scene bores the living daylights out of you, consider a more exciting (and potentially crippling or life-threatening) option of working as a stuntperson, instead.

Stuntpeople perform all the dangerous tasks you see in movies and TV shows, such as jumping a car over a ditch, falling down a flight of stairs, walking on an airplane wing, catching on fire, getting blown up, crashing a motorcycle into a wall, scaling a skyscraper, getting punched in the face, wrestling a shark underwater, and doing any other task that normally would cause serious injury to the person involved.

Of course, working as a stuntperson isn't as easy as working as an extra, but the pay is much better and the work far more exciting. Stuntpeople even have their own training schools (to teach people different types of stunts, such as falling through a window or lighting themselves on fire) and their own union that ensures they're paid well for their work.

Stuntpeople tend to be young, athletic, and highly proficient in a variety of different skills, including horseback riding, martial arts, alligator wrestling, or some other unique talent that threatens the life and safety of the participant.

Generally, you break into the stunt business by first doing simple actions, such as falling off a building or getting punched in the face. As you gain experience, you eventually graduate to the more dangerous stunts, such as falling off a building just as it blows up or getting punched in the face and falling through a window.

Just remember that stunt work is highly dangerous, and nearly every stuntperson suffers broken bones or serious injuries at some point in his or her career. A small handful of stuntpeople get killed, lose a limb, or get paralyzed every year, so if risking your life just to do something highly dangerous that you never get public recognition for still appeals to you, then, by all means, consider working as a stuntperson instead of as an extra.

Getting work as an extra

Extras, like all types of actors, have agents, too. When a studio needs extras to fill out a scene, they contact agencies that specialize in extras. Most agencies use all physical types, age ranges, and ethnicities who want to work as extras.

Show business loves sprinkling clearly recognizable nationalities in the background as extras, so if you fit into a specific ethnic niche, your chances of getting a job as an extra are extremely good. It's too bad your chances of getting a higher-paying speaking role aren't just as easy!

Unlike regular casting agencies, extras-casting agencies are rarely picky. If you're willing to work, these agencies are willing to put you on a set somewhere to work as an extra. Often, a studio needs an extra at the last minute, which in show business terms means tomorrow morning. So if you sign up with an extras-casting agency, don't be surprised to get a call late at night to report for work as an extra early the next morning.

Although anyone can be an extra, you can't just show up at an extras-casting agency during your vacation in Hollywood and expect to get a role in a movie or TV show. Studios need to plan for the number and types of extras they need, which means if you don't live near the studios, an extras-casting agency probably won't want to use you.

Extras-casting agencies specialize in filling a set with live bodies, and that's it. Head shots, resumes, and any acting experience you may have are irrelevant to these agencies. As long as you're alive and willing to work, an extras-casting agency will be happy to use you.

You can get a taste of extra work anywhere you live. Extra work done in movies, TV shows, industrial films, commercials, and music videos may be filmed anywhere, either in a studio or on location. When film productions travel to far-off locations, directors often hire the locals as extras and advertise in the newspapers to attract participants. If you happen to be in a location where a movie is being filmed, you can apply to work as an extra without going through an agency at all. To find out more about extra work in your area, contact your state's film commission.

Examining a day in the life of an extra

Because extras are treated as little more than living props who have the unfortunate tendency to get bored without having anything to do for ten hours at a time, the typical day for an extra closely follows that of a typical movie or TV actor but without the money, fame, or prestige.

The first thing you do as an extra is arrive early to check in so that the director knows you're available. Next, you may need to get fitted for any costumes or report to makeup, whatever the director deems necessary. This process usually starts early in the morning (7:00 a.m. start times are typical) and continues until all the extras are properly dressed and ready to go.

After you're dressed, you usually have to wait around until the stars are dressed, made up, and ready to go, which usually takes most of the morning. If you're lucky, you may get a chance to watch the camera operators film one scene that you probably won't be in, so you have to sit around and wait some more. (The extras often have to stay in one part of the set, so the director will know where to find them when he needs them. This restriction means that you usually can't wander around and watch the filming.)

About this time, lunch will be ready. The stars, director, producer, and anyone else with a lot of clout and money get to eat first and find a place to sit. Then the minor actors get to stand in line, followed by the camera operators, the carpenters, the gaffers, the security officers, and anyone else who actually has a productive job to do. Finally, the extras get to eat. (Don't forget to let a big star or director cut in line ahead of you if he or she wants seconds before you've even had firsts.)

The food served on the set is usually excellent and plentiful. If you're a starving actor, getting extra work can be a way to eat decent meals for the entire day while getting paid for it at the same time.

After lunch, the director may film another scene that you probably won't be in, either. So you'll get plenty of time to mill around with the other extras and stare blindly into space. To keep yourself amused, you may want to hang around the catering truck (affectionately known among business circles as the "roach coach"), which constantly dishes out cold drinks, sandwiches, and bags of potato chips for the amusement of the camera crew and anyone else who believes in eating continually.

After another scene change and possibly another costume change for the major actors, the time may finally arrive for you to take your role in a scene where you'll be standing in the background where nobody will be able to recognize your face, let alone recognize that you're actually a living human being. If you're lucky, the actors won't mess up their lines, but more likely, the actors will forget a line, a light bulb will suddenly burn out, a plane will fly overhead and ruin the sound, or the director will be just plain unhappy with the way the scene looks, so you'll have to do it all over again.

If you're one of the lucky extras in the scene, you'll be sitting down. If you're one of the unlucky extras, you'll be forced to continue standing in one place. More troublesome is when extras have the job of walking around. Not only do these extras need to get into position again, but they also need to walk past the major actors in the exact same way each time the director wants to reshoot the scene. This exactness provides continuity to the scene.

As an extra, you have full access to the studio lot or shooting location, so spotting famous movie and TV stars walking around is inevitable. Whatever you do, don't disturb the stars! The last thing these stars want is to have an extra bug them for an autograph. When actors are on the set, they want to concentrate on working, not on satisfying an autograph hound. If you annoy the stars or the director, they have the power to get you thrown off the set immediately.

Finally, you may be done with filming your particular scene, and then you can go back and wait with the other extras until the director decides to use you again later that day (which may be never, but you're expected to wait until the end of the day, anyway). In show business terms, no one stops work after an 8-hour day. Expect a 10-, 12-, or 14-hour day, most of it spent sitting around watching other people work (or also sitting around).

When filming finally wraps up for that day, extras can go home. You may be hired to work another day or two. Eventually, when all filming is done, chances are good that you either won't be able to recognize yourself in any of the scenes or that all of the scenes you appeared in will be cut from the final film. If you're lucky, you may be able to spot yourself in a film, although no one else will likely notice you.

Isn't life as an extra fun?

Extra work is completely unpredictable. Sometimes, you appear in several scenes. Sometimes, you appear briefly in one short scene. And sometimes, you never get used at all. If the director never uses you, you still get paid, but you have to sit around the whole day in hopes that you actually get used in a scene or two.

To kill time, many extras bring books, crossword puzzles, portable stereos, or any other type of device to amuse themselves for hours at a time. Rather than trying to kill time, use the time to learn more about acting by either watching the film crew, reading books about acting, or networking with other actors. You can read a book or do a crossword puzzle anywhere, so make your time on the set useful and productive in boosting your acting career — no matter how much or how little you may be able to accomplish each day.

Appreciating the Advantages of Being an Extra

Working as an extra means long hours, low pay, lack of recognition, and (perhaps) minimal acting skills. Despite those rather underwhelming attributes, consider some of the advantages to being an extra: You get a behind-the-scenes look at filmmaking and a chance to network with fellow actors (not to mention all that free food).

Investigating the technical business of show business

One reason people pay money to tour the Universal Studios back lot is because they want to get an insider's peek at show business. As an extra, you're actually part of show business (albeit a very tiny part), so you can use this valuable opportunity to explore the technical side of filmmaking.

Novices, as well as actors, coming from a theatrical background are often astounded at the amount of time camera operators need to film a five-minute scene. Commercial shoots, which may capture only 30 seconds to a minute, often take one or more days to film. The reason is simple: If you want to capture the best scene possible, you may as well take the time to do it right rather than do a lousy job in ten minutes and be forced to reshoot it all over again the next day.

The technical side of filmmaking involves moving props around, checking the sound, adjusting the lighting, and arranging different camera angles. When the camera crew thinks they're ready, *stand-ins* go through the actions that the principal actors will follow. These actions may include walking through a door, sitting in a chair, and picking up a cup of coffee. (See the sidebar "Stands-ins: The extras nobody knows about" in this section.)

Stand-ins: The extras nobody knows about

If working as an extra seems like a relatively anonymous business, consider the role of stand-ins. A *stand-in* is someone who has a similar height, build, and look of a major star or principal actor. Instead of wasting the movie star's or principal actor's time by having her stand on the set while the camera and lighting crew adjusts the lighting and prepares the cameras, a stand-in does this job instead.

As the name implies, a stand-in simply stands where the movie star is going to stand while the crew makes sure that the lighting and camera angles are okay. If the scene involves walking or moving in any way, the director may ask the stand-in to move in the same way that the star will move during filming. If any shadows, echoes, or additional disturbances threaten to wreck the scene, the director wants to find out about them now before calling the stars in (and dealing with their sometimes temperamental egos).

When the camera crew is ready, the stand-in walks off the set, and the big star replaces her to do the actual filming. As a result, stand-ins have no chance of being seen in the film. To offset this slight disadvantage, stand-ins do get paid better than regular extras, and they have guaranteed work for as long as the filming takes place.

So if you happen to look like someone famous, consider working as a stand-in, instead. As a stand-in, you can get paid to stand around and do nothing without having to work for the government first.

While the stand-ins go through these motions, the camera crew rechecks to make sure that shadows don't accidentally cover an actor's face, the door doesn't squeak too loudly when opened, the cup of coffee doesn't stick to the table, and so on. Any minor problem must get fixed immediately and the entire scene retested again (and again, and again).

By watching this endless parade of actions occur over and over again, you can take note of what problems and difficulties an actor may encounter on a film set. By becoming aware of these difficulties, you can understand and prepare yourself when you (hopefully) get a role as one of the principal actors on a film or TV set one day.

All the people on the set have a job to do, even if most of the time they appear to be doing nothing at all. Whatever you do, don't offer to help lift equipment or move props around, because your help won't be welcome — it's against union regulations, and you'll just make a nuisance of yourself anyway. As an extra, your job is to stay out of everyone else's way and do what the director tells you to do.

Studying the acting side of filmmaking

Most of the time, when the principal actors (the big names) start filming a scene, the extras get herded out of the way like a bunch of unwanted stray cats. The reason for this segregation is to keep the set as quiet and as uncluttered as possible — and having a bunch of gawking extras standing in everybody's way helps no one.

Still, if you're lucky enough, you may be able to quietly tuck yourself away from the set in a spot where you can still observe the filming from a distance. Take advantage of this opportunity! By watching experienced actors work, you can see what they do right (and what they may do wrong). Also, try to listen and watch how the director may adjust their acting and how the actors modify their performances accordingly.

As an extra, you have the unique opportunity of seeing how a TV show, commercial, or movie is filmed; you can then study the final product when it's released to the unsuspecting public. By watching and absorbing when an actual scene is being filmed, you can become familiar with television and film acting. When the happy day arrives when you're chosen for a principal role in a TV show or movie, you'll know what to expect on the set and why.

Networking with fellow actors

As long as you're trapped on a set for many hours at a time, you may as well strike up a conversation with your fellow extras. Rather than chat mindlessly about sports or the weather, take this opportunity to network with the other extras and swap information about agents, upcoming auditions, tips for acting, suggestions for hiring a photographer to take your head shots, and anything else you can think of that can help you out as an aspiring actor.

Some extras may be outright hostile to sharing any information with you, whom they view as competition. If you run across a tight-lipped, insecure actor like that, just walk away and spend your time with someone more interesting. Communication goes both ways, though: Try to share your own information with the other extras, instead of constantly asking them to cough up information for you. With this approach, you won't be seen as selfish and greedy.

Making a little (emphasis on "little") money

Working as an extra requires nothing more than being alive, so you may want to work as an extra for a little spare cash. In return for working (waiting around) for 10 to 14 hours at a time, you get paid a small amount of money (ranging anywhere from $50 to $100 or more), lunch, and lots of time to sit around to wonder why you wanted to work as an extra in the first place.

Working as a technical advisor

Rather than stand around in front of the camera as an extra, you may be more interested in standing around behind the camera as a technical advisor. As the name implies, a technical advisor offers tips to the actors and director for making a particular scene more realistic, whether it means changing the dialogue, altering the props, or rewriting an entire scene. The next time you see a movie or TV show involving doctors, lawyers, soldiers, police officers, or con artists, chances are the director used a technical advisor's insight to make the scene as authentic as possible.

To work as a technical advisor, you (obviously) need a special skill that's in demand, whether it's working as a brain surgeon or as a member of a SWAT team. Technical advisors must analyze a script and watch the filming. Fortunately, technical advisors get paid a lot more than ordinary extras. Technical advisors also can continue working in a normal job while spending their free time dabbling in the wacky world of show business.

If you have an important skill that filmmakers may need, consider working as a technical advisor. Although this job won't help your acting career much, it can help pay your bills and enable you to make valuable contacts. You also gain exposure to show business — you'll see whether this is an industry you really want to get more involved in after all!

The myth of sudden stardom

A persistent rumor among extras is that if the director or producer notices you, she may suddenly give you a speaking role so that you can make a lot more money and become a star. This myth, much like Big Foot, UFOs, and the Loch Ness monster, does have some element of truth to it.

The director or producer really does have the power to elevate someone from a lowly extra role to a speaking role that allows that person to be seen rather than shuffled into the background to share screen time with a potted fern. But truthfully, most directors and producers are too busy working with their stars, camera operators, and assistants to take more than a cursory glance at the motley crew of extras, huddled to one side, hoping to be recognized. Even if a star suddenly falls ill or fails to perform properly (shows up late, can't stay sober, and so on), chances are good the producer will simply wait until the star or any of the principal actors is feeling better rather than take a chance on dragging an extra into the spotlight.

So yes, it's theoretically possible that working as an extra can be your path to stardom, but realistically, your odds of striking it rich are probably better if you buy a lottery ticket instead. Just as you wouldn't bet your future on the outcome of a lottery drawing, you shouldn't base the future of your acting career on the off chance that someone will discover you as an extra.

If you have lots of spare time on your hands and don't mind sitting around doing nothing, by all means, try to work as an extra as often as possible. If you're truly aspiring to be an actor, however, working as an extra may be worthwhile only occasionally so that you can study the art of filmmaking and acting.

Advancing Your Career Beyond an Extra

The main reason you don't want to work one extra job after another is because you should want to be the star, and working as an extra isn't going to help you achieve that goal. Many people do extra work out of boredom, to keep themselves amused (especially popular with some retirees). Perhaps you have the misguided belief that you can work as an extra and magically be discovered on the set where you'll be elevated to a starring role. (See the sidebar "The myth of sudden stardom" in this chapter.)

The goal of an actor is to get a speaking role. Not only does that job pay better, but it also allows you to be seen and heard, which extra work will never do for you. On rare occasions, a director may want an extra to shout out a word or two, such as "Hey!" or "He went that way!" If you speak even just one word, you'll no longer be considered an extra, and you'll have a speaking (and acting) credit that you can add to your resume.

The moment you have a speaking role in a union production, even if it's just one word, you automatically qualify for joining the Screen Actors Guild (a process known as being "Taft-Hartleyed").

Four additional reasons why you shouldn't aspire to be an extra include

- Not much money
- No fame
- The stigma of being "just an extra"
- No noticeable presence on screen

You could work as an extra every day for the rest of your life and be lucky if you make just enough money to scrape by. If you want to get rich as an actor, working as an extra is probably the last job you want. (Even waiting tables pays better per hour than working as an extra.)

In addition to the lack of money, extra work doesn't provide you with any acting credits you can use to build your resume. Saying that you worked as an extra in the top ten movies of the past decade is about as meaningful as having an aspiring quarterback say that he emptied the trash for the past ten Super Bowl teams. Basically, nobody in show business cares what type of extra work you've done because it shows only that you're skilled enough not to wave at the camera like an enthusiastic passerby when it points in your general direction.

If you work too often as an extra, you may also earn the unwanted reputation of being nothing more than "just another extra." As soon as directors start recognizing you as an extra, they may never be able to picture you as anything else no matter how talented you may be.

Perhaps the biggest disadvantage is that the time spent (wasted) working as an extra means time taken away from attending acting classes, going to auditions for real roles, and making phone calls to learn about new opportunities as an actor.

Ultimately, working as an extra can be amusing, interesting, and actually fun; but if you're serious about succeeding as an actor, you should pursue extra work sparingly and devote your time to discovering more about acting so that you can get the high-profile (and high-paying) jobs, instead. But if you like getting a behind-the-scenes peek at how show business works, you just may find that working as an extra can be interesting and fun.

Chapter 15

Getting Your Kid into Show Biz

In This Chapter

- Deciding whether to make the commitment
- Looking at acting roles for kids
- Exploring the business side of the child acting biz

Show business offers plenty of work for child actors for the simple reason that the current batch of talented and experienced child actors will eventually grow up and become adults. As a result, film, television, and theater need to find new faces all the time, and child actors are always in demand.

Show business uses all types of child actors, ranging in ages from newborn babies to teenagers who still aren't old enough to buy beer legally. So whatever age your child may be, he or she can always start an acting career at any time.

If your child happens to look younger than he or she really is, you can use that baby face to your advantage! Show business worships youth, not just for the physical attractiveness but because an older child actor who can pass himself off as younger child should (theoretically) be easier to manage on the set. Getting a 3-year-old to cooperate may be difficult, but getting a 5-year-old who looks like a 3-year-old is (hopefully) much easier on the director and the rest of the cast.

If you think that your child has what it takes to make it big as a child actor, this chapter gives you the tips that you need to help make his acting dreams come true. For starters, you need to ask yourself and your child whether you're willing to sacrifice time and money to help your kid become an actor. This chapter then describes the array of acting gigs your kid can try out for. Finally, you'll discover the laws and regulations you need to be aware of when your child gets called for an audition or arrives on the set for filming.

Considering the Commitment

Pursuing a career in acting is time-consuming, whether you're a kid or an adult. What makes acting tougher for children, though, is that not only do they need to continue going to school, but they also must sacrifice their free time by trying to live a normal life while going to auditions as well.

So before you rush out and throw your pride and joy to the sharks of show business and pray for the best, take a moment and ask yourself these two questions:

- Does your kid really want to become an actor?
- Do you really want to spend the time and money helping your kid to become an actor?

Does your kid really want to do this?

Being a child actor doesn't mean that you have to give up being a child. You *can* juggle between an acting career and being a kid. Some kids may totally love acting for a few years and then suddenly take an equally great interest in soccer, skateboarding, or oil painting. If the kid's acting career takes off, great. If not, the kid still has a normal life as a human being.

Generally, aspiring child actors fall into one of three categories:

- Kids who want to act more than anything else in the world. If your child fits in this category and would love nothing more than a chance to act on stage, TV, or the movies, feel free to skip to the next section, "Do you really want to do this?"
- Kids who think that acting may be fun but also want to pursue other interests in life. If your child fits in this category, you may want to pursue acting less aggressively so that your child has time to pursue other activities as well.
- Kids whose parents are trying to force them to become actors against their will. If you fear that you may be pressuring your child into a career in acting, think about what you're doing. If a child doesn't want to pursue an acting career, he or she definitely won't act very well, making auditioning and the pursuit of an acting career a complete waste of time for everyone.

Some children may *love* the idea of acting — until they're faced with the reality of long hours, reading the same line over and over again, spending so much time away from their friends and activities, and so on. Sit down and have a heart-to-heart with your child to explain up front the commitment that he or she is agreeing to make. If your child seems legitimately committed to pursuing an acting career (as committed as he or she can be at age 5 or 10), the next question you have to ask yourself is how much support you're able to give your child to succeed in show business.

Child actors, just like adults, often pursue acting for all the wrong reasons, such as thinking that becoming a star will make them more popular, get them rich, make other people respect them, and so on. Unless your child really loves acting, all the fame and money in the world isn't going to make your child's life (or your life) any better. Many former child actors go on to a life of alcohol or drug abuse after the fame and money run out. But as long as your child truly loves acting and as long as you're willing to support your little actor 100 percent, all the hardships, pain, and obstacles in the way will be nothing more than amusing stories that you and your child will be able to tell your friends and family one day.

Beware of the stereotypical stage mother (or father)

Don't ever force your kid to go into acting (or any type of career for that matter). Your child — not you — should choose his or her life. If you try to sacrifice your child's happiness to make yourself feel better about your own pitiful existence, you don't need a child with an acting career; you need a psychiatrist, preferably one who isn't afraid to use excessive electric shock therapy to help you see the error of your ways.

Even if you manage to force, threaten, or otherwise coerce a child into acting when he or she really doesn't want to, guess what? When your child auditions (and most children audition alone, out of sight of the parents), casting directors and producers can spot a browbeaten child within seconds and won't even consider using that child for two reasons:

- First, if the child doesn't want to act, he or she won't be very good at it no matter how much the parents may threaten or bribe the child.
- Secondly, producers and directors know that even the best child actor is useless if accompanied by an obnoxious stage mother or father who constantly annoys them and interferes with the taping or rehearsal of the play.

No matter how much you may believe otherwise, child actors can be replaced. In many cases, a producer chooses one child actor and later fires him or her because of the obnoxious behavior of that child's parents. When this happens, producers look back at the handful of child actors whom they thought would also be perfect for the part and uses one of those children instead.

On the flip side, if your child ever fails to win an audition, don't give up hope. The ultimate winner of that particular audition may possibly have parents who annoy the director or producer so much that the producer winds up using your child after all. If this happens, you can thank some other child's parents for not having the common sense and professionalism that you (hopefully) already possess.

Do you really want to do this?

How many people are willing to pay someone else's expenses, chauffeur someone else around town, and sacrifice a good chunk of their own free time just on the off chance of making money for your children? Well, that's exactly what you'll be doing. If this thought makes you cringe, you may want to seriously consider keeping your kid out of show business.

Getting your child into show business requires a massive commitment of extra time, money, and patience. Although adult actors can support themselves and find a way to get themselves to an audition, child actors need a parent or guardian to drive them to the auditions, help them with their homework, and still do all the other regular parent stuff, too. If you think that your life doesn't have enough time right now, you'll definitely have much less time for everything as soon as you try to help your kid break into show business. And if you have two or more kids who want to break into show business, you've just doubled or tripled your already overburdened schedule.

Because children may get discouraged easily or change their minds literally overnight, make sure that your child knows that it's okay to stop acting at any time. But also make sure that the child isn't quitting out of discouragement but truly desires not to pursue acting anymore (or at least for the time being). Remember, a child can always return to acting later in life, either as a child actor or an adult actor.

When faced with this additional burden on your time and resources, you, as the parent, need to be just as committed to your child's acting career as your child. Plus, you have to give your child every right to stop pursuing acting whenever it no longer makes him or her happy — no matter how much money and time you may have invested in photographers, acting lessons, and resumes. So if the prospect of running around and trying to do five different things at once already makes you dizzy, maybe you should put your child in something that will cause you less stress and anxiety — like sky diving or alligator wrestling.

Setting goals for you and your child

Although you can never predict how much success your child will achieve, you can set goals early in your child's acting career that are completely independent of what success (or lack of success) your child may encounter. For example, the initial goal may be to find an agent for your child and start going out on auditions.

If you think that show business is competitive . . .

Raising a child is tough enough. But try raising a child actor, being around for your spouse, and raising one or two other kids who may not want anything to do with the rigors of show business. After you pile on so many obstacles, even the potential multimillion-dollar windfall may not seem as attractive as it once did. Perhaps the toughest part about raising a child in show business is sharing your time with any other children you may have.

Siblings naturally fight with one another and vie for their parents' attention, and show business only aggravates that situation. (Children may also resent their sibling's "star" status, so be prepared to deal with this form of sibling rivalry as well). If you're spending most of your time driving one child to auditions, you still need to set aside some time to spend with your other children. Many parents make the mistake of lavishing all their attention and love for their "star" child while indirectly sending the message to their other children that, somehow, they're not as important. This kind of lopsided attention will only be a recipe for resentment, anger, jealousy, and years of therapy for everyone in the future. Remember, all your children are stars in their own right, and you should treat them all equally.

Besides devoting time to any other children you may have, you also need to set aside time to spend with your spouse, so that he or she doesn't feel neglected and left behind. Finally, you still need to set aside time for yourself as well to keep from going totally crazy after dealing with some of the people you'll inevitably meet in show business.

Remember, your child's well-being always comes first. If an acting career threatens to destabilize your relationship with the other members of your family, the time's come to take a serious look at how important an acting career really is for your child. Getting a child in show business requires determination from the child, support from the parents, and acceptance from the rest of the family. You can squeeze your child's acting career into any busy schedule as long as everyone is willing to negotiate, make sacrifices, and work together.

A second goal may be that after your child auditions for a certain number of roles, such as five (or whatever seems reasonable for you), both you and your child will sit down and honestly evaluate whether an acting career is something that both parent and child really want to pursue. If not, great. At least you've had the fun of getting a sneak peek into show business, and both of you will have plenty of memories (happy, bizarre, and otherwise) to remind you about your child's short acting career.

Don't give your child a fixed deadline for him or her to succeed as an actor. For example, if your child goes to five auditions and doesn't get any of them, don't automatically assume that your child should get out of acting. He or she may wind up passing the sixth and seventh audition. You can never predict when or how success will come in the world of show business. On the flip side, you also can't predict when success may go away for a while.

Childhood is full of major changes; children get and lose teeth, they get acne, they may need braces, and voices change. All these changes can play havoc with a child's normal life, not to mention an acting career. These changes don't necessarily mean that the time's come to throw in the towel, though. As long as your child is enjoying the experience and wants to keep trying, you need to help him or her see it through.

If both you and your child want to continue pursuing acting after a certain number of auditions, make a plan to determine how much time both of you will be willing to sacrifice from your day to pursue your child's acting career. Your plan should be clearly stated and easy to measure, such as saying your child will always do his or her homework in return for the parents always being available to take the child to an audition. If from the beginning you define clearly stated goals that every family member can see, discuss, and accept (or negotiate around), you can create a healthy family environment where everyone knows what's expected of them ahead of time.

Exploring the Acting Options

If you've read this far, you and your child must be serious about pursuing an acting career. Your next question may be what types of roles are open to a child actor. You can read about your options — ranging from modeling to theater — in the following sections.

If you're also an actor, be sure to bring your own head shot and resume to every audition that your child goes to. A casting director possibly may also cast you to play the parent of your own child in a TV commercial, film, or play. (Of course, acting with your child can be a fun and enjoyable experience, or it can be a recipe that lays the groundwork for years of therapy between you and your child in the future.)

Print ads

Print ads are snapshots that appear in magazines, newspapers, catalogues, and even on Web sites. These ads show actors sitting or standing near a product being advertised, such as a box of diapers. For clothing ads, the actor may pose to model certain clothes.

The younger the actors, the harder it can be to get them to cooperate to do anything for an extended period of time. As a result, babies and toddlers are often better suited for print ads rather than commercials or films because the director needs only a snapshot to capture the child in action as opposed to an entire commercial or TV show. (This logic explains why you rarely see babies on TV shows on a regular basis.)

For babies and toddlers appearing in print ads, size and appearance aren't that crucial. (Most babies always look cute anyway.) But for teenagers, print ads tend to prefer boys and girls who are more slender and taller and have attractive features.

Many teenagers, especially girls, starve themselves to look as thin as the models they see in print ads. Make sure that your teenager eats a healthy diet and maintains a positive self-image to prevent her from becoming bulimic or anorexic.

One of the more unusual modeling assignments available is modeling part of your body, such as a foot or a hand. Many hand and foot models earn plenty of money just for displaying a perfectly shaped body part to advertise a particular product. Although most hand and foot models are adults, occasionally, a print ad for a child's product may need a child's hand to hold a product or wear a child's shoes. So if your child has distinct body features, this type of modeling may be an additional avenue to explore.

TV commercials

Many child actors get their start working in TV commercials for two reasons:

- TV commercials are usually shot in short segments, so child actors aren't forced to memorize lengthy lines.
- TV commercials provide massive exposure in return for a relatively short amount of work (often just a day or two on the set), which can boost a child's acting career tremendously.

Of course, the drawback is that commercials often require child actors to do the same thing over and over and over . . .

The most sought-after commercials are national commercials run on the major networks. On the next tier down are the regional commercials (broadcast through a certain area, such as the Southwest) and, finally, the local commercials (usually broadcast in one city).

If your child is fortunate enough to land a TV commercial (no matter what kind it may be), make sure that you get a copy of that commercial for your child's portfolio. Appearances in TV commercials can often lead to bigger roles in TV shows and movies, so having a copy of all your child's commercials can give future casting directors another chance to view your child's acting ability. Also, the more tape you can collect showing your child's acting ability, the more credibility your child will have in the eyes of casting directors and agents.

Film and TV shows

For many people, film and TV roles represent the pinnacle of success in show business. Both opportunities offer your child worldwide exposure — in addition to the chance of massive amounts of cash in the form of salaries and *residuals* (also known as *royalties*), where your child gets paid each time a TV network airs that movie or TV show again.

Although films and TV shows offer the greatest financial rewards and exposure, they also demand the most time commitment. A single episode of a TV show often takes an entire week to rehearse, rewrite, and finally tape. (A typical TV show season lasts for several months, such as 26 weeks for a full season.) During the taping of a TV show, your child will likely spend every day at the studio, which means that you, as the parent, will spend every day at the studio. The only difference is that your child actually has a job to do to keep him or her busy, while your job is to be around for your child and to stay out of everyone else's way. (Now may be a good time to take up knitting or catch up on all those novels you keep meaning to read.)

As the parent of a child actor, your job is to deliver your child to the set and then stay out of the way, so the director can tell your child what to do next. Don't interfere with the director (unless you feel that your child's safety is threatened), and don't bring any other family members to the set without the director's permission. The director has enough to worry about without having to deal with unruly siblings or nosy relatives running around and getting in everyone's way.

Unlike TV shows that are often filmed in a studio (usually in Los Angeles or New York, if the show's made in the United States), movies may be filmed anywhere in the world — or even in several different parts of the world. As a result, getting a child in a film will likely require travel for both you and your child (paid for by the production company, of course). Depending on the film, you and your child may find yourselves in downtown Chicago one week, in the middle of Death Valley the next, and, finally, freezing to death in the tundra of northern Canada for the final month of shooting.

Because films often require constant travel, expect your child and one of the parents to be separated from the rest of the family for long periods of time. Films take anywhere from a few months to a year or more to film, and depending on your child's role, he or she may be required to be on the set during the entire length of filming.

Due to the unpredictable nature of babies and young children, films and TV shows tend to avoid relying on them because of the need to finish filming on a tight schedule. If a film or TV show needs to use a baby in a major role, the director tends to prefer using identical twins. (See the upcoming sidebar, "Twins: Your fast track to show business.")

Twins: Your fast track to show business

If you happen to be the parent of identical twins (or even triplets), you've just doubled (or tripled) your chances of breaking into show business.

The reason is simple. Getting children to do what you, the parents, ask them is tough enough, but directors, who are often on a very tight schedule, may find it even more exasperating. With identical twins, directors can simply use whichever twin feels like cooperating at any given time. While one twin is throwing a tantrum or wanting to go to sleep, the second twin may be laughing and ready to step in front of the camera. Then, when this second twin gets bored and wants to wander off and play somewhere, the first twin can step right in and take over.

Many directors also like using twins at the same time to achieve certain visual effects that involve two identical people standing or sitting side by side. So if you have identical twins, you may find the doors to show business opening up for you faster than for most other children.

Theater

Theater experience is the most valuable of all for learning the craft of acting. Theater offers a child experience in dealing with a live audience and the chance to play (and hopefully perfect) the same role night after night.

Because plays are performed live, child actors are chosen less for their looks and more for their actual talent and discipline. Theaters can't afford to deal with children (or their parents) who may be moody, irritable, or unreliable. As a result, most plays tend to rely on older, more mature children, with only bit parts (if any) given to younger children. Instead of using real babies, theater productions use dolls because dolls are more reliable and won't cry at the wrong time.

Appearing in a stage play requires long hours of rehearsals followed by the actual performances. The performances can range from a few days to a few weeks for community theater to several years for major touring Broadway productions.

If your child lands a role with a touring Broadway production, a parent or guardian must accompany the child actor, which means both the child and the parent are likely to spend long periods away from home and the rest of the family.

The Business of Child Actors

Although child actors are considered equals on a set, they do have completely different needs than adult actors. Although most adult actors can (usually) be counted on to show up on time, work as long as necessary, and take care of themselves on and off the set, child actors don't have that ability. Some of the unique situations involving child actors deal with labor laws, schooling requirements, and money management.

Getting started as a proud parent of a child actor

Getting a child into show business is similar to, but still slightly different from, the process that an adult needs to follow to break into show business. For example, child actors don't need a large investment in head shots and photographer fees, simply because a child's appearance changes so fast. To get your child in show business, you just need a decent-quality photograph that you or a friend can take at any time. (School pictures are a nice idea, but even a simple snapshot will work.) When your child starts reaching the teenage years, that's when you should start considering professional-quality head shots.

Another difference is that adult actors may be expected to perform a memorized monologue, but casting directors don't expect a child actor to memorize a monologue of any kind. Instead, casting directors want to see a child act naturally in front of the camera. (In many cases, even acting lessons can destroy a child's natural spontaneity and turn that child into an unnatural drone who overacts.)

Of course, child actors share similarities with adult actors in that they should try to get an agent as soon as possible because an agent can help them find work that they may not otherwise know about. In addition, both child and adult actors should collect their past film and television work on a videotape so that they can show their acting performances to casting directors.

Procuring the paperwork

Most minors need a special work permit to work as an actor on a project. Although laws regulating minors vary from state to state (and country to country), an actor typically has to apply for a work permit by filling out an application that verifies the following:

- The child is being offered a job (signed by the employer, in this case, the studio or production company).
- The child has a C grade average or higher (signed by the child's school).
- The child is physically fit to work (signed by a physician).

After the proper paperwork has been filled out, your child will get a work permit that's good for a fixed amount of time, such as one month or more. If necessary, you can always renew the work permit for another few months. The idea behind a work permit is to keep your child from being abused and exploited by unscrupulous employers.

Watching out for your child's welfare

To protect the welfare of children, studios must provide three different types of workers on the set: a child welfare worker, a nurse, and a teacher. These workers are present to make sure that your child's time, health, and educational needs are met.

- The child welfare worker makes sure that the studio is obeying child labor laws and acts as a liaison between parents and the studio. If you feel that your child is being overworked or put in physical danger, talk to the child welfare worker on the set. Child welfare workers know how to talk to the studio people, so you don't look like an interfering stage mother or father. (Anytime children are on a set, a child welfare worker must be nearby.)
- The nurse protects the welfare of babies. (A nurse may not be required if the child actors are old enough to be able to take care of their own body functions.)
- The teacher ensures that children receive a required amount of schooling in a separate room or area on the set. Studios must pay for teachers on the set if a child actor has to be on the set for more than three days. These teachers must be fully qualified and have proper teaching credentials, which means that the director's girlfriend isn't allowed to work as a teacher to justify her presence on the set.

Restricting time on the set

To prevent unscrupulous show business producers from turning child actors into sweatshop entertainers, national, state, and union regulators have established rules for the maximum amount of time a child actor may spend on a set before he or she must be allowed to go home.

Child actors may only work a specific number of hours a day, depending on the age of the child. Table 15-1 lists typical working restrictions for children.

The exact number of working hours for children varies from state to state and in other countries, such as Canada. Check with local labor laws to determine the exact number of hours that child actors may legally work every day.

Table 15-1 Typical Time Restrictions on Child Actors

Child's Age	*Typical Daily Time Restrictions*
15 days to 6 months	2-hour maximum; no work session may last longer than 20 minutes
6 months to 2 years	4-hour maximum with 2 hours devoted to rest
2 to 6 years	6-hour maximum with 3 hours devoted to rest and school
6 to 9 years	8-hour maximum with 3 hours devoted to school and 1 hour devoted to rest
9 to 16 years	9-hour maximum with 3 hours devoted to school and 1 hour devoted to rest
16 to 18 years	10-hour maximum with 3 hours devoted to school and 1 hour devoted to rest

Two additional time restrictions may govern child actors, depending on the geographical region:

- Twelve hours must elapse between the time the child actor leaves the set and the time the child actor must return to the set the next day.
- All time spent traveling from the studio to another set location counts toward the child's working day.

Educating on the set

Just because your child may be working in a hit play or TV show (and probably making a lot more money than you) doesn't mean that your child doesn't need to go to school anymore. From a legal point of view, children need to stay in school until they're old enough to take responsibility for their own actions (which could mean dropping out of school).

Success in show business can be short and fleeting. Wise actors get an education and develop other skills to fall back on in case their acting careers suddenly nosedive or disappear altogether. Many child actors fail to graduate to adult roles, forever burdened being typecast as that cute little kid that everyone knew about ten years ago. For that reason, children really need to complete their education and pursue other interests for an alternate career if necessary.

Whenever possible, auditions for child actors are often held in the afternoons or evenings, so children aren't forced to leave school every time they want to audition for another role. (However, you may still need to take your child out of school in the middle of the day for some auditions.) If your child is lucky enough to land a role in a TV commercial or print ad, the work will likely take a day or two. Missing one or two days of school to work is no different from missing a day or two for sickness, so you, as the parent, should contact the school and obtain makeup work for your child to do after the taping is done on the set.

The big conflict between attending school and work really occurs if your child lands a major role in a film, TV show, or play that requires that the child be taken out of school for long periods of time (such as several months). In these cases, your child will be required to continue his or her education with the aid of a fully qualified teacher (at the production's expense) in a classroom on the set. (Studio or location classrooms range from a separate room or building to a tent in the middle of a field.) All studios must set aside a special area for schooling and provide a qualified teacher. In some cases, your child may be the only child on the set. In other cases, large groups of children may be around. Generally, studios provide one teacher for every ten child actors.

By law, your child must attend classes set up by the studio. Class time isn't a time for children to rehearse lines, change their costumes, or take a nap. This time is specifically set aside for learning, and your child and everyone else on the set must treat it that way.

Despite the often bizarre locations to which a TV or movie set may take your child, studios try to set up as normal a learning environment as possible. Teachers are required by law to submit reports covering a child's grades, attendance, and attitude, which will later be forwarded to the child's regular school.

If a child's grades fall below a C average, your child may be forced to return to a regular classroom and lose his or her acting role, so your child really needs to work to keep his or her grades up.

Managing all that money

The real money problems occur when nobody has enough of it. However, in the world of show business and child actors, the more prominent money problems occur when a child suddenly makes a ton of money, forcing the parents to figure out what to do with it.

The origin of Coogan's law

Jackie Coogan began his acting career at the age of 5, starring opposite Charlie Chaplin in the movie *The Kid.* He later went on to appear in other movies, including *Robinson Crusoe* and *Oliver Twist.* In his short acting career, Jackie Coogan amassed a fortune estimated to have been worth more than $4 million. (Considering that the average movie theater ticket cost a nickel back then, this meant that Jackie could have seen his own movie several million times, or slightly less than the number of times the average *Star Wars* fanatic has seen the first *Star Wars* movie.) Unfortunately, before Jackie's father had a chance to establish a trust fund for Jackie, he died in a tragic car accident.

Jackie's mother took control over Jackie Coogan Productions, which was Jackie's production company that received all of Jackie's money. Shortly after her husband's death, Jackie's mother married the family's business manager. When Jackie grew up and planned to marry actress Betty Grable, he naturally expected that all the money he'd earned as a child was stored away someplace where he could withdraw it anytime he needed it. But when he discovered that he was actually broke while his mother and stepfather were living well, Jackie filed a lawsuit against his own mother and stepfather.

The big question was where did Jackie's millions go? During Jackie's most lucrative acting years, he'd received a paltry allowance of $6.25 a week, with an occasional $1,000 gift tossed in for Christmas or his birthday. The bulk of Jackie's millions had disappeared under his stepfather's gambling debts and excessive spending habits. By this time, Jackie's fortune had shrunk to a mere $291,715. Jackie and his mother decided to settle out of court where Jackie's mother paid him $126,307.50, a hefty sum back then but a far cry from the millions Jackie should've received.

So in 1939, California passed the Child Actor's Bill, also known as "Coogan's law," which gave the courts the power to set up to half a child's earnings in a trust fund. Although this law still hasn't kept parents of child actors from fighting over, spending, and wasting their children's money, it does provide some measure of protection to ensure that no child actor winds up losing a fortune due to the parent's incompetence, mismanagement, or greed — as more-recent child actors Gary Coleman and Macaulay Culkin can tell you.

If your child happens to land a lucrative role in a TV show or movie, you may be tempted to quit your job and live off your child's earnings. Be careful! Fame and money may last for only a few years, and a child's income can dry up literally overnight. Enjoy your child's money, but for your child's sake (and your own sake), don't waste it. Otherwise, you may find yourself getting sued in court by your own child. (See the upcoming sidebar, "The origin of Coogan's law.")

Although child actors rarely blow all their money on luxury items, their parents often do. Hollywood is full of parents who immediately spent all their child's money and wound up bankrupting their child and themselves in the process. So before your child starts making a sizable income from acting, make a plan now to set aside a certain percentage of the money for your child's future (such as for college, to create a fixed income for the rest of the child's life, and so on) — and make sure that you stick to your plan. Think of your child's income as money devoted solely for your child's future and welfare, not as a treasure for the parents to plunder. Any money that parents take from their child's income should be used to cover both the parents' and the child's reasonable (note the emphasis on *reasonable*) expenses. If your child is fortunate enough to start earning incomes of six or seven figures, talk to a financial planner immediately.

Although a million dollars may sound like a lot of money (and it is), the truth is that actors never get all the money. Before an actor gets *any* money, the actor's agent and manager (if he or she has one has one) take out their shares of the money. Next, the actor must set aside money to pay state and federal income taxes. Then the parents need to set aside a certain percentage of the remainder in the child's trust fund. Finally, what's left is the money that the parents may actually spend, which is often a mere fraction of the original actor's income. So the lesson is simple. If your child earns a million dollars, you can't go out and buy a million dollars' worth of houses, fancy cars, jewelry, or electronic appliances. Ultimately, what's important is your relationship with your child, not the money that he or she brings in. If money is your overriding concern, no amount of money will ever keep you happy anyway.

Helping Your Child Deal with the Ups and Downs of Show Business

Many adult actors aren't very good at handling sudden fame, so you shouldn't be surprised that overnight success can drastically alter a child actor's life as well. When adult actors start acting arrogant, haughty, and overly obnoxious, studios often tolerate their tantrums simply because they make too much money off these actors to get rid of them. However, if child actors (or their stage mothers or fathers) start acting the same way, the quickest solution is to replace the child with someone more tolerable.

The following list includes tips on keeping your successful child actor humble, normal, and relatively sane (as sane as anyone can remain while working in show business):

- Make sure that your child leads as normal a life as possible, which may include taking out the trash, going to school, walking the dog, washing the dishes, and perhaps even volunteering in community activities.
- Make sure that your child has the opportunity to make and keep plenty of friends who have nothing to do with acting or show business whatsoever. That way, your child can grow up learning how to live in the real world rather than the artificial glitter of Hollywood or Broadway.

Also, consider enrolling your child in group activities where the child's peers may not care about or even be aware of a classmate's "star" status.

- Children (and people in general) will act rude as long as they can get away with it, so if your child starts behaving badly, make sure that you let your child know right away that that kind of behavior isn't acceptable.
- If your child's ego gets inflated and his or her "star" status becomes difficult to deal with, go out on fewer audition calls (or stop going altogether) until your child starts behaving and understanding that star status isn't an excuse for treating other people poorly.

Keep your gushing in check. Don't overlook the parent's role in creating an egomaniac. If the parents constantly gush over their child "star" in public, the child will naturally accept an inflated view of his own importance in the universe. Sometimes, the problem isn't correcting the child's behavior as much as it may be correcting the parents' behavior instead.

Of course, your child may suffer from a deflated ego rather than an inflated one if he or she constantly gets rejected at auditions and never gets any parts. If this is the case, be sure to let the child know that rejection is nothing to take personally. Remember, the way the parents handle rejection can determine how the child perceives rejection, so don't express disappointment and anger at a child's failure to land a role. Instead, help the child understand that there's more to life than winning a role in a dog food or laundry detergent commercial. This type of attitude and example can help your child grow up with a proper perspective on life.

When talking to your child, your body language tells how you really feel, regardless of what words come out of your mouth. By being honest, you can maintain a healthy relationship with your child now and in the future.

The more you allow your child to live a normal childhood and grow up being a kid, the more likely your child will grow up and become a decent adult. Children only have one childhood, so let your child live as normal a childhood as possible. Worldwide fame and million-dollar paychecks ultimately mean nothing if your child isn't happy — a lesson that many adults still struggle to understand every day.

Part V
Managing Your Money as an Actor

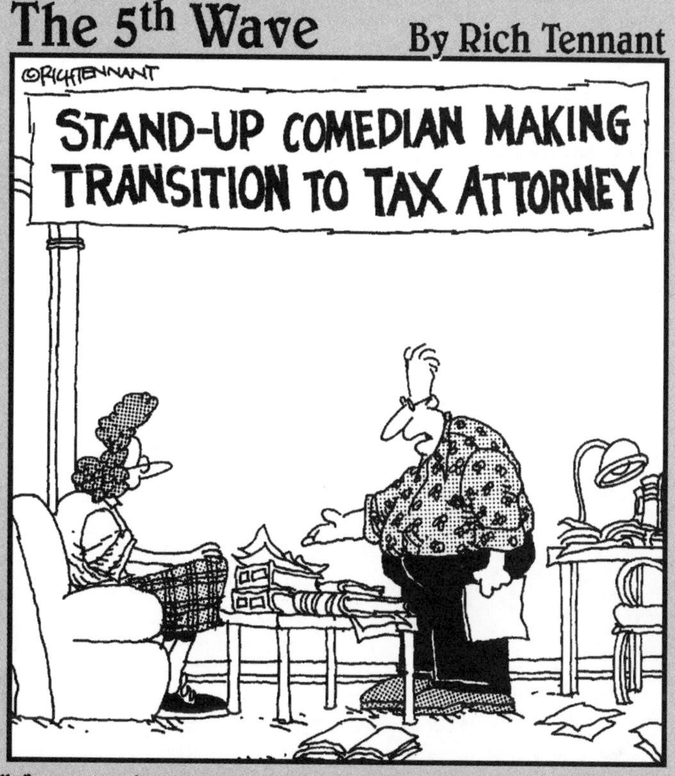
The 5th Wave
By Rich Tennant
©RICHTENNANT
STAND-UP COMEDIAN MAKING TRANSITION TO TAX ATTORNEY

"Hey – what's the deal with all these statutes? Hey – what's the deal with all these books? Hey – what's the deal with the Bar Exam? Hey – and what if I don't pass it... ?"

In this part . . .

No matter how much you may consider acting to be an art, you also have to take care of the financial side of acting. This part of the book explains how to keep your money to yourself by avoiding common show business scams, how to get a day job to support your acting career, and how to handle your money after you start earning it on a regular basis.

By reading the information in this part of the book, you can discover how to pursue an acting career without becoming the stereotypical "starving artist." Starving for your art may sound poetic, but, in reality, nothing is more likely to kill an acting career than poverty. The smarter you are with your money, the more likely you'll be able to have fun while pursuing acting with the comfort of financial security and freedom.

Chapter 16

Don't Get Ripped Off! Avoiding Con Games, Scams, and Self-Destruction

In This Chapter

- Examining the anatomy of a hoax
- Recognizing typical show business swindles
- Handling deceit from within the industry
- Avoiding self-destruction
- Looking out for Number One — you!

Every year, thousands of hopefuls from all over the world descend upon Los Angeles and New York, intent on becoming the next superstar of tomorrow. Many of these aspiring actors arrive with little more than their luggage and their dreams — which makes them tempting targets for the hundreds of con artists looking to take advantage of these actors' ignorance, gullibility, and foolhardiness.

The goal of a con artist is simple: to separate you from your money as quickly as possible. Not only do the better con artists steal from you once, but they keep stealing from you again and again without your even realizing it. As soon as your money runs out, these swindlers disappear to look for fresh prey, leaving you broken emotionally, spiritually, and financially.

Fortunately, with a bit of insight from the information in this chapter, you can make yourself a much tougher target for these scam artists. If someone tries to snare you with phony promises of success, you'll have the foresight to run, not walk, as quickly as you can in the opposite direction.

Identifying the Elements of a Con Game

Con artists use a variety of different tricks to fleece their victims. Unfortunately, as soon as someone discovers the con, the swindlers come up with a new one. To avoid getting fleeced, you need to know both the common types of con games and the elements of a con game so you can spot them before the con artists can separate you from your money. The following sections describe the hook, line, and sinker approach that most show business con artists use.

The hook: baiting the suckers

Before a con artist can get his hands on your money, he has to get your attention first. In the world of show business, the most common bait is the promise of a shortcut or secret to guarantee you success in show business. The con artist may wax eloquent about previous people who succeeded by listening to him and rattle off a seemingly impressive list of credentials that make him sound like an authority on the subject.

Shortcuts to success don't exist. Any time someone offers you a faster route to fame, she is either lying or setting you up for a swindle. Ask yourself, if this person is so interested in helping me succeed, what's in it for her?

Con artists operate by using ambition and ignorance against you. Your desire to succeed draws you toward the con artist while your ignorance makes you believe that the con artist really can help you (for a price, of course). When the con artist captures your attention, the next step is to make you commit to some foolhardy action, which usually involves handing over money.

The line: exploiting your trust

Getting a victim to fall for the bait is the con artist's first step toward getting your money. When the con artist sees that you've fallen for his lies, the next step is to exploit your trust.

A con artist wants you to act right away, so he may claim that he has only one more opening left in his "class" or "seminar" where you can meet a star. The goal is to convince you that if you don't act now, you may miss out on some incredible opportunity. (The real goal, however, is to convince you to fall for the con game right away so the con artist can take your money and run.)

Whenever someone wants you to act immediately, without time to think about what you're doing, be sure to do the opposite and take time to consider what you're doing. You just may save yourself from becoming a victim.

The sinker: taking your money

Ultimately, all con games end by taking your money (or worse). All too often, the con artist takes your money and leaves before you even realize you've been conned.

Most often, these con games promise something that never existed in the first place. For example, a con artist may promise to set up a meeting with a "hot" casting director for a fee. When you pay that fee, the con artist disappears, and you never receive your promised meeting with the casting director — who doesn't even know that you or the con artist exist.

A second, and more deceptive, con game involves taking your money without your even being aware that you are being fleeced. For example, a con artist may pose as a photographer offering to take pictures for head shots that virtually "guarantee" employment. (Refer to Chapter 4 for more info on head shots.) After you pay your money, the con artist hands you a bunch of poorly photographed and, ultimately, useless images that you can never use. In this case, the con artist delivers a product but the result isn't quite what you expected.

Often, the con artist blames outside circumstances or even the victim for the poor quality of his promised services or product: "The weather was bad, and that's what ruined your expensive head shots," or "You didn't use the makeup artist I 'approved,' so that's why your face doesn't look right." Whatever the excuse, the con artist's goal is to lead you into believing that he is innocent when he's really not.

Exposing Common Show Business Con Games

Being able to tell the difference between a con artist and a legitimate businessperson can be extremely difficult. When you understand the basic elements of a con game, however, you can become an expert at spotting and avoiding the more common ruses that plague the show business world.

Almost all show business swindles use the promise of stardom to lure victims and then take the victims' money while delivering a mediocre or nonexistent product in return. By avoiding outright theft, show business con artists can stay in business for years to fleece each new wave of hopefuls searching for stardom every year. The following sections reveal many of the con artists' favorite scams. Read these sections closely to guard yourself against these tricky schemes.

Fake screen tests

Con artists often advertise a fake screen test to search for new talent. A *screen test* is a recorded audition to determine a person's suitability as an actor for film or television. Some con artists go so far as to charge an "evaluation" fee to take their phony screen test in the first place.

Inevitably, everyone who shows up for this screen test miraculously does "a fantastic job, darling." Of course, each candidate (sucker) now needs head shots, resumes, and an agent. Here's where the real con game begins. The con artist uses this opportunity to bilk the victim out of more money by steering the victim to other con artists, usually toward specific photographers or agents who have promised this con artist a cut of the profit for sending gullible actors their way.

To avoid being tricked into doing a fake screen test and later dealings with unprofessional photographers and agents, keep up your guard by avoiding any screen test that requires money up front. If someone tries to steer you towards a particular photographer or agent, be careful. Evaluate that person's credentials and get some recommendations from your fellow actors.

Phony agents

An agent has the power to find work for an actor, so don't be surprised to find that one of the most popular and most common con games involves phony agents. To help you avoid phony agents, you need to know the key characteristics of legitimate ones. Legitimate agents:

- **Work on commission.** These agents make money only when you make money.
- **Are registered with the state and with one or more unions, such as the Screen Actors Guild (SAG) or the Actors' Equity Association (Equity).** Registration ensures that the agent abides by specific union rules that protect an actor's rights.

Contact one of the unions, such as SAG or Equity, and ask for its list of registered agencies. Never sign or visit with an agent who isn't registered with an actors' union. If you have a problem with a registered agency, the union can help you resolve the problem even if you aren't yet a member of an actors' union.

Note, however, that some agents may appear on a list of union-approved agencies, but they can still be dishonest, sleazy, or outright con artists. Just because an agent appears on a union list doesn't mean you can stop being suspicious of them.

Phony agents spend their time searching for new prey (by placing misleading classified ads or even cold calling potential actors), charging upfront fees, and promising exposure and success, but for a price.

Enticing classified ads

Browse through any newspaper and you'll find ads for agencies claiming that they're "looking for new faces" and promising big money for people with "no experience necessary." All you have to do is call for an appointment, and you can get started in show business. It's that easy!

Watch out! First of all, agents make money when their clients make money, so it's in the agent's best interest to sign only those actors who have the greatest potential for getting work. As a result, agents can select who they want to represent — and they want to represent the best, most promising actors that they can get. Aspiring actors bombard reputable agents with phone calls and resumes all the time, so these agents never need to resort to advertising for actors in the classified ads.

Classified ads that promise big money for actors are designed to lure you into the so-called agent's office where the second part of the con game can continue, usually involving an upfront fee of some kind.

Cold calls

Shady agents entice victims to their office by *cold calling*, where they call people at random as a telemarketer does. While reputable agents spend most of their time on the phone contacting casting directors and studios in an effort to find work for their clients, shady agents spend most of their time trying to find prospective victims, instead.

During a cold call, a shady agent may claim that his agency is "seeking new faces and is scheduling appointments for people right now, and would you be interested in a free evaluation of yourself or your child's potential?" Reputable agents have plenty of actors knocking on their doors, mailing them head shots, and calling them every day, so they never need to resort to cold calling.

If you're gullible enough to show up, the con artist has already won half the battle. Now all he has to do is take your money through one of many ways, such as a "registration" fee or by referring you to "photographers" or "acting coaches" who provide the shady agent a *kickback,* or cut of the profit.

Upfront fees

When a shady "agent" succeeds in getting you into her office, she may dazzle you with stories of famous people she's helped in the past and promise that she can do the same for you — for a fee, of course. The agent may justify this upfront fee so that you can "prove" that you're serious as an actor.

Other times, an agent may claim that she already has a contract with a studio to hire actors and that you need to pay the agent a casting fee. Don't do it! Be aware that the studio pays casting directors, not the actors; and agents should never take money from any actor unless that agent has found work and money for that actor first.

Reputable agents never charge fees of any kind, so any hint of a fee should be your first warning that you should leave that agent immediately.

Promises of additional exposure

Instead of or in addition to an upfront "registration" fee of some sort, phony agents may also offer or request that you pay an additional fee to have your photograph included in a book, on the agent's Web site, or on videotape. These agents promise that having the photos in a book increases your exposure and the chances that a high-powered casting director will see you.

Theoretically, these outcomes are possible, but realistically, most casting directors don't peruse one agent's book or Web site of photographs looking for actors to cast. Nor are casting directors likely to view the agent's videotape of you either, which means paying for these so-called "services" likely does nothing but make the agent money while not increasing your chances of getting work one bit.

The only book that your head shot needs to appear in is the Academy of Players Directory (`www.acadpd.org`), published by the Academy of Motion Picture Arts and Sciences, 8949 Wilshire Blvd., Beverly Hills, CA 90211; (310) 247-3058. This directory of actors is the only one that reputable casting directors use.

Another variation of this scam requires you to purchase additional publicity materials, which might include postcards and brochures with your head shot on them. By purchasing these extra publicity tools, the shady agent assures you that you can increase the chances that a casting director sees your face. The truth is, the agent makes money selling you overpriced publicity material and never has to make money the legitimate way — by getting you work.

Anytime an agent (reputable or phony) tries to make money off of you without getting you a job, you're more likely to lose that money than get any work out of it.

Shoddy photographers

Not all photographers are equal. Some photographers may specialize in taking family portraits and then decide to branch out into taking head shots for actors to make a little extra money. Because these photographers often don't know what casting directors look for in a head shot, the pictures they take may look beautiful — if you want a picture suitable for framing or for your high school yearbook.

Get your head shot pictures taken only by a photographer who is familiar with the world of show business. Getting your picture taken by a photographer who has no clue what a head shot should look like is just a waste of time and money. Before hiring a photographer, ask to see sample head shots that he's taken before, or get a recommendation for a photographer from another actor.

Many times, an agent may request that you get new head shots because your current head shots are poorly done or because they no longer look like you. Reputable agents give you a list of photographers whose work they trust. Phony agents often give you the name of just one photographer — who happens to be secretly working with the agent. Photographers who rely on this shady source of income are rarely any good. The photographs they take may be mediocre at best and absolutely useless at worst.

Also be wary of any photographer who tries to pressure you into agreeing to use him or her right away. Reputable photographers know that head shots are a big investment, so they understand that you need to take your time to evaluate several photographers until you find one that you feel comfortable using.

If you're trying to get your child into show business, many shoddy photographers will try to take expensive photographs of your child, which the photographer may claim is necessary for show business. Don't believe it. Children grow rapidly, and their appearances change just as quickly, so spending a lot of money on head shots for a child (especially babies and toddlers) doesn't make any sense. For kids, you need just a decent, inexpensive photograph. Children's head shots aren't as crucial as an adult actor's head shots, so save your money and don't buy expensive head shots for your child. (For more information on what your child needs to break into show business, see Chapter 17.)

Although price isn't always a reflection of a photographer's quality, don't be too frugal. Your head shot is your calling card, and getting the best head shot as possible is important. (For more information on head shots, refer to Chapter 4.)

Worthless acting schools

Before you can even hope to get a job as an actor, you need to develop and hone your acting skills. While some people are just natural born actors, most people need additional training through acting classes or coaches. Because so many actors sign up for acting classes every day, it's no surprise that con artists set themselves up as acting teachers.

When looking into any acting class or instructor, do the following:

- **Investigate the acting teacher's credentials.** Some acting teachers are simply former actors who never succeeded as an actor, so they make their money teaching instead. Taking acting lessons from someone like this would be like taking navigation lessons from the captain of the Titanic.
- **Ask to sit in on one session for free.** Sampling a session before you sign on the dotted line, helps you determine if the class format and the teacher's style is for you.
- **Determine how many students the teacher instructs in each class.** Some acting teachers limit the number of students so they can effectively teach everyone. Others try to cram in as many students as possible just for the money, regardless of the effect it may have on the quality of the class.
- **Ask if any of the acting teacher's former students have done anything notable after taking the class.** While the answer may be more of a reflection of that student's persistence and determination, it is still evidence of the acting teacher's ability.
- **Make sure the school offers a refund policy.** Reputable acting schools know that not everyone will like a particular class or instructor, so they offer full or partial refunds, based on how many classes you've already attended. Shady schools don't offer refunds because they want only your money in the first place.

In addition to getting kickbacks from shoddy photographers, phony agents may also work with disreputable acting teachers who (unknown to you) provide a kickback to the agent for referring gullible victims to them. Reputable agents know that even the best acting teacher may not be right for certain actors, so any time an agent tries to coerce you into signing up with a particular acting teacher, do your best to avoid both that agent and the recommended acting teacher.

In case you're trying to get your child into show business, you can pretty much ignore acting classes for your child. Casting directors want to capture the natural spontaneity of a child, and forcing your child to endure acting classes is a waste of time and money. If your child is a teenager, however, acting lessons may help. (See Chapter 17 for more helpful advice on furthering your child's acting career.)

No one can guarantee you success in show business. If an acting teacher "guarantees" that you will be successful in acting, that's a sure sign you're dealing with a con artist, not a reputable acting teacher.

Sleazy casting directors

Actors often think of casting directors as the gatekeepers to show business. As a result, many con artists pass themselves off as casting directors and advertise in newspapers that they're responsible for casting a huge new role in a potential blockbuster film, and they're holding open auditions right now.

When you show up at these phony auditions, the "casting director" evaluates your potential, finds you acceptable (in fact, the con artist finds *everyone* acceptable in order to scam as much money out of as many people as possible), and then claims that you need to pay him a *casting fee* (which the con artist assures you is tax-deductible). As soon as you pay this casting fee (presumably to pay for the cost of your audition), the con artist disappears.

Obviously, actors never pay casting directors. Reputable casting directors get their payments from the studios who hire them, so you should never give money to anyone involved in making a film or play.

Legitimate casting directors are usually members of the *Casting Society of America* (CSA) (`www.castingsociety.com`). Don't be alarmed if you meet a producer or casting director who seems to have worked for numerous studios or production companies over the years. Many casting directors and producers are independent, which means that studios and production companies hire them for a given project, and then when they're done, they may work the next day for a completely different studio or production company.

Useless 1-900 casting hotlines

Another hoax involves useless 1-900 casting hotlines. These hotlines promise that for a fee (of course), you can get inside information about the latest casting information for films, TV, plays, and commercials.

These casting hotlines make their money by keeping you on the phone for as long as possible. After you dial in, you often have to listen to a long recorded message explaining how the casting hotline works, or perhaps the voice repeats casting information slowly (to give you time to write down the information, naturally).

Sometimes, these 1-900 casting hotlines might actually have valid information (if you have the patience to wait long enough to hear it), but more likely than not, they are simply ways to scam money out of desperate actors.

All of the actors' unions — SAG, AFTRA (American Federation of Television & Radio Artists), Equity, and so on — offer their own audition hotlines (none of which is a 1-900 number) that you can call and find out about the latest auditions.

Meaningless beauty pageants

One con game that specifically targets women and children are beauty pageants where the prizes are meaningless. Many con artists run beauty pageants that promise the winner a trophy (which anyone could just buy from a trophy shop) and the chance to meet a casting director or agent (both of whom are usually con artists themselves). In return for the opportunity to win a five-dollar trophy and a chance to meet another con artist, beauty pageant contestants are asked to pay a registration or entry fee.

The con artist makes his money charging every contestant this entry fee. The money collected from the entry fee winds up paying for the trophies and lining the con artist's pockets. While only one person can win the meaningless trophy, every contestant is usually "discovered" by a phony agent or casting director, who then steers the victim toward paying for unnecessary head shots, classes, or additional registration fees of some sort.

Avoid any beauty pageant where the grand prize is nothing more than a trophy and an empty title. Legitimate beauty pageants usually include a variety of prizes such as scholarships, cars, and cash. Also be wary of any entry fee.

Shady get-rich-quick schemes

Many actors worry about paying their monthly bills, so it's no surprise they fall prey to ordinary get-rich-quick con games that promise a lot of money for doing relatively nothing.

The most common "bait" for get-rich-quick schemes involves the promise of making huge amounts of cash in exchange for a trivial amount of work, such as stuffing envelopes, manufacturing jewelry, or sending out chain letters.

Although the lure of easy money may seem promising, ask yourself two questions. First, if it's so easy to make a lot of money doing so little work, why isn't everyone doing it? Second, even if you could make a lot of money doing trivial work, is this the type of work that you really want to do anyway?

Rather than fall for get-rich-quick schemes, focus on your acting career instead. Look for ways to make money that either:

- Help you improve your acting skills (such as by acting in a show at an amusement park)
- Help you increase your chances of making contacts among casting directors, agents, directors, producers, and other actors (such as working as an administrative assistant at a major studio)

If you pursue any job or activity simply because it makes you happy, you naturally steer clear of most con games that lurk around the fringes of show business.

Dealing with Dishonesty

When you understand the basic principles of a con game (which are to exploit your gullibility, lure you in with promises, and take your money before you have time to think), you can avoid most schemes that might target you. While you can always avoid con games, you may have more trouble avoiding dishonesty within the world of show business itself.

Unlike con artists, who are 100 percent crooked, many working professionals in show business may only be 10 percent, 30 percent, or 85 percent crooked. Because they're not outright con artists, these dishonest people may take advantage of people only when the opportunity looks too good to pass by, much like the proverbial honest bank teller who works for years as a trusted employee, only to embezzle millions of dollars on a whim. Show business has loads of celebrities suing their relatives, long-time friends, and spouses over missing money, so just because you've worked with and trusted someone for years, that is still no guarantee they won't steal from you later. Isn't show business fun?

Potential problems with non-union productions

Unions exist to protect their members. If anything goes wrong during filming or rehearsals, you can always complain to the appropriate union and it will send out a representative to protect your rights.

Unfortunately, if you work on a non-union production, you won't enjoy any such protection. Even if you sign a contract, you have no guarantee that the production company will honor that contract. (Good luck spending time and money on suing someone in court!) Sometimes you won't get paid everything owed to you, other times you won't get paid at all, despite promises that you would be.

Even worse, some non-union production companies have been known to travel to another city or country, run out of money, and strand all the actors in a strange land without giving anyone return airfare back home.

In these cases, the non-union production company never sets out to deliberately rip off the actors. This type of situation arises when the non-union production company runs out of money through mismanagement or outright stupidity, which has nothing to do with the actors or the quality of the show.

When working on non-union productions, always be prepared for anything to go drastically wrong. If your work requires travel out of town, make sure that the non-union production company has purchased a prepaid ticket for you to get back home. Otherwise, set aside enough money to get you back home if necessary — or at least know someone you can contact at any time (parents, friends, relatives, and so on) who can bail you out of any emergency at the last minute.

Unscrupulous business managers

Actors aren't always the best money managers in the world, so when an actor starts earning money on a regular basis, many of them turn their finances over to another person, such as a professional business manager, a spouse, or a relative. The idea is that this other person takes care of paying your bills and taxes, invests your money, and gives you plenty of cash to enjoy your newfound stardom.

Watch out! While many people are completely honest, the temptation to control someone else's money without any form of auditing or outside supervision may prove too tempting. If an actor doesn't know how much money he's making or how much his bills may be, a business manager may be tempted to steal a little extra money for himself — and the actor may never know it for years.

No one has more interest in your money than you do. If you must turn over control of your money to someone else, spend the extra money to hire an outside auditor, lawyer, or accountant to keep your business manager honest.

Casting and networking parties

Even when someone has a legitimate show business credential (such as starring in a hit film), she can still abuse that credential by taking part in a casting or networking party. The idea is that actors pay a fee to attend a party where you get a chance to mingle with one or more legitimate (or phony) casting directors, agents, or producers.

While actors may get a chance to talk to a reputable casting director or producer, chances are that she is getting a percentage of the fees that the actors have paid to attend the party. (That percentage of the fee explains why this person would lend her name to help promote the party in the first place.) As a result, that person tries talking with as many people as possible to keep everyone happy, but the chances that anyone will actually get cast for a role through such a casting or networking party is slim.

Any time you have to pay money for a chance to be discovered, you can safely assume that you won't be discovered.

Missing residuals

Anytime you appear in a film, TV show, or commercial that airs on a television network, whether that network is a local TV station or an international TV station, you may qualify for *residuals* (also known as *royalties*), which is additional money paid to you for your performance. Your agent negotiates residuals before you sign a contract. Many actors, such as extras, never earn residuals no matter how many times they may appear on TV. (Refer to Chapter 15 for more information on working as an extra.)

If you live and work in the United States and appear in a film or TV commercial that airs on a TV station in Japan, how would you know? Ironically, the production company knows, and they're the ones responsible for paying you. The production company tries to be honest because if it gets caught deliberately cheating actors out of their residuals, the union can take harsh action against that company.

Anytime you appear in a TV show or commercial, tell all your friends and relatives about it. That way, if people you know spot you on TV in a local market and you later find out that you never got paid for it, you can contact your agent or the actor's union, which will definitely contact the production company, to make sure you get all the money legally owed to you.

Protect Yourself: Beating the Con at His Own Game

In show business, protecting yourself against all types of dishonest dealings and con games is important. Spotting a con artist requires doing a little bit of thinking and research, which is exactly why con artists try to rush you into giving them money as quickly as possible so you won't have time to do either research or thinking.

When in doubt, take your time and ask for help, which are two moves con artists don't want you to do.

If you fear that you're dealing with a dishonest person, you can find out of the person is truly who she claims to be:

- If an agent claims to represent a celebrity, call the local union chapter (SAG, Equity, AFTRA, and so on) and ask, "Who's the agent for so-and-so?" Not only will the union give you the name of that actor's agent, but it will also give you the phone number and address. If those names, addresses, and phone numbers don't match up with a suspicious agent that you're investigating, congratulations! You've just spotted a con artist.
- If a casting director or producer claims to be working for a well-known studio, call that studio and ask for verification. Legitimate casting directors and producers don't care if you want to verify their credentials because it only shows them that you're serious and cautious, which they can understand.
- If a person appears to be using a misleading company name to trick actors into thinking she is a representative of a well-known studio or organization (such as MGM Production Associates instead of the legitimate MGM Pictures, or DreamWorking Productions instead of Steven Spielberg's legitimate DreamWorks SKG), look up that studio or organization in the phone book or on the Internet. Call the legitimate organization and ask if it has a representative located at a specific phone number and address. If the well-known studio can't verify the so-called agent or casting director's name, address, and phone number, you've probably spotted a con artist.
- Consult directories for lists of show business professionals. (***Note:*** Just because someone is listed in a directory doesn't mean that person couldn't still be dishonest or even a con artist. So be wary of everyone you meet.)
    - **The Casting Society of America** (`www.castingsociety.com`) lists all legitimate casting directors.
    - **The Hollywood Creative Directory** (`www.hcdonline.com`) sells directories that list all legitimate producers, agents, and managers.
- Contact the police or the Better Business Bureau if a photographer, company, or organization sounds suspicious to you.
- Ask the advice of other actors. With so many con artists and shady people lurking around the fringes of show business, chances are good that other actors have either been victimized by a similar con game or heard of someone who has.

The moment you find a con artist, spread the word to fellow actors to keep them from being victimized. If the con artist advertises in a newspaper or magazine, contact the publisher and request that they remove the con artist's ad. The more people who can spot and run con artists out of business, the safer the world of acting will be for everybody.

Being Your Own Worst Enemy

Nobody can wreck an actor's career faster than the actor himself. Although many people in show business may deliberately or inadvertently help kill your career, self-destruction is often the most fatal career killer simply because if you don't take steps to protect your career, no one else will do it for you.

If your career dies or goes into a fatal tail-spin, you'll see that, suddenly, all types of show business people whom you thought were your friends may no longer return your calls, meet you in person, or associate with you in any way. Before you have the chance to watch the show business world abandon you, make sure that you have a solid support system of true friends, relatives, and spouses (hopefully, not more than one) who will stand by you at all times. With this supportive network, you can still lead a normal life after your show business career winds down for whatever reason that may or may not be in your control.

Life is more than money and fame. Just ask all those dead actors how much they're currently enjoying their money and fame. Your acting career is just part of your life; it's not your entire life. If you try to substitute acting for a well-balanced life, you'll be disappointed with the results every time. So do yourself and the world a favor and do your best as an actor, but also spend additional time establishing a sane life for yourself outside the world of show business such as starting a career outside of show business. You'll be glad you did.

Some of the worst forms of self-destruction that plague show business personalities include excessive amounts of drugs, sex, and alcohol, along with money problems and outright criminal behavior.

Dealing with drug abuse

At some point in your career as an actor, you may have to confront the temptation of using drugs. You may be greatly tempted to "fit in" and take drugs for social reasons, or you may be tempted by the quick escape from the pressures of show business.

Ideally, stay away from all types of recreational drugs so you can spend the time and money focusing on boosting your acting career, instead. After all, what will likely help your career in the future: buying and using drugs or taking that money and using it to pay for acting lessons, improvisational classes, voice lessons, and additional publicity for yourself?

Ignoring any judgments of morality, drugs ultimately distract you from focusing on your acting career. If that's a choice you want to make, then make it knowing this: Every time you take a drug for recreational reasons, you may be harming your acting career, either now or in the future.

Separating sex from show business

Along with drugs, show business tends to enjoy flirting with promiscuous sex. Sex poses two problems for beginning actors: Some actors may be tempted to exchange sex for the unwritten promise of future acting roles, and some actors also look toward the relatively easy money that the pornography industry offers. Watch out!

Reputable casting directors will never cast you for a role because of any sexual favors you may give them. These directors know their careers are on the line, and if they cast a totally inappropriate actor just because that person slept with him, the casting director's career could be ruined. Any time a casting director asks you to do something that sounds suspicious, there's a good chance that casting director isn't legitimate.

Acting is a tough business, so having a strong spouse or partner by your side can do wonders for your emotional and psychological well being. Likewise, relying on random sex partners to substitute for meaningful relationships probably isn't going to help your acting career.

Getting into the adult entertainment industry (a euphemism for pornography) is easy for any actor to do. Leaving that same industry, however, is much tougher. As soon as you enter this arena, you emphatically eliminate yourself from appearing in any TV commercials (a lucrative source of income for many actors), and you seriously hamper any chance of landing a major TV, film, or theater role. In addition, no director or producer is likely to take you seriously as an actor or want the negative publicity that you may bring to a project (which potentially could kill the success of a million-dollar-plus production).

Dealing with alcohol addiction

Because alcohol is legal, readily available, and socially acceptable, it's one of the most widely abused drugs. As a result, alcohol abuse runs rampant throughout society and the show business community, as well. Some people rely on a few drinks just to relax and unwind while others depend on a few drinks to just make it through the day.

Drinking alcohol carries not only the risk of alcohol addiction, but excessive consumption can lead to health-related problems. Being sick certainly doesn't help you become a better actor or get those cherished roles you want. Even a few drinks can hurt your career if you wind up attending too many auditions with an obvious hangover.

If you drink alcohol, do it responsibly and always keep in mind that your ultimate goal as an actor is to get work, not to get drunk. If you can remember this short bit of advice, you'll already be ahead of many other acting hopefuls whose careers will either spiral out of control and smash into the ground or never take off in the first place.

Curbing excessive spending

Many actors spend the early part of their careers struggling just to pay their bills, so as soon as they start earning more money in one week than they used to make all year, they lose complete control over their common sense when it comes to money management. Often, beginning actors spend more than they make (like many people do) until their bills far exceed their current income and even whatever their future income could be.

When an actor gets a financial windfall from a hit TV show, popular commercial, or blockbuster film or Broadway play, the first goal should be to save as much money as possible — stash it away in savings or make safe investments for retirement. Then, if your income plummets dramatically, these savings and investments help you to live comfortably while you look for work. You're in a position of stability and comfort rather than hunger and desperation.

One of the principles of money management is paying yourself first, such as 10 percent of your income, before paying any of your bills. Only after you have paid yourself and paid off all your bills should you even consider using the remaining money for luxury items. (For the full scoop on handling your money, get a copy of *Personal Finance For Dummies, 3rd Edition,* by Eric Tyson, or *Save Smart for a Secure Future,* by William T. Spitz, both published by Wiley.)

Avoiding criminal activities

To survive, actors often develop thick skins to shield themselves from the harsh criticism they inevitably garner throughout their careers. Conversely, when success arrives, many actors soon develop inflated egos and an exaggerated sense of importance. While being arrogant isn't necessarily a crime, too many actors believe that their celebrity status puts them above the law in minor or major ways.

Minor crimes expose you to negative publicity that you may not necessarily want to live down for the rest of your life. Major crimes will likely end your career faster than any amount of sex, drugs, or alcohol could ever do.

For both personal and career reasons, stay within the confines of the law and avoid taking yourself and your reputation too seriously. Conduct yourself in life as a reasonable person, and your career should be secure. Conduct yourself with the temperamental childish attitude of an adolescent, and you'll likely find yourself plastered on the front page of every trashy tabloid, which probably won't translate into future acting roles.

All it takes is one fit or uncontrolled emotional outburst to turn your life from an interesting career with lots of potential to a legal and emotional nightmare that can lead only to disgrace, at best, and prison time, at worst. If you're ever tempted to commit a crime, don't. The consequences to your life and career simply aren't worth it.

Handling emotional and psychological problems

Many people go into show business to fulfill unsatisfied or hidden emotional or psychological needs that linger from their childhood and falsely believe that achieving stardom in show business will meet those needs.

Unfortunately, when these actors become successful, they discover that whatever voids exist in their life still exist no matter what amount of fame or money they may achieve. Usually, at this point, actors turn to drugs, sex, or alcohol to fill the psychological gaps in their lives.

Before turning to the false psychological therapies of drug, sex, or alcohol addiction, involve yourself in activities that may include attending self-help workshops or motivational seminars. Don't be afraid to visit therapists, psychologists, psychiatrists, past-life birth regression specialists, or anyone else who you feel can honestly help you achieve the emotional and spiritual balance you need. (Ask your fellow actors for recommendations of people they may have used to help them.) Life is too short to allow the emotional trauma of the past to interfere with the present and spoil your chance for happiness in the future.

Chapter 17

Working to Pay Your Bills Until You Hit It Big

In This Chapter

- Don't quit your day job
- Working for yourself
- Getting an entertainment-related job

Unless you happen to be independently wealthy or have someone (a spouse, relative, friend, or lover) who's willing to pay all your bills while you pursue acting, you probably need to get a job. Unlike most people who look for a job as a way to support *themselves,* you should look for a job as a way to support your *acting career.*

Ideally, you want a job that pays fabulous amounts of money while leaving you plenty of free time to pursue acting. Unfortunately, that type of job is usually called "being a star." For actors who aren't yet stars, an outside job is often necessary to provide income during those inevitable periods when acting roles suddenly seem to disappear for weeks or months at a time.

Maintaining a steady source of income is important. When you aren't worried about paying your rent next week or wondering if you have enough money to buy food for tomorrow, you can approach auditions in a much more relaxed manner, which will only increase your chances of landing a role.

This chapter explores different ways to juggle a day job with an acting career without having to wait on tables to do it (although that's still an option, too).

Making the move to the big city

If you feel that you can only succeed as an actor if you move to one of the big cities, take some time to think your plans through. Cities such as Los Angeles, New York, and London are extremely expensive places to live, which means that you'll need to find a decent-paying job in a hurry — unless you have a huge savings account that you can live on for several months while you find a place to live, get settled in, and start making the rounds as one of many aspiring actors.

Instead of packing your bags and moving, you may be better off staying right where you are and pursuing an acting career from your home town. If you think that breaking into acting in a smaller city such as Miami or Memphis is difficult, the competition simply gets hundreds of times worse if you move to a large city such as Los Angeles without any acting training or experience whatsoever. After you get enough acting experience and training in your home town, you may be ready to move to a bigger city in search of more lucrative acting roles.

If you insist on moving to Los Angeles or New York or beyond, the best preparation you can do is to develop marketable skills. Getting a minimum-wage job flipping burgers at a fast food restaurant may earn you spending money in your home town, but it's never going to support you and your acting career in an expensive city.

Learn typing and word processing, plumbing, construction, massage therapy, cooking, driving a forklift, accounting, fixing cars, translating foreign languages, or any skill that can help you get a job (either on a permanent or part-time basis) in a hurry. Scan the classified ads in the city newspapers to see what kind of opportunities may be available for someone with your skills. The more specialized and marketable your skills are, the easier it can be for you to find a job that allows you to live and pursue acting at the same time.

Deciding Between a Full-time and a Part-time Job

If you've ever tried to live on a beginning actor's salary, you surely have an appreciation for the term "starving artist."

While getting started in acting, you absolutely need another source of income to ensure that you can pay your bills on time. Any leftover money can help pay for the cost of acting classes, head shots, and postage for mailing your promotional material to casting directors.

For the countless actors who don't make millions of dollars from their acting debut, there are temporary, full-time, and part-time positions to apply for.

When you can consistently and reliably earn nearly as much money as you earn from your day job, that may be a good time to quit your day job. (See Chapter 20 for more advice on when you can safely quit your day job.)

Getting temporary work

One of the most popular methods that actors use to support themselves is working as a temporary employee (also known as a *temp*). The main advantage of temp work is that it leaves the bulk of your time free to pursue acting. Then again, the disadvantage of temp work is that you never know when (or if) you'll be working again, much like having a second career as an actor.

To work as a temp, you need to sign up with a temporary employment agency (also known as a *temp agency*), which may give you a test to measure your skills, such as typing speed or familiarity with some commonly used computer programs such as Windows XP or Microsoft Word.

When you sign on with a temp agency, you're essentially an employee of that temp agency. When a company needs a secretary, for example, they call the temp agency, and the temp agency calls you (if you're skilled in secretarial work). You do the job, and then the company pays the temp agency for your services. The temp agency takes out their fee from your check and then writes you a check.

Just as the name implies, temp work may only be for a day or two, several weeks, or even several months or longer. Working with a temp agency is similar to working with your agent. You call your temp agency to inform them of the dates you're available. If the temp agency finds a job for you, they give you a call and tell you the time and place of your next job. If you haven't heard from your temp agency for a while, you can call them and ask if they've found any work for you.

Some temp agencies offer to train you in certain office and clerical skills — take them up on it! This training is free and gives you a chance to develop skills that can help you get better paying temp jobs in the future.

Many temp agencies even provide healthcare benefits to their workers. Take advantage of these and any other benefits that a temp agency may offer you.

Make sure that your temp agency is aware that you're an aspiring actor and request all types of work related to the entertainment industry. (Some temp agencies even specialize in just filing positions within the entertainment industry.) You just may get a temp job working as a receptionist for an agent or casting director who you may not otherwise have gotten to meet on your own.

If you do a particularly good job at a company, that company may offer you a full-time position. Weigh the pros and cons of taking a full-time job versus working as a temp. If your new employer is willing to work with your acting schedule, you may want the security of a full-time job. But if an employer demands that you work for the company first, regardless of your acting career, you should seriously look for another job that's more accommodating to your schedule.

Because temp work will likely take you to different types of companies in different parts of town, be sure to let everyone know that you're an aspiring actor. Someone may happen to have a friend who's an agent or director, which could lead you into meeting someone in show business who can help jump-start your acting career.

Temp work will likely put you in places where you have access to a computer, printer, copy machine, and office supplies, but don't take advantage of your temp job to help your acting career in any way, shape, or form. Never use company equipment or supplies for personal use! For example, don't make photocopies of your resume on the company copy machine. Don't rewrite and print your resume, using the company computer and their really cool inkjet printer. Don't bring copies of your head shot and resume and use the company stapler to attach your head shot to your resume during your spare time. And definitely don't take pens, paper clips, glue sticks, or any other type of office supplies home with you that may come in handy for your acting career.

Considering the benefits of apartment management

If you're a handyman (or handywoman) who knows how to patch up holes in plaster, fix leaky faucets and broken doorbells, unclog toilets and sinks, straighten out broken screen doors, and repair cranky water heaters and faulty air conditioners, you may have the skills necessary to become a manager of an apartment complex.

The two biggest benefits of managing an apartment complex are that you can get paid and live rent-free (or at the very least, at a greatly reduced monthly cost). In exchange for a salary and free or reduced rent, you have to take care of all the minor problems that crop up around the apartment complex during any given day. If Mrs. Smith down the hall complains that the neighbor's dog has torn a hole in her screen door, you have to be part diplomat and part repairman and fix the problem as quickly as possible (or as quickly as you can after you get back from an audition).

Because you can arrange your own schedule to handle the majority of the routine and non-emergency situations that pop up in an apartment complex, you can focus on acting instead of worrying about what your boss will say when you inform her that you need to take *even more* time off to go to yet another audition.

Getting full or part-time work

Rather than relying on the whims of a temp agency to pay your bills, you may prefer just getting a part-time or full-time job, which can give you the added advantage of a steady income along with possible benefits like medical and dental care.

A part-time job can leave most of your time free for acting while still giving you a reliable source of income at the same time. But a part-time job may not earn you enough money to pay your bills. You can always get two or more part-time jobs, but you may want to consider getting one well-paying, full-time job instead.

Before taking any full-time job, let your boss know that you may need to take time off to attend auditions. As long as bosses know about your acting career, they can arrange your work schedule to everyone's satisfaction. You're getting a job to support your acting career, not interfere with it — if a boss refuses to hire you unless you commit to spending every day working, spare yourself the anguish and just look for another job elsewhere. If you absolutely must get a job where you'll be tied down in one place for long periods of time, consider working an evening shift to leave your days free for auditioning (or sleeping).

Whether working at a part-time or full-time job, be the best worker possible. If your boss needs you to stay late, stay late — as long as doing so doesn't interfere with any acting classes or auditions you need to attend. By working hard for your boss, you increase the chances that your boss will be more lenient towards you when you need to skip out during the middle of work to attend an audition.

Working for Yourself

Rather than deal with the headaches of begging for time off to attend an audition in the middle of the day, work for yourself! By being your own boss, you can set your own working hours (which you can schedule around your acting classes and audition times), and you can (hopefully) establish a reliable source of income that depends only on you and not on an incompetent boss.

To work for yourself, you need a marketable skill that you can sell to others. Scooping French fries into a paper cup isn't a marketable skill. Graphic design, plumbing, resume-writing, carpentry, fitness training, and photography are marketable skills.

Working for yourself takes time and discipline. Not only do you need to market your services, but you also need to do the work, collect payment, and do your bookkeeping. As your business expands, you can always hire people to do these jobs for you (maybe even fellow actors who need to make a spare buck or two), but initially, you have to do all these things yourself. You may want to check out *Freelancing For Dummies,* by Susan M. Drake (Wiley), for info on everything from getting freelance jobs to handling your bookkeeping.

If you have a skill that others are willing to pay for, consider freelancing your services to other companies. For example, people with a medical background and word processing skills can often work at home doing medical transcription where they listen to tape recordings from a doctor and then type and print the doctor's reports on their computer. If you have accounting experience, you can offer your bookkeeping skills to other businesses. If you have enough experience, you can earn a decent living through *consulting.* Consulting involves advising a business on how to improve its efficiency. To discover more about consulting, pick up *Consulting For Dummies,* by Bob Nelson and Peter Economy (Wiley).

Companies often hire freelancers because it's cheaper than hiring someone full-time to do the job for them. So if you have a specialized skill that other businesses can use, such as Web page designing, you can freelance your skills, work around your auditioning and acting class schedule, and earn a decent living while pursuing acting.

Getting a Job That Pays You to Be Entertaining

Whether you work as a temp, at a part-time or full-time job, or in your own business, you still have the problem of splitting your life between your acting career and your income-producing job that has nothing to do with your acting career. To avoid dividing your time and energy in two different directions, try to combine the two as best you can and get a job in the entertainment industry.

By working in the entertainment industry, whether it's out in the spotlights where you can practice performing in front of people, or behind the scenes where you can make valuable contacts and network with powerful show business people, you can focus your life towards your acting career. Best of all, the show business industry understands the chaotic schedule of aspiring actors, so when you tell your boss that you need to go out on an audition, your boss will likely understand.

Teaching traffic school

When people break a traffic law for the first time (or the first time in a long time), the court will often give them a choice between having the infraction stored on their driving record (which drives up their insurance rates, pun intended) or attending traffic school. Not surprisingly, most people choose traffic school.

Traffic school classes are usually taught in the evenings or on Saturdays, freeing up your weekdays to audition and interview for acting roles.

Teaching traffic school doesn't necessarily make you a lot of money, but it can be a handy day job that gives you a chance to practice performing at the same time. Because traffic school instructors have to find a way to keep a diverse group of people engaged for eight entire hours, it's a perfect job for actors to practice their public speaking and performing skills in front of a captive audience.

You have to spend the eight hours reviewing traffic laws, but no one said that you can't have fun with it at the same time. To attract customers, many traffic schools advertise *comedy traffic school,* and the classes are often taught by stand-up comedians or actors who want to practice their comedy or improv skills. So between teaching traffic laws, you can toss in a joke or two or create a humorous skit that somehow teaches the students traffic regulations.

Performing on the street

One great way to make money and practice your entertainment skills at the same time is to perform on the street where lots of people are walking around, such as near a busy beach or park. Acts most suitable for street performing include anything *visual,* such as juggling, riding a unicycle, doing gymnastics, miming, playing a musical instrument, or improvising by yourself or with others.

Street performing can often be lucrative because if you're good, people will often toss in a dollar or two. By the end of the day, you may get paid over 100 dollars to practice performing. And you get to set your own hours at the same time.

In certain places, you may need a permit from the city to perform on the street. Find this out beforehand, or else you could be forced to pay a fine.

Amusing patrons at an amusement park

Amusement parks offer a wide range of entertainment-related jobs, including park performers in charge of keeping people amused while they wait in line (so they forget how long they've been waiting for a ride that lasts less than a minute), tour guides, show performers, and giant costumed animals that little kids can mob.

When you work for an amusement park, you have to make sure that you keep your act within the moral standards of the park. If you do anything that anyone might consider to be even remotely offensive or insulting, you can get fired immediately.

Summer is the peak season for amusement parks. But they often start hiring months in advance, especially for unique specialty acts, such as performers for regularly scheduled shows in the park. If you're talented in singing, dancing, miming, or any other type of performing skill that can amuse both senior citizens and little kids alike, working full- or part-time at an amusement park can be a fun way to pay your bills.

Entertaining the kiddies

If you have clowning, puppeteer, or magic skills, consider hiring yourself out for children's parties. Knowing how to keep small children (and their parents) amused is a specialized skill all in itself. And although it may not directly translate into a show business career, it can teach you how to perform in front of an audience that has an extremely short attention span. That way, when you start performing in front of the general public, you'll already be used to entertaining people who may not be paying attention.

If you get particularly good at entertaining children, consider getting a job as a *baby wrangler* on a film set. When a film, television show, or commercial uses small children, the production company often hires a baby wrangler to keep the children amused, so they'll be happy when the camera starts filming them. Working as a baby wrangler also gives you a chance to study filmmaking and to network with the other people on the set, such as other actors, directors, or producers.

Catering to the acting crowd

Although it's not necessarily an entertainment-related job, catering can often get you behind the scenes on film sets, award ceremonies, or private parties hosted by high-powered show business executives. During the event, your attention must be focused on your catering duties, but at the very least, you can eavesdrop on scraps of conversation and perhaps pick up information that may prove useful later on in your acting career (such as finding out that a director is going to start auditioning actors for a new project with a role that you might be able to fill).

If you happen to be a chef, try getting a job at one of the fancy restaurants that show business people visit on a regular basis. You'll be in the kitchen most of the time, but you can pop out occasionally to make something "special" for a particularly important person you're trying to meet, such as an agent. When that person sees your head shot and resume later, they'll remember you and will be more likely to look them over rather than toss them aside.

Working in a film or television studio

If you decide to take a job where you don't get paid to perform, such as a janitor or a receptionist, try to work inside the entertainment industry. And what better way to get an inside peek at the industry than by working in a film or television studio?

Studios employ a variety of people from security guards and janitors to cooks and secretaries. Naturally, these types of jobs are highly coveted because they can give you access to the offices of casting directors where you can conveniently drop by and leave your head shot and resume.

Many studios offer tours, so if you speak a foreign language, you can increase your chances of getting a job as a studio tour guide. As a guide you can get paid to roam around behind the scenes and speak to different people working in show business.

Perusing scripts for payment

When aspiring screenwriters submit their masterpiece to studios, the first people to read their scripts are specially hired people called *script readers* or just *readers*. The job of a script reader is to analyze some of the several hundred scripts received by studios each week and write a quick summary of that script (called *coverage*), noting the good and bad points with a final recommendation on whether the script should be considered.

After a script reader analyzes a script, someone else (usually a junior executive or assistant of some sort) reads the script reader's coverage. Based on the script reader's recommendation and the person's own cursory examination of the script, he or she may reject the script (and return it to the screenwriter) or pass the script further along the corporate chain to someone else in the studio who has a little more executive power and prestige. This other person (who may be a director or producer) may read the script and either reject it or decide to purchase it.

By working as a script reader either full- or part-time, you can get paid to analyze scripts and possibly be the first to spot a blockbuster script long before anyone else in Hollywood even knows of its existence. If you decide to expand your skills towards screenwriting, you can also learn the common mistakes that script readers catch all the time. So if you ever write a script with yourself as the star, you can (hopefully) write a script that will actually get made into a film rather than be rejected.

Winning big on a game show

Here's a secret. Many of the people who appear on game shows aren't just ordinary people who hope to win fabulous prizes. Many of the people who appear on game shows (and reality-based shows, for that matter) are actually aspiring actors who want to win fabulous prizes while also appearing on national television.

Game shows generally look for bubbly, enthusiastic, excitable people. They want people who will squeal with joy and hug and kiss the game show host the moment they discover they just won a year's supply of insecticide for knowing that one of the colors in the American flag is blue. And who better to play the part than an aspiring actor?

But when you try out for a game show, keep your acting aspirations a secret. Game shows like to foster the delusion that its players are ordinary people and for some reason, no one (not even actors) considers actors to be ordinary people.

Before trying out for a game show, watch the show (or if possible, attend a taping of the show in person; the tickets are usually free). Study the types of people that are selected to appear on the show. The people who appear on *Wheel of Fortune* are much different than the people who appear on *Jeopardy.*

With a little bit of luck, you may get on a game show and win enough money to pay your rent for a few months or more. With a lot of luck, you could win a lot of money, appear on the show for several days in a row, and see what you look like on a major television network. Even if you lose, you still get a consolation prize of some sort, which could be a trip to some really cool place or (even better) a home version of the game that just made you look like a loser in front of millions of people across the country.

If you're a member of the *Screen Actors Guild* (SAG), you can only appear on three game shows for your entire life. If you're not a member of SAG, you can appear on as many game shows as you like.

Do a song and dance in a casino

To take people's minds off of the fact that they're losing their Social Security checks or their children's college funds in a slot machine, many casinos offer their patrons both afternoon and evening shows.

These shows offer work for magicians, stand-up comedians, singers, dancers, jugglers, musicians, clowns, animal trainers, and impersonators. Typically, these shows run six days a week, up to two shows a night, so you can get plenty of practice performing while getting paid a hefty annual salary at the same time. If your act starts becoming popular, you may even attract a big show business producer to come in and watch your performance.

If you're a magician, you can also find work in the magic shop that's found in many casinos and shopping malls. Magic shops sell trick cards and devices and hire magicians to demonstrate the products to customers.

Performing in a casino offers steady, year-round work and a decent salary but may limit your access to any auditions in New York or Los Angeles. Fortunately, many films shoot in Las Vegas, so you can audition and land a role in one of these major films.

As an alternative to working full-time in a casino, consider working there for a week at a time instead. Most of the larger casinos bring in new talent for a day, a week, or several weeks at a time. This way, you get a chance to perform in a casino, get paid for doing it, and audition for acting roles on your days off without having to make a long-term commitment.

Performing on a cruise ship

Many cruise ships offer Las Vegas-style entertainment, such as magicians, singers, dancers, musicians, comedians, and more. By working on a cruise ship, you can get paid to perform and get a free cruise at the same time. Unlike casino work where you must live near the casino (such as in Las Vegas or Atlantic City), cruise ships give you the chance to live anywhere and spend your time between cruises auditioning for roles in your home town — whether that home town is Los Angeles, New York, or practically any other city in the country.

When you work on a cruise ship, you typically live and eat in the area reserved for the rest of the ship's crew, but you may be expected to mingle and socialize with the passengers throughout the voyage. As a performer, you must entertain the passengers both during your show and while you're just walking around the ship and running into passengers at random. Consider this time as practice. If you can be charming and captivating to guests, you can do the same when you're being interviewed during an audition.

On some cruise lines, the performers will only be asked to come back if they receive enough positive recommendations from the passengers, so you need to remember to be upbeat and energetic whenever you're in a part of the ship where you could come into contact with the guests.

When you perform on a cruise ship, the entire cruise may last a week or two, but you may only be hired to perform for one or two nights. The rest of the time, you're essentially trapped on the ship and literally out to sea because you'll miss any auditions that pop up while you're floating around the ocean on a cruise ship.

Cruise ships, like amusement parks, expect their performers to adhere to strict moral standards because you're considered a representative of the cruise line. If you do anything to offend or upset a passenger, the cruise line may very well fly a helicopter to the cruise ship, pluck you off the ship, and ban you from ever working for that cruise line again.

If the idea of being stranded out to sea on a cruise ship bothers you, consider working at a resort. Many resorts hire Las Vegas-style entertainment to entertain their guests, so you may be able to work at one of these places without having to be out to sea (literally) every day.

Acting in an interactive play

One of the latest forms of theatrical entertainment is the *interactive play.* In an interactive play, the performers follow a script, but they include members of the audience as part of the show. These types of performances combine acting with improv to create an unpredictable and different type of show every night, based on the members of the audience.

Most of these interactive plays are either comedies or murder mysteries, where audience members try to guess which actor is the murderer. No matter what kind of interactive play you join, the emphasis is on fun and improvisation, making this kind of acting an especially enjoyable way to get paid.

Becoming a professional reader during auditions

When auditioning for a role, you have to act and read lines of dialogue from a script. The scene may be nothing more than a few lines of dialogue, or it may be an entire scene. In any case, the script will likely involve two or more characters. Because the auditioning actor will only read lines from one character, casting directors sometimes hire a professional actor, called a *reader*, to read the lines of any other characters in the script. That way, auditioning actors can read their lines and react to an actual person rather than running through only their portion of the script.

By working as a professional reader, you can get an inside peek at how auditions are run from the casting director's point of view. Because auditions may involve half a dozen or more actors, working as a professional reader gives you plenty of experience figuring out how to audition, act, and work with different types of people.

Even better, as a professional reader. you can watch what other actors do right during the audition and what they do wrong. By studying the casting director, you can also discover how that particular casting director works (in case you audition for that person in the future).

Because you'll likely be reading the lines of two or more characters, you can practice accents, different manners of speaking, and just performing different roles without fear of blowing an audition. (You already got the job. What have you got to lose?)

After spending an entire day reading the same lines to different actors, you can't help but be a little bit stronger and smarter as an actor. Best of all, you can get paid for doing this, too.

Getting "extra" time in the studio

Perhaps one of the easiest entertainment-related jobs to get is working as an extra in film, television, commercials, and music videos. (Refer to Chapter 16 for more information about working as an extra.) Extra work doesn't pay much (anywhere from $50 to $100 a day), but it does give you a chance to study filmmaking by actually being on the set. Plus, you get all the free food you can eat (or stuff in your pockets), so consider extra work as chance to make money, gain inside information about the business of film or television production, and get a free meal or two at the same time.

One of the best reasons to work as an extra is the potential that the director may give you a line or two to speak, which can be as simple as "Hey, you!" or "Yeah, dude." Even if you utter a single syllable, you've just elevated yourself from the teeming masses of extras into a speaking role, which may even qualify you for that coveted membership into the Screen Actor's Guild (refer to Chapter 3 for info on why membership is so desirable).

Working as an extra means spending the entire day on the film or television set. So be careful about working too much as an extra because you really want to spend your days auditioning for roles, not just sitting around in the background all day.

Chapter 18

Managing Your Finances

In This Chapter

- Managing your earnings
- Emerging from the dark hole of debt
- Knowing when to quit your day job

Landing any acting job is a big accomplishment, which means that all those long hours of calling agents and casting directors, auditioning for numerous parts, and taking classes in everything from acting and improv to singing and dancing have finally paid off. After you get that first job, you'll have the experience, confidence, and credibility to help you get that next job. And eventually, with a little bit of luck and a whole lot of talent, you'll begin landing more lucrative acting jobs. But until that day comes, you need to focus on managing the money that you earn now.

In this chapter, you can find out ways to manage your money — from saving to investing to digging yourself out of debt to reaching the point where you can one day even quit your day job.

Handling Your Money

At any given time, more than half of all actors (including veterans who may have appeared in countless TV commercials, films, plays, and television shows) are out of work. Acting is a business in which job security is virtually nonexistent. One month you can be basking in the success of a hit play or blockbuster film, and the next month you can be out of work with no future acting prospects in sight. Welcome to the insecure world of acting. If you want a career with more stability, go into medicine, law, accounting, or engineering — like your parents wanted you to do in the first place. But if you're committed to a career in acting, be ready to live on a tight budget until you hit it big.

To help you track where your money is coming from and what you may be spending it on, consider using a money management program, such as Quicken or Microsoft Money. After using one of these programs for a few months, you may be surprised at how much (or how little) money you're earning and how much money you're wasting. Also, for more information about managing your finances, pick up a copy of *Personal Finance For Dummies,* 3rd Edition, by Eric Tyson (published by Wiley).

Two of the best ways to keep yourself financially stable are to save money and eliminate your debts as much as possible.

To make ends meet, many actors get two day jobs. Be careful, though, because holding down two day jobs simply doubles the problems that you may encounter when you need to take time off to audition.

Saving it!

The secret to handling money is always to spend less than you earn. After all, if you earn only $500 a week, you can't spend more than $500 a week, or you'll gradually go into debt. Earning more money is rarely the solution, either, because many people who can't handle $500 a week aren't likely to be any better at handling $500,000 a week.

The best way to stop yourself from spending more money than you make is to deposit a certain percentage of each paycheck into a savings account. Then use the remaining part of your paycheck to pay your bills. (Most people use their entire paycheck to pay their bills and then wonder why they don't have any money left over for themselves.)

The percentage of each paycheck that you save should remain consistent, such as always saving 10 percent. So, for example, if you earn $1,000, save $100 for yourself and use the remaining $900 to pay your bills.

You need to allocate part of every paycheck toward developing your future acting career. That may include paying for minor (or major) cosmetic surgery, buying new head shots, traveling to auditions in other cities, or taking additional classes in acting, voice, singing, dancing, or improvisation.

Always saving a certain percentage of every paycheck takes discipline, which is something that every professional actor should try to develop. The more money you're committed to saving, the more financially secure you can be. That way if an emergency strikes, such as your car breaking down, your acting career won't go into a tailspin because you can't afford to get your car fixed, and without a car, you can't get to as many auditions as you'd like.

Having money in the bank also removes that aura of desperation that often plagues actors who have less than two weeks to come up with their rent money or face eviction. The more desperate you are, the more likely it will taint any audition you do. The more relaxed and confident you are, the more likely you'll succeed at your next audition. For that reason alone, you simply can't afford not to save money to provide a cushion to finance your acting career.

After you're a member of one of the actors' unions, you're eligible to join the Actors Federal Credit Union (`www.actorsfcu.com`), located in New York City. Like most credit unions, the Actors Federal Credit Union generally pays a slightly higher interest rate on savings accounts and charges slightly lower interest rates on loans. Best of all, because the Actors Federal Credit Union caters to actors, it understands the often bizarre nature of the entertainment industry. So although a regular bank may frown upon loaning money to someone without a regular history of work, the Actors Federal Credit Union may be more understanding. (That doesn't necessarily mean that it'll loan you any money; it'll just be more understanding.)

Dealing with income taxes

Whether we like it or not, we all have to pay taxes. But paying taxes on your acting income can be a little trickier than paying taxes on your income as a janitor or bank teller or computer programmer. For example, the company that you work for as a computer programmer probably automatically deducts state and federal income taxes out of your paycheck. As an actor, it's up to you to set aside a certain amount of your acting paycheck to cover any income taxes that you may owe. If you forget to set aside a portion of each paycheck for income taxes, guess what? By the end of the year when you file your tax returns, you may find that you suddenly owe the government a huge chunk of money that you're not prepared to pay. Luckily, you can legally reduce how much you pay in income tax on your acting income each year through a little bit of planning and bookkeeping.

Acting is a business. Therefore the government allows you to write off all types of acting expenses up to the income you earned through acting. So if you earned $1,000 for the year, the government may allow you to claim up to $1,000 in acting expenses. (Consult a tax advisor for more details.)

Keep accurate records of your acting expenses or anything remotely related to acting, including the cost of head shots; printing up your resume; travel expenses to and from auditions; makeup; any meal and lodging expenses incurred while working as an actor; the cost of acting, improv, singing, dancing, and auditioning classes; dry-cleaning costs; postage; gym membership; and anything else that you spend to help your acting career. (See the Cheat Sheet at the front of this book for more deduction ideas.)

Note: Any expenses must be used *exclusively* for your acting career. You can't buy a new wardrobe or a new computer and claim that they're acting expenses, because they can also be considered personal items.

For more information about taxes, pick up a copy of the latest edition of *Taxes For Dummies* by Eric Tyson and David J. Silverman (published by Wiley).

Talk to your fellow actors and find out whom they hire to help them prepare their taxes. An accountant who's familiar with an actor's expenses may be able to save you money on your income taxes.

Digging yourself out of debt

If you don't owe any money to anyone for any reason, congratulations! You've just become part of an elite group of the population who wouldn't be thrown into the debtor's prison if they happened to live in another period of time. But if you're like most people, you may owe hundreds (if not thousands) of dollars for credit card bills, car loans, student loans, or any number of payment plans that promised low monthly payments only to bury you beneath a mountain of debt before you realize that your total monthly payments represent more money than you happen to make every month.

The question of bankruptcy

As a last resort (or sometimes as a first resort), many people turn to bankruptcy. Essentially, bankruptcy tells your creditors, "Remember all that money I borrowed from you a while back? Well, I'm not going to pay you back, so there!" Sometimes, bankruptcy allows you to wipe out a debt by paying just part of it, such as paying $5,000 to wipe out a $20,000 debt, and sometimes, you can just wipe out a debt without paying any money at all.

A milder form of bankruptcy, known as Chapter 11, allows temporary protection from creditors. The theory is that by giving you a chance to avoid paying your debts for a while, you can reorganize your finances and set up a payment schedule to your debtors that you can handle without losing your mind in the process.

Although initially appealing, bankruptcy has serious drawbacks. After you've avoided paying your past creditors, you'll have an extremely difficult time re-establishing your credit. Also after you declare bankruptcy once, you'd better change your spending habits right away because you may find it tougher to declare bankruptcy ever again.

Because actors have never been considered the best loan risks throughout history, adding a history of bankruptcy is simply going to make credit even tougher to get. In general, try to avoid bankruptcy by not going too far into debt at all. Then again, sometimes bankruptcy may be the *only* way to pull yourself out of a financial nightmare. You may want to talk to a lawyer and get legal advice. (Unfortunately, you can't declare bankruptcy to avoid paying your fee to your bankruptcy lawyer, too.)

Investing in yourself

As an actor, your body (often referred to by actors as their *instrument*) is your main source of income, so you really need to take care of your body no matter what your financial status may be. At the most basic level, you should eat a healthy diet, exercise on a regular basis (regular meaning more than once a year), and get plenty of rest so that you can look your best everyday. (Baggy-eyed, hung-over, sleepy actors don't tend to attend, let alone do well in, too many auditions that could lead to work.) You need to take care of your body as best you can. If you fail to do so, your acting career can suffer as a result.

Before you can focus on getting out of debt, first make a promise to yourself to stop accumulating more debt. Ask yourself what's more important — your acting career or buying lots of stuff that you probably don't really need? One way to avoid accumulating more debt is to cut up all but one credit card and use it only when absolutely necessary, such as for renting a car or making an airline or hotel reservation.

As soon as you make the decision to stop accumulating more debt (a big step for most people), you need a plan for eliminating your existing debt. The following list contains tips on how you can do just that:

- **Make paying off loans and credit card bills a priority.** Allocate a percentage of each paycheck to paying off a loan or large credit card bill and pay more than the minimum amount each month. (Ideally, pay it all off, so you don't wind up getting charged 18.5 percent interest for a pizza you bought three weeks ago with your credit card.) After you get into the habit of paying off your bills early, you can use that extra money previously earmarked for one debt to speed up payments off another debt.
- **Consolidate your debts.** If you owe money to a dozen different people, you can often save money by consolidating your debt into a single new loan. *Debt consolidation* works by getting a borrower to pay off all your debts. So instead of owing money to half a dozen different companies, you now owe money to a single company. Not only does this loan make tracking your bills easier, but the new loan often charges a substantially lower interest rate than the combination of your previous loans, thereby saving you money in the long run.

Many credit card companies may offer to pay off your other credit card debt if you switch to their credit card instead. Although this service is a form of debt consolidation, watch out. Often your new credit card account will offer a low introductory interest rate, such as 4.9 percent, but after a few months, that interest rate could suddenly skyrocket to 19.5 percent or more.

- **Curb compulsive shopping.** If you're a compulsive shopper, chances are good that you're using shopping as a way to make up for a deficiency elsewhere in your life, whether it be a miserable marriage, a job you can't stand, or just an overall feeling of low self-esteem. Try to correct the underlying reason that you got into debt in the first place.
- **Contact Debtors Anonymous (`www.debtorsanonymous.org`).** If you're in over your head, this organization can help you get out of debt by using the same principles that work for organizations such as Alcoholics Anonymous.

Investing your earnings

Over time, you can squirrel away a decent amount of money in your savings account. To make that money do more for you, consider getting in touch with a financial advisor who can help you invest some of your savings in either high-risk or low-risk options, depending on how much of a risk taker you are. Or pick up a copy of *Investing For Dummies* by Eric Tyson (published by Wiley) for more advice on investing.

Investing your savings

Low-risk investment options include money market accounts, certificates of deposit, and savings bonds. These options offer a higher rate of return on your money than your ordinary savings account offers.

If you don't mind taking risks, consider investing part of your savings in mutual funds and stocks. *Mutual funds* invest in a variety of companies, thereby spreading the risk so they won't lose too much money. Mutual funds generally provide higher rates of return than ordinary savings accounts, but you can't know for sure that they'll increase in value. In fact, many mutual funds even go down in value over time.

Buying stock means that you buy a share of a company and become part owner. When the company makes money, you share in those profits. When the company loses money, the value of your stock goes down. Investing in stocks is riskier than investing in mutual funds. But stocks often promise higher rates of return through an increase of the stock's value and through *dividends*, which are part of the company's profits paid out occasionally to the stockholders.

Real estate, especially in the lucrative Los Angeles and New York areas, can be a risky but attractive investment. Many people in these cities buy a house or condominium and rent out spare rooms.

Of course, you can take on even riskier investments, ranging from ostrich farms and oil wells to race horses and fine art. Before you invest in anything, though, first get advice from several reputable financial advisors. Anything promising you extraordinarily high rates of return for low risk is usually a con game. (For more information about con games, see Chapter 16.)

Living Well Without Going Broke

No matter how little you may be earning, with a little imagination and creativity, you can still live reasonably well and manage to cover the three biggest expenses: housing, food, and clothing.

To help yourself live frugally and still get the things you need in life, check out the following Web sites that provide information and sell newsletters loaded with money-saving tips for living cheaply and well:

- Cheapskate Monthly (`www.cheapskatemonthly.com`)
- The Dollar Stretcher (`www.stretcher.com`)
- The Frugal Corner (`www.frugalcorner.com`)

Dealing with housing expenses

Everyone has to live somewhere, and for most actors, that usually means starting out in an apartment. Although the cost of monthly rent should be a major factor when looking for an apartment, don't forget to check out the safety of the apartment, its proximity to the areas you need to travel to, and its access to public transportation or highways.

Saving a few bucks for a cheaper apartment doesn't do you any good if your apartment is located in the middle of a gang-infested neighborhood. The money you save on lower rent will be more than offset by the higher cost of car insurance, the risk of getting robbed, burglarized, or physically harmed, and the demoralizing effect on your peace of mind.

In many cities, especially Los Angeles, you absolutely must have a car if you hope to travel around to different auditions. Because most auditions are held in the same parts of town, you should try to find an apartment nearby. Not only will you save wear and tear on your car, but you can avoid the congested highways and arrive at an audition on time.

In other cities, such as New York, San Francisco, or London, you can rely completely on public transportation. So look for any apartment located near a subway station or bus stop. To save even more money, you can often buy a monthly pass that gives you unlimited rides per month or a reduced fare per ride.

Because the monthly rent for apartments in the larger cities can often exceed the monthly mortgage that a family of four might spend for a house in a more isolated part of the country, getting your own apartment may not be feasible. Instead, you may need to share an apartment with one or more roommates.

Local actors' union branches often have bulletin boards where fellow actors can advertise that they have a room available or that they need a room. By sharing an apartment with a fellow actor, you can pool your resources to split the cost of subscribing to a trade publication, such as *Variety* or *Backstage,* and share tips about agents, casting directors, and auditions with each other. Best of all, a fellow actor roommate is more likely to understand the chaotic and emotional pursuit of show business more than a roommate who's a mail carrier or a college student.

If you're handy with tools, you may be able to live at a reduced rent or even for free if you work as an apartment manager. Sometimes people may rent out rooms in their house and offer reduced rent if you agree to help out with certain chores, such as taking care of the lawn and garden or walking the dog every day.

You may be able to live in a really nice neighborhood cheaply, such as living in someone's guest house (remember Kato Kalin living in O. J. Simpson's guest house?) or in someone's home as their house-sitter. Just because you're paying low rent doesn't mean that you have to live in a seedy neighborhood. With a little creativity, you can live in a nice neighborhood while paying a monthly rent that would normally get you a cockroach-infested studio apartment.

Eating cheaply

Obviously, you have to eat, but *what* you eat and *where* you eat can determine how much you have to pay for food. Eating in restaurants (even fast-food restaurants) is the most expensive way to eat; buying raw ingredients that you cook yourself is the cheapest way.

If you don't know how to cook, start with a cookbook that teaches you how to fix quick and simple meals. You can save enormous amounts of money over the years if you buy unprocessed ingredients and eat at home.

Before you head to the grocery store, clip coupons and keep an eye out for double-coupon days at certain stores. Also, buy certain items in bulk, such as pasta and toilet paper. Join your local supermarket's savings club to get extra savings on certain items each week.

If you work in a restaurant, you can often eat any extra food for free, such as hamburgers left too long under the heat lamp or pizzas that somebody ordered but never picked up. Some restaurants also offer employee discounts on food. If you can get a job at a casino, employees often get the leftover buffet food at no charge.

Try working as an extra because that can give you a glimpse behind the world of show business and also give you access to the food that the catering service provides to the film crew. On any film set, hot meals are served for breakfast, lunch, and dinner, and in between, the catering service often provides bags of potato chips, sandwiches wrapped in plastic, and bottles of water, juice, and soda. As an extra, you're entitled to gorge yourself all you want (and if you sneak off with a few sandwiches in your pockets, no one is likely to complain).

Buying clothes

Until you're a big Hollywood or Broadway star, you probably won't have enough money to shop for the latest fashions on Rodeo Drive. In fact, you may not even have enough money to shop for clothes at your local discount store, either. As an alternative, consider shopping at thrift stores.

Thrift stores (often run by charities, such as the Salvation Army or Goodwill Industries) sell used items that people have discarded, and many of those items are either brand-new or barely worn. Other sources for clothes are garage sales and outlet stores, which often sell slightly damaged or imperfect clothes.

If you wear your own clothes during some of the larger theatrical productions, you can get paid for providing your own costume and have the production company pay for any necessary dry cleaning.

Deciding When to Quit Your Day Job

Inevitably, one question that haunts all artists is when they should quit their day jobs. Generally, you should begin thinking about giving up your day job in the following circumstances:

- You start spending more time working as an actor than working at your day job.
- Your acting income — including any residuals (also known as royalties) — equals or exceeds your day-job income.

Be *very* careful about quitting your day job to become an actor. You easily can go years (or even decades) without steady acting work. When you can consistently and reliably earn money through acting, you can safely quit your day job.

Being an actor married to a working spouse can give you a small measure of security. Between acting roles, your wife or husband can support the both of you so that neither of you goes hungry. With a bit of creative juggling of your finances, you can be married, raise a family, and still pursue an acting career.

Before quitting your day job, you should have several months of savings accumulated so that, if you don't land any acting jobs during that time, you can still pay your bills. After you quit your day job, you can also always work part-time, work at home, or start your own business.

The main point is that you should never let finances stop you from pursuing your dream of acting. If you really want to act, work to find a way to do it, and maybe you'll be able to make a little (or a lot) of money doing it as well. Sometimes the pursuit of a goal can be nearly as enjoyable and memorable as achieving that goal, so make sure that you enjoy your journey into acting. When you reach the point where you truly enjoy the lifestyle of an actor, you may not even care whether you have a day job or not.

Part VI

The Part of Tens

"I know it's a Furby, Ronald. Just work with it until we can get a skull."

In this part . . .

The world of show business can be laden with all sorts of self-defeating ideas that people may try to convince you are true. Even worse are the many unsavory individuals who prey on show business hopefuls as they pursue an acting career. This part of the book dispels some of the more common myths about show business and shows you how to overcome or avoid the traps that keep many actors from succeeding in show business.

This part also discusses ways to improve yourself as an actor and identifies common traits found in successful actors. On the surface, many of these traits appear to be common sense, but as you may notice in the real world, common sense is less common than you might think. So browse through the different traits of successful actors and figure out how to imitate their actions. You just may find yourself becoming more successful as a result.

Finally, you may be interested in pursuing acting as a hobby, so this part concludes with ten different ways to act just for the fun of it. Acting can be a career, a part-time job, a hobby, or just something you dabble in every now and then. As long as you're having fun, who cares what anybody else thinks?

Chapter 19

Ten Myths of Show Business

In This Chapter

- Pulling the curtain on ten major show business myths
- Arming yourself with enlightening realities

Because show business is such a mysterious, secretive entity for most people (even to those who live in Los Angeles or New York), many aspiring actors often fall prey to one of the many myths surrounding show business.

These myths have common themes:

- A special "magic bullet" or secret can make you into a star automatically.
- You can succeed by putting forth little or no effort.
- Other people control your destiny.

Rather than taking action and working to improve their craft, many aspiring actors simply hope that one of these myths will make them into a star. One reason these myths persist is that, in rare cases, they actually can turn a complete unknown into a star. But unless you want to place your acting career completely in the hands of chance, you're better off avoiding these myths and just working to make yourself into the best actor you possibly can be — no matter how long it may take to do it.

Myth #1: Show Business Is Closed to Outsiders

Many people think that show business has all the talent it needs and has firmly shut the door on finding and discovering any new talent. Don't believe this myth one bit! In reality, show business needs new talent all the time, so a fresh new opening for a talented actor is always becoming available, and that actor could be you.

Actors fade in and out of popularity all the time. Some actors are lucky enough to get a second chance at stardom (think of John Travolta), while others are even luckier never to have lost their appeal in the first place (think of Tom Hanks or Julia Roberts, although by the time you read this, even these names may seem like the answers to some obscure Hollywood trivia question). The point is that show business needs a constant influx of new stars to replace or supplement the fading glow of their current stars all the time.

Show business isn't just about highlighting the current batch of stars. It's also about discovering new ones. In fact, many studios and casting agencies hire *talent scouts* whose jobs are solely to scour the world, looking for the next big star who will capture the public's attention and make tons of money for everyone involved in show business — including the producers, directors, and television and movie studios.

Making it into show business has no set rules. Nearly every successful actor has found a different path to success. As long as you can weather the inevitable rejections, maintain a positive attitude about yourself and your acting career, and treat acting as a business, you increase your odds for success (and a little bit of luck can't hurt, either!).

Myth #2: It's Who You Know, Not What You Know

Similar to the myth that show business is closed to outsiders is the belief that you have to know somebody to break into show business. The truth is, you do and you don't.

Yes, your show business career can certainly get a boost if your dad or sister is a rich and powerful Hollywood or Broadway producer, director, or actor who can insist on getting you a role. You must realize, however, that having a relative in show business simply makes it easier for you to step through the doors into show business; to succeed, you still have to have enough talent (and a special look) to appeal to the general public.

Most people know who Sylvester Stallone, Tom Hanks, and Julia Roberts are, but does anyone know that each of them has a brother who is an actor, too? If this is news to you, it only proves that being related to someone famous isn't a guaranteed ticket to success.

Myth #3: Only the Young and the Beautiful Get Work

Being young and beautiful is definitely a plus in a business that puts a premium on what you look like, but just being young and beautiful is no guarantee that you'll ever succeed — just as being old and ugly won't necessarily keep you out of acting, either. (Of course, attractiveness is in the eye of the beholder, and as soon as someone becomes famous, even the homeliest person suddenly can become an international film star. Do you think anyone would've given Mick Jagger acting roles in films if he was just a bus driver?)

If you're relying on being young and beautiful to succeed in show business, get in line behind thousands of other young and beautiful people who think that their looks will magically open the doors of show business to them as well. While all these young and beautiful people are busy waiting and hoping, everyone else is busy hustling for auditions, taking acting classes, and sharpening their craft — and getting the parts!

Myth #4: You Have to Move to L.A., London, or New York to Succeed

Many aspiring actors believe that they absolutely must move to Los Angeles, London, or New York to work, so they pack their bags, show up at the airport, train station, or bus terminal, and spend the next few years working menial jobs like waiting or busing tables or walking a beat as a security guard while living in substandard housing (meaning dirty and downright dangerous neighborhoods).

If living in Los Angeles, London, or New York could guarantee you success as an actor, every Los Angeles, London, or New York resident would be a major star by now. Smart actors know that you don't have to move to Los Angeles, London, or New York to get work. No matter where you live, you can find work as an actor in local community theaters or regional TV commercials.

After you have experience acting, you may want to advance your acting career one step at a time and move to the nearest big city to start auditioning for bigger theater and TV commercial roles. (A large city like Chicago, Washington, D.C., or Dallas offers infinitely more acting possibilities than a tiny town like Findlay, Ohio, or Deming, New Mexico.) When you establish a credible track record of success in these big city markets, you're in a much stronger position to move to Los Angeles, London, or New York with years of experience behind you.

Almost every city has a theater of some type, and many Hollywood films or TV shows film in other cities, such as Vancouver (to take advantage of the cheaper Canadian dollar), San Diego, Baltimore, or Chicago. By contacting your state's film commission, you can find out which films or TV shows may be shooting in your area so that you can audition for a role in a major film or TV show right in your own backyard.

Myth #5: Plastic Surgery and Body Implants Get You Work

The only thing you can rely on about major plastic surgery and body implants is that they cost serious money and give you scars. If you think that bigger breasts or a face-lift guarantees you work as an actor, you probably really need a full frontal lobotomy instead.

Although using plastic surgery and body implants to drastically alter your appearance probably won't increase your chances of getting work as an actor, don't overlook the value of having minor cosmetic surgery, such as dental work or scar and tattoo removal, or getting contact lenses. The goal behind minor cosmetic surgery is to make you look more natural and, thus, more appealing. Straightening, whitening, or capping your teeth improves the image you present to others, but major cosmetic surgery, such as breast implants or face-lifts, can just make you look like a freak if not done properly.

Whether you get major or minor cosmetic surgery, just remember that even if you alter your appearance to look perfect, you still need to know how to act to land a role. Good looks are no substitute for acting, although attractive actors are definitely more likely to get work than blatantly ugly ones.

Sometimes, what appears to be a character flaw can actually be a trademark. For years, Hollywood told Jay Leno to get plastic surgery to reduce the size of his chin. He refused, and now his prominent chin is an integral part of his personality.

Myth #6: You Have to Sacrifice Your Principles

In acting, as in other types of work, being honest and polite rather than an obnoxious, greedy, self-centered moron will get you farther in the long run.

Although show business abounds with horror stories of dishonest people who stole someone else's idea or cheated someone out of millions, guess what? Show business is a small community where most everyone knows everyone else, and as soon as word gets around what type of person you really are, any success you may have managed to grab in the short term will be more than offset by the lack of trust and friends in the long term.

So yes, sacrificing your principles may initially give you some small measure of success as you stomp other people out of the way, but in the long run, show business is a vicious world where you need all the friends you can get. If you wind up making too many enemies, you can be sure your enemies will take great delight in stepping on you when you're down to the point where you may never have enough strength or support to get back up again.

If you're actually nice to people and easy to work with, you can advance your career a lot faster than by stabbing people in the back. When you're nice to people, they may take the time to look out for opportunities for you, but if you hurt everyone you meet, no one will want to help you at all.

Myth #7: You Can Break into Show Business by Taking Off Your Clothes

For some odd reason, many female actors (and some male ones, as well) think that taking off their clothes is a sure-fire shortcut to succeeding in show business. If this were true, then Hollywood and Broadway casting directors would be looking for the next big star by scouting out nudist colonies and beaches.

The myth of posing nude

For women, posing nude in a prestigious men's magazine like *Playboy* or *Penthouse* may seem like one way to break into show business. But if none of the top actresses of the past century got their break by posing as a centerfold, what makes you think you're suddenly going to be the exception?

People become stars because of their talent and their looks, not just their looks alone. In addition, trying to break into a magazine like *Playboy* or *Penthouse* is extremely competitive, which means the time you waste trying to pose nude could be better spent trying to break into show business as an actor instead.

If you want to pose nude, work toward that goal without any expectations that doing so will help boost your acting career. If you want to be an actor, work toward becoming an actor. After you succeed as an actor, you can always decide to pose nude later, but just posing nude won't necessarily help you land an acting role.

The myth of sleeping with someone famous or powerful

Some aspiring performers think that if you sleep with the right people, they'll be able to open doors for you in show business. Getting a role by sleeping with someone is possible, but it's not likely. Instead, you could spend a good chunk of your life sleeping with people who will simply take advantage of you and waste your time when you could be studying acting and landing roles instead.

The myth of appearing in adult movies

Many starving actors and actresses often believe that one way to break into show business is to start out by appearing in adult movies. The logic is that it's better to have a job somewhat involved in show business than to work as a waiter while getting no experience whatsoever with show business (other than serving lunch to the people who are already in show business).

Starring in adult movies will likely kill your acting career, not advance it, so don't fool yourself and believe that you can work in these movies until something better comes along, because nothing better will. You'll be stuck in adult films until you're too old to be useful anymore.

Myth #8: You Can Be "Discovered" and Made into a Star

Show business loves to perpetuate the myth that a casting director will one day walk into a restaurant or store and suddenly decide to make the cashier or janitor of that place into the next big star.

Although you certainly can be discovered anywhere, don't use this as an excuse for not taking acting classes, pursuing auditions, and staying in contact with agents, as well. Just because you have a billion-to-one chance that someone may discover you on the street doesn't mean that you should suddenly stop pursuing other avenues that could boost your acting career.

Myth #9: The Right Agent/Manager/ Coach Can Get You Work

Surrounding yourself with the right people can definitely boost your acting career, but the only person who can get you work is you. No one can stand in front of the camera or be on the stage for you. No matter how many doors someone may open for you and how many opportunities someone may give you, you still need to display the presence and acting skill necessary to turn the film or play into a blockbuster smash hit. If you can't do that, then nobody will want to waste time opening doors for you when they could be making more money opening doors for someone else who can make them money.

No one has as much interest in your future as you do. As long as you remember that, you'll never fall for the trap that someone else controls your destiny.

Myth #10: Show Business Will Destroy You

Browse through the headlines of any trashy tabloid newspaper at the supermarket check-out stands, and you'll never fail to read about the latest bitter movie star divorce, the latest extramarital affairs of the stars, the alcohol or drug abuse problems of celebrities, or the criminal trials of once-famous people. (While tabloids exploit, exaggerate, and sometimes just plain lie about the private lives of celebrities just to sell newspapers, keep in mind that famous actors are under intense public scrutiny at all times.)

The truth is that show business never destroys anyone — people destroy themselves. The weak, the foolish, and the emotionally unbalanced believe their own publicity and feel that their stardom makes them invincible — until they do something really stupid that destroys their career, such as developing a raging drug problem, drinking themselves into a stupor, or committing a felony.

If you think being rich and famous will make you happy, think again (and keep thinking until you come up with the right reasons for going into acting). If you think acting will be fun and make you happy, then no amount (or lack of) success and riches will ever change that — and you'll wind up being a success no matter what ultimately happens.

Chapter 20

Ten Traits of Successful Actors

In This Chapter

- Being professional from start to finish
- Believing in yourself and never giving up

Acting isn't always fair. (Then again, neither is life, so welcome to reality.) Sometimes, a completely unknown, talentless individual skyrockets to stardom while an acting veteran slaves away for decades and never becomes an artistic success.

Despite this pessimism about the acting business, you still have a chance to succeed at any time. Like any endeavor, the best way to succeed is to study successful people and then emulate what makes them successful. Although studying the traits of successful people won't necessarily make you as successful as they are, doing so can often help you become more successful than you are right now.

Don't measure success by fame or money. Some of the wealthiest and most famous actors are completely lonely and miserable people. On the other hand, many unknown actors may not be basking in fame and riches, but they're having a lot of fun just being on stage or in front of the camera. If you measure success by the amount of money you have, you're following a near-perfect formula for unhappiness and failure. But if you truly love acting more than anything else in the world, you'll always be a success because every part of the acting process will fascinate you no matter what the final outcome may be.

Respecting Other People's Time

The world of show business never has enough time. Everybody is busy, and nobody has time to waste. So the most important trait an actor needs is respect for other people's time.

Respecting other people's time means always (yes, always) showing up early wherever you go. If you have an appointment to meet an agent or casting director, get there early. (Fifteen to 20 minutes early is fine.) Not only will your early arrival make the agent or casting director more receptive to you, but it may also give you a little bit of extra time to spend with that agent or casting director to demonstrate your acting abilities, too. (If you show up late, an agent or casting director will likely be upset — not exactly the ideal frame of mind for someone who has the potential to boost your career.)

Showing up early is crucial after you get a role as well. On a film or television set, arriving early gives you enough time to get dressed and get into makeup. For a theater performance, showing up early ensures that you're ready to perform when the curtain goes up. When a director can rely on you to be ready on time, you'll be classified as an actor who is easy to work with, and that reputation can only help you land additional roles in the future.

Besides showing up early, you can also respect other people's time by taking up as little of their time as possible. For example, if you call an agent, keep your phone call short and to the point. If you visit an agent in his or her office, don't waste the agent's time by complaining about the traffic on the way over there. Do what you set out to do — whether that's dropping off your resume and head shot or performing a monologue — and then leave.

Planning Ahead

Being on time and using up as little of other people's time as possible leads toward another important trait of successful actors: being prepared by planning ahead. Preparation by planning ahead means that when someone asks you to do something, you're ready to do it right away and do it well. Some examples of being prepared include

- Carrying enough head shots and resumes to hand out to anyone (reputable) who asks.
- Making sure that your head shot is always attached (glued or stapled) to your resume.
- Knowing all your lines.
- Memorizing your monologues or knowing your music so well that you can start performing them immediately anywhere.
- Consistently checking your answering machine, voice mail, and answering service so that you can return a call as quickly as possible.
- Carrying enough everyday makeup (women only) and changes of clothes for every audition you go to.

- Getting enough rest and exercise so that you physically look and feel your very best at all times.
- Finding the location of an office, studio, or set ahead of time so that you can arrive early despite any traffic or transportation delays.
- Improving your acting skills by studying other actors or taking classes.

Nothing in the world of acting is ever easy. If a casting director wants you to perform a monologue in his office, a construction crew will inevitably be busting up concrete outside of his window. If you need to drive to an audition, traffic will always be jammed and parking spots nonexistent. No matter what, you always run into situations that are completely outside your control, so the only way you can overcome this problem is by being prepared to deal with any and all adverse situations. The more prepared you are to handle the minor problems that pop up, the more time you have to prepare for dealing with the major aspects of acting, such as performing during your audition.

Being Flexible and Adaptable

Acting is an unpredictable business, so be prepared for change at all times. The more flexible and adaptable you are for different types of roles, the more likely you are to eventually get a role.

You may have your heart set on performing Shakespeare, but for some odd reason, you keep getting hired to perform in television commercials instead, advertising everything from laxatives to luggage. You may dream of performing only in soap operas, yet a single audition can turn your career around by casting you in a hit TV sitcom instead. In the world of show business, nothing stays the same (including the people in charge), so you need to be flexible and ready to change and adapt literally overnight.

Many actors become producers, directors, agents, managers, and writers. So consider taking screenwriting classes or directing workshops in case you want to change careers but still stay in show business.

By exposing yourself to the world outside of acting, you can find out how people of different levels of education, cultures, and ages think, work, and act — which can only provide additional ideas for ways you can behave the next time you go out on an audition. No matter how much you may love acting, take some classes outside of the acting world. Acting is about accurately portraying people who may have different backgrounds, so by learning different skills, you can study people you may never normally have met before.

For example, take a few sailing or skiing lessons, and you suddenly find yourself immersed in a new world with a culture all its own. Take a history class at your local community college and gain a background understanding of people from other times. Coach a Little League team and meet baseball fanatics and children with varying backgrounds and attitudes and face unusual situations that you may never have dreamed could exist (such as trying to break up a fight between irate parents and obstinate umpires).

Being Professional

Even if you're a beginner, you can still act like a professional. (And if you've been in the acting business for a while, you better act like a professional, or you may find yourself one day acting like you enjoy being unemployed.)

How a professional actor behaves

Being professional simply means that you understand your role as an actor and your business relationship to other people around you. As a professional actor, you must do the following:

- Continually look for new auditions to go to.
- Improve your acting ability through classes and other learning experiences.
- Know how to act and take direction when you actually get a role.

Unprofessional actors sit around and wait for their agents to find them work (and then complain when they don't get enough work), never take classes to improve their acting skills, and disrupt the production of a project by being hard to work with or incompetent (or both). Don't be that guy!

Acting professionally with your agent

Professional actors also understand their relationship with their agents. As part of this relationship, you must do the following:

- Listen to any advice that your agent gives you. (If you don't agree with your agent, it's okay to say so, but at least first listen to your agent's reasons for telling you something.)

- Inform your agent of any auditions that may be perfect for you, so your agent can get you a chance to meet the casting director.
- Keep your agent informed about your availability at all times. (If you go on vacation, let your agent know the dates when you'll be gone.)

Make sure that you contact your agent only for legitimate purposes. Think of your agent as a business partner — not a therapist, parent, or a miracle worker. If you hear of an audition for a part that you could play, that's a legitimate reason to call your agent. If you stub your toe or break up with your girlfriend, don't call your agent. If you annoy your agent with too many phone calls, your agent may just start ignoring you in return.

Agents make money only when a client gets a role, so agents are naturally more open and receptive to actors who consistently get work (and thus earn them money). If you want your agent to do more for you, first work hard and start earning more money for your agent.

Acting professionally with casting directors

Casting directors may see hundreds of actors for a single role, so it's important that you both conform and yet still stand out. Conforming means following standard business practices, including the following:

- Showing up for your audition on time (or preferably early)
- Acting to the best of your ability during your audition and taking direction from the casting director if you're asked
- Sending thank-you notes to every casting director you meet

By just treating each audition professionally, you automatically separate yourself from the vast majority of actors. After you know how to behave correctly during an audition, you need to rely on your acting abilities to separate you from the rest of the actors who also know how to act professionally during an audition.

A casting director may absolutely love the way you look and the way you act — yet still choose someone else for a particular role. Acting professionally toward casting directors doesn't guarantee that you'll land a role, but acting unprofessionally does virtually guarantee that you won't even be considered.

Acting professionally on the set

Just because you survived an audition doesn't mean that you're home free. Many actors have lost their jobs by acting like boneheads on the set. Actors who habitually show up late, get into fights with the director or their fellow actors, interfere with other people working on the set, or show up drunk or high may be written out of a show or just fired outright.

You can lose an acting job about a million different ways, but you can get one only by acting professionally at all times to everyone on the set. Professionalism simply means being courteous and polite to everyone, whether you like them or not. Sometimes, a person who appears to be the lowliest assistant on the set may one day become a high-powered director. So being nice to everyone is a good business practice — as well as just a good way to live your life altogether.

Acting professionally on the set means doing the following:

- Showing up at the set on time (or early)
- Knowing your lines and being willing to help your fellow actors perform well
- Treating everyone around you with politeness and courtesy

Directors and producers don't always hire the best actor for the role, but rather the actor whom they like the best. Although you should always strive to be the best actor for a role, you should also make sure that you work easily with different directors and producers no matter who they are. That way, you can become one of the few actors whom directors and producers both like.

Being Yourself

The only certainty in show business is that nobody knows what the big fad will be next year. Because predicting what people will want to see at any given time is impossible, actors should avoid trying to guess trends and just be themselves.

So when you show up at an audition, don't try to be the type of actor that you *think* the casting director wants to see. (You can't know for sure and will almost always guess wrong anyway.) Just be who you really are. Casting directors want to see someone who can act, but they also want to see someone who's interesting and likeable. If you're too busy trying to act like somebody you're not, you risk coming across as phony and artificial, and the world of show business is full of enough phony and artificial people already.

Being Well-Groomed

Auditions are like going out on a blind date. You never know who you're going to meet, so you want to look and act your best when you finally meet them. Likewise, in the world of auditions, you should look and act your best, including being well-groomed. Being well-groomed means the following:

- Your body is physically clean and neat.
- Your clothes are clean and appropriate.

If you know that you're going out on an audition, prepare for it the night before. Get plenty of rest, lay out the clothes you plan to wear, and wake up early enough to make sure that you can shower, shave, and brush your teeth in plenty of time to still arrive at your audition early. Being well-rested, early, and prepared helps relax you so that you can concentrate on actually performing during your audition. Auditioning is hard enough without the added stress of oversleeping and rushing to your audition, worrying all the while whether you're going to make it there on time.

Make sure that you have a clean change of clothes with you at all times. That way, if you accidentally spill coffee in your lap or tear your sleeve, you can change into fresh clothes right away.

Being Persistent

Nobody has more interest in your success than you do. Therefore, the only sure way to guarantee success in the world of acting is to take full responsibility for your own career. And the best way to control your own destiny is to remain persistent in your goal to make a living as an actor.

Persistence means developing a tough skin to protect your ego from the inevitable rejections you're going to face. Every actor hears the word *no* many times, but only those actors who continue to work on their craft and look for work eventually hear their first *yes*. After you get that first *yes*, you'll hear a lot more people telling you *yes* — as long as you continue getting better.

Persistence is what separates professionals from the amateurs and wannabes. If having doors slammed in your face and hearing phones slammed down while you're talking discourages you from acting, you probably don't really want to *act* so much as you want the money and fame. But if you truly enjoy the craft of acting, you'll see rejection as part of the game that every actor has to play.

When people tell you *no,* they aren't rejecting you personally (although it may feel that way). They're simply rejecting you as an actor for that particular role. Chances are good that the person who rejected you today may hire you for a different role tomorrow. Unless you remain persistent in your quest to become an actor, you may never know how many times people would've said *yes* to you if only you'd stayed in acting a little while longer.

There's a fine line between persistence and stupidity. Persistence means finding out what works and what doesn't work and then continuing to do only what works. Stupidity means doing what doesn't work over and over again, getting rejected, and then wondering why you're not getting anywhere. Be persistent, not stupid, and you'll go a lot farther in any career you choose — whether it's acting, writing, skateboarding, or computer programming.

Avoiding Mind-Altering Substances

Most successful people in show business don't start out as alcoholics and drug addicts (although many of them end up that way). Casting directors may see hundreds of people for every role, so they're looking both for a reason to choose you and a reason to *pass* on you (the show business term for *rejecting* you).

If you show up at an audition drunk or high, the casting director can only assume that you behave this way on a daily basis. Therefore, he or she will likely pass on you because you're too much of a risk to the project.

If you find yourself overindulging in drugs or alcohol, consider entering a treatment program. Doing so should help you free up your life so that you can focus on your acting career.

Being Willing to Learn and Improve Yourself

If you're an absolute beginner, you need to learn how to act by getting as much experience as you can through workshops, classes, or (best of all) actual roles in anything ranging from church plays or community theater productions all the way up to film, TV, and stage roles. Still, no matter how good you may become as an actor, you'll always be stronger in certain areas and weaker in others. So rather than do nothing and hope that your current set of acting skills will be adequate for the rest of your life, be willing to keep learning as much about acting and about life as possible.

Besides accepting the fact that life always changes dramatically from one day to the next, you can prepare for change by doing the following:

- Continually improving your acting abilities
- Developing acting-related skills
- Learning non-acting skills

If you've traditionally done serious, dramatic roles, take an improv or comedy workshop. If you've always done stage plays, take a television commercial workshop. By learning additional types of acting skills, you'll learn new techniques and understand the nuances of different acting mediums (film, television, and stage). That way, the next time you suddenly find yourself in an unfamiliar setting, you won't be totally at a loss as to how to behave.

Besides focusing on acting, focus on yourself as a person by pursuing non-acting skills. Exercise, take yoga classes, learn to meditate, take up jogging, learn a martial art, and do whatever it takes to keep your body and mind limber, strong, and in shape. Even if you never become a Hollywood or Broadway superstar, at the very least, you'll be in great physical condition to do any other activities that you may enjoy.

Believing in Yourself

Perhaps the most important trait is believing in yourself. No matter what your friends and relatives may say and no matter how many agents and casting directors turn you down, if you truly believe in yourself and desire to be an actor, nothing can stop you from reaching your dream. (Of course, your dream may take years or even decades to realize, but if you really want something, you can get it if you keep trying hard enough.)

Believing in yourself is the stuff that fantasies are made of. Unfortunately, for too many people, fantasies are all they'll ever get from their dreams — unless they take action to make their dreams come true. So besides believing that you can succeed, you have to take action. Keep trying to get those roles (the more auditions you go to, the better your chances), and keep striving to make yourself a better actor.

Each time you get back from an audition, analyze your mistakes, correct your defects, and then go out on another audition as an improved actor. If you take the time to get better, you simply increase your odds of success even more.

The three keys to success are luck, timing, and longevity. You can't control luck or timing, but you can control longevity by simply believing in yourself and trying over and over again until you finally find a path to success.

Ultimately, the only person truly responsible for your acting career is you. You can't guarantee the level of success that you'll reach as an actor, but you can guarantee that you'll never fail as long as you continue to believe in yourself. If you truly enjoy what you're doing, you'll always be a success in whatever you choose to do.

Chapter 21

Ten Tips for Improving as an Actor

In This Chapter

- Becoming captivating and confident
- Keeping food on the table
- Exercising your mind, body, and attitude

Acting is a demanding craft that can take years to learn and a lifetime to master. No matter how good you are (or think you are), you can always get better. The better you become as an actor, the better your chances that you'll never have to work in a job that requires handling someone else's food again.

This chapter offers tips to help you keep your acting skills sharply honed so that you can make sure that your acting career never stagnates. Now all you need is that one opportunity for the right producer, director, or casting agent to notice you and help the world recognize your talent.

Mastering the Art of Auditioning

Many actors spend years taking acting classes, studying drama or theater in schools, and still wonder why they don't land a role. Here's a little secret: Actors with the most talent don't always get the roles. The actors who know how to audition are the ones who get the roles. (For more specific information on auditioning, see Chapter 9.)

Casting directors may choose another actor over you for a million different reasons, and none of these reasons are in your control. So rather than dwell on situations you can't control, focus on the aspects of your audition that you *can* control, such as

- **Overcoming your nervousness:** To bring out the best of your abilities, you need to relax. If you allow your nervousness to overwhelm your acting skills, you aren't likely to give a decent performance. You need to find a way to relax that works for you — whether it be deep breathing exercises, yoga, meditation, or even prayer before each audition.

- **Being prepared:** Know what to expect during an audition. The more familiar you are with the auditioning process, the less you'll need to focus on the process of auditioning, and the more you can focus on performing. To gain auditioning experience, go to as many auditions as possible. Inevitably, you're going to make mistakes (and see others make mistakes), so learn from your mistakes and the mistakes of others.

  Besides going to as many auditions as possible, take an auditioning class as well. An audition class can familiarize you with the typical process of auditioning so that you'll know what to expect.
- **Acting to your best ability:** If you make a mistake during an audition, don't call attention to it by criticizing yourself. Just keep performing to the best of your ability.

Knowing How to Audition and Act for the Camera

Acting for a live audience and acting for the camera are very different. If you don't understand these differences, you won't know how to properly act at an audition for film, television, and theater roles.

Auditioning for the camera

Take a class to learn how to audition in front of a camera. Camera acting techniques can teach you what types of clothes look best (and worst) when captured on-camera and can give you valuable practice performing and seeing how you look from the camera's point of view. (If you think that your own voice sounds funny when captured on audiotape, just wait until you see how your acting looks when captured on videotape.)

When you audition on-camera, remember that the camera captures every movement from a nervous twitch in your eye to a slight motion to scratch the back of your leg with your foot. Such minor motions can be distracting and sabotage your appearance on-camera. An auditioning class can show you how these minor movements can appear annoying on tape so that you can be aware of everything you do when standing in front of a camera.

Even if you want to act only in theater, learn how to act in front of the camera anyway. Because acting is an unpredictable business, you don't want to limit yourself to any particular acting field.

Acting for the camera

Many acting classes teach camera techniques so that actors know how to "cheat" (move their face slightly towards the camera). That way, their faces appear in view of the camera at all times even when they're supposed to be looking directly at another actor.

Learning camera techniques for acting can also teach you how to block your movement with other actors (so that everyone remains visible to the camera lens at all times) and how to "play" towards the camera at all times. For example, watch every actor pull out a gun, and you notice that they always choose the hand closest (and thus most visible) to the camera. See Chapter 10 for more on these techniques.

Expecting the Unexpected: Improvising

In the world of show business (and life in general), things hardly ever go according to plan. In an audition, you may not have time to prepare for the part that you're trying out for. And during a film or production, technical difficulties, missed cues, and skipped lines can all throw any scene into disarray. Because you can never predict or plan for any last-minute changes or disruptions, you can only prepare yourself to deal with any problems whenever they pop up.

One of the best ways to train yourself to handle the unexpected during an audition is to take an improvisation class. In some auditions, the casting director may just give you a general direction, such as, "You're a housewife, and you've just discovered that you have a headache while preparing lunch for your husband," to see how you react and perform an impromptu scene. You have to be ready to run with it.

In some commercial auditions, the casting director just needs actors to perform certain actions without any dialogue at all, such as playing with a child or walking down the street. The more interesting you make your performance, the better your odds of getting the role. Improvisational classes can help you prepare by teaching you to be comfortable in unfamiliar situations and act naturally and spontaneously no matter what the circumstances.

Improvisation can also come in handy during an actual performance, too. Inevitably, actors (sometimes even you) may forget a line or accidentally skip over entire chunks of dialogue. In a play, these mistakes can be fatal unless the actors can quickly improvise dialogue to get the play back on track.

During a film, television show, or commercial, improvisation can be useful for experimenting with different scenes. Sometimes, a director deliberately keeps the cameras rolling after a scene has been shot, just to see if anything interesting occurs. With improvisation skills, you can stay in character and possibly create a new scene that strengthens the overall story.

Developing a Sense of Humor

Acting may be a serious business, but that doesn't mean that you have to be serious all the time. With the inevitable problems, disappointments, and frustration associated with show business, having a sense of humor helps you to endure your pursuit of an acting career. Even serious, dramatic roles call for a touch of humor once in a while, and casting directors and producers tend to prefer working with people whose company they enjoy. So having a sense of humor can help your acting career both on and off the stage.

Improvisation classes can help you develop a sense of humor, but consider taking a stand-up comedy workshop, too. Even if you have no intention of working as a stand-up comedian, familiarizing yourself with the art of stand-up comedy can teach you two valuable skills: how to face an audience by yourself without the support of a script, scenery, costumes, or other actors and how to develop a sense of comedic timing to make people laugh. By learning to face a hostile, indifferent, or bored audience and keep them amused, you can sharpen your own skills for when you perform during an audition as well.

Situation comedies need comedic actors all the time, and many commercials rely on some form of humor, too. So developing a sense of humor can broaden the number of acting opportunities open to you.

Overcoming Stage Fright

Even the best and most experienced actors get a little bit nervous about performing. No matter how experienced you may be, that nagging thought in the back of your mind that you may do something foolish is always there, whether you're at an audition or in the middle of a paid performance.

Stage fright is different from just plain nervousness. Even seasoned actors get nervous performing in public, but they manage to perform despite their anxiety. Stage fright is when your body freezes and your mind shifts into a "fight or flight" panic mode that prevents you from performing at all.

Stage fright occurs when your thoughts focus on yourself and how you appear to others. So the quickest way to overcome stage fright is to focus your thoughts on the other actors. By placing your focus off yourself and on other people, you can minimize the paralyzing effect that stage fright can have over your performance. By thinking of others first, you can actually use stage fright as an additional tool to enhance your acting performance. For example, think about ways to make your fellow actors look good by listening to what they say (rather than just waiting to recite your memorized lines) and responding to the other actors' actions. Or, if you're doing a reading by yourself, you can focus on the audience and concentrate on ways to make the audience (whether it's a single casting director or an entire room full of people) interested in what you're saying.

The best way to overcome stage fright is to keep throwing yourself into situations that give you stage fright. To overcome the fear of public speaking, many people join a group such as Toastmasters (`www.toastmasters.org`). If you get nervous during auditions, take an auditioning class to help you face your fear and eventually overcome it so that you can perform to the best of your ability.

Stage fright is partly the fear of facing the unknown, so the more familiar you become with situations such as performing or auditioning, the more confident you become in those same situations. That doesn't necessarily mean that stage fright will ever go away. But the more you face your fears, the more you realize that you can survive and still perform without letting your fears paralyze you.

Understanding Human Psychology

Acting is about playing a role. If you're a 17-year-old kid and you're given a role playing a 17-year-old kid, you can pretty much draw from your own experience to make your acting appear realistic. But if you're given the role of playing an astronaut stranded on the surface of Mars, how do you act out that role? Because you can't draw from experience, you have to rely on your knowledge of human psychology instead, which can help you understand the ways people react to different situations.

Consider taking a course in human psychology at a community college or university to discover how different types of people tend to behave, and become a people-watcher whenever you're in public. Look at the ways different people dress, act, and behave, and you'll notice similarities that you can use for portraying those people as an actor. The more you can draw upon the behavior of people, the more realistic your acting can become when portraying different roles.

Developing Your Voice and Improving Your Body

As an actor, your job is to communicate to an audience with your voice and your body.

Your voice

If no one can understand what you're saying, no amount of acting ability can help you land a role.

Voice lessons can be as simple as learning how to breathe and project your voice. By learning these techniques, you can speak clearly for long periods of time without straining your voice. For added versatility, you may also want to consider taking singing lessons. Singing lessons can teach you how to control your voice, while also giving you the chance to audition and perform in musicals or commercial roles that may require a trained singer.

If you have an accent of any kind, visit a dialect coach who can help you eliminate regional speech patterns. But don't forget your dialect completely because, sometimes, a certain dialect (such as a Southern or Bostonian accent) can help you land a role. For that reason, many actors also use a dialect coach to teach them different types of dialects. The more dialects you can speak, the greater the chances that you'll be able to land a role that specifically requires certain types of accents.

Your body

Besides developing and training your voice, you also need to develop and train your body. At the simplest level, start a regular exercise program to keep your body in good shape so that you'll be healthy enough to attend auditions and play any role you can get. At a more complicated level, you may want to take training such as movement classes to help you improve the body gestures that are part of your acting.

Learning the art of miming can teach you how to express yourself without relying on words. Dance lessons not only exercise your body but also improve the chances of landing a role in a musical.

Because many films and television shows emphasize the martial arts, sign up for martial arts classes to get your exercise and also to gain yet another important skill that may help you land a particular acting role. Fencing classes can improve your coordination while teaching you to use a sword in case you get a role that requires a sword fight.

Without a strong and healthy body, you won't be able to enjoy much of what life has to offer you, let alone pursue an acting career. Even money and fame won't do you any good if you're too sick to enjoy any of it.

Maintaining a Reliable Source of Income

If you're desperate, it'll show in the way you look, act, and behave. Desperation keeps actors from relaxing and focusing on their performance, making them less likeable as a result. If you go into every audition with the desperate feeling that you need the role or else you'll be evicted from your apartment, you can probably plan on being evicted.

The best way to avoid a sense of desperation is to develop a reliable source of income, either through an outside business or job, through the support of a spouse or generous relative, or through a savings account that can tide you over when acting roles seem sparse and unavailable.

Avoiding Guaranteed Failure

Life is rarely fair. Sometimes, you don't get a role because the casting director is from a small town and wants to give an actor from that same small town a role that you should have gotten. Other times, the casting director may be in a bad mood and too busy fuming about the fight he just had with his wife that morning to even notice the brilliant audition you just gave. That's life. It's not fair, but as long as you keep trying and keep improving, eventually someone will notice your talent and give you a chance. And one chance is all you need to further your acting career.

Although nothing can guarantee success, certain actions and attitudes can guarantee failure. Keep the following tips in mind, and you're bound to go far (well, farther than the late, unprepared, lazy guy auditioning after you).

- **Be early.** Directors, producers, and agents hate nothing more than someone who's perpetually late, thereby forcing everyone to adapt their schedule to accommodate the late arrival. Perpetually late actors are often rewarded by never having the chance to show up late again — because they may never get another acting job again. Don't be that person — show up early.

- **Be prepared.** The best way to show that you really want to work is to be prepared. When you show up at an audition, bring head shots and copies of your resume. On the set, show up prepared by reviewing the script ahead of time so that you can give a credible acting performance.
- **Be available and easy to contact.** Agents often get frantic phone calls from casting directors who suddenly need a certain type of actor by tomorrow morning. So if you're too busy partying to answer your phone, check your answering machine, or check your answering service, you may miss the chance to audition for any last-minute roles.
- **Treat acting as an important part of your life.** When you treat acting as if it's a nuisance to your path to fame and fabulous wealth, you naturally sabotage yourself. Never taking acting lessons or classes, failing to learn from your mistakes, being disrespectful, showing up late, never returning phone calls, and giving sloppy performances at auditions give people the impression that you're not serious about your career.
- **Don't lie.** Making up phony credits on your resume or lying about certain talents you don't have, such as speaking French fluently or knowing how to ride a unicycle, tells a casting director that you aren't a person to be trusted, especially when you show up on a set and can't perform the skills that you claimed to possess.
- **Never wait for others to bring success to you.** Look for acting jobs on you own. Don't sit at home and wait for your agent or your friends to notify you of them. The more you rely on others to bring you success, the more likely others will focus on their own careers and forget about yours.

Staying Sharp

Acting is a skill. You can always find ways to improve your existing acting skills, develop new skills, and learn from others, both in and out of the acting field. Watch movies, television shows, and plays to see what other actors do right and wrong. Read scripts and plays to understand the different ways to tell a story. Study the works of directors to figure out their techniques and methods. Attend acting seminars and classes to gain knowledge from others and network with your fellow classmates.

In any career, whether it's acting or accounting, you can never stop learning if you hope to be one of the best in your field one day. More importantly, don't just learn for the sake of your career. Learn for your own enjoyment. If you truly love acting, your passion will shine through during all your auditions and performances, and that passion will likely translate into greater success for your career.

Chapter 22

Ten Ways to Act Just for the Fun of It

In This Chapter

- Acting and volunteering in school and community theaters
- Getting your film fix by acting in student films or working as an extra on the big screen
- Producing shows via public access TV or the Internet

Acting can be a demanding and intense career. However, you don't have to sacrifice your life to move to Los Angeles, London, or New York to act. In fact, you don't even have to give up your job or alter your lifestyle if you want to act, either.

Despite the promises and lure of money and fame, many people just want to enjoy acting without the hassle of depending on acting for their income. For many people, acting can be an enjoyable hobby, much like figure skating or scuba diving. If they can get paid for doing it, great. If not, that's great, too. If you feel this way, acting can be a fun way to keep yourself amused and express yourself at the same time.

(If you're devoting your life to acting full-time, you may also find that some of the ideas in this chapter can help you practice and expand your acting range by performing in different situations.)

If you really find that you enjoy acting, you can always devote yourself to it part-time or full-time as a career at any time. Likewise, if you get tired of acting full-time, you can always scale back and act part-time or just as a hobby. Let your life dictate your acting career, not the other way around.

If you're already a member of an actors' union, you may not be able to participate in one or more of the acting opportunities listed in this chapter, such as performing in a community theater or a student film. When in doubt, talk to a union representative because violation of union rules can result in harsh penalties or outright banishment from the union.

Join a Community Theater Group

Getting involved in a community theater allows you to experience show business without leaving the comfort of your neighborhood. Community theater groups generally consist of a group of interested people who enjoy acting in plays for their own amusement. The cast members don't get paid, and they often do double or triple duty, making sets and costumes, selling tickets, marketing the plays, baking and selling cookies to raise money, and cleaning up the theater after each show.

Despite their amateur status, community theaters offer actors an excellent chance to participate in all aspects of theater in a (normally) friendly environment. Due to their low budgets, community theaters tend to produce plays that require minimal costumes (typically ordinary clothes that cast members are likely to have hidden in their closets), props, and sets (often old furniture that someone is willing to loan to the theater for a few weeks).

Don't feel bad about listing community theater experience on your resume because it shows that you at least have some acting experience, which is better than no acting experience at all. But to avoid the community theater label (which many people associate with rank amateurs), many actors eliminate the word "community" when listing the theater on their resume. For example, instead of saying that you performed at the Rochester Community Theater, you may say that you performed at the Rochester Theater.

Part of the fun of community theater is that it gives you a chance to be involved in a theatrical production from start to finish. As a result, you gain a better understanding of the process of producing a play. Because members of a community theater choose the plays that they want to perform, members can experiment with different types of plays that can challenge their acting abilities. By joining a community theater, you can get valuable acting experience that you may never get anywhere else.

If you don't find a community theater group near you, or the one that is near you doesn't produce the type of plays you enjoy, nothing's stopping you from starting your own community theater group. To find out more about starting and running a community theater, visit the Community Theater Green Room Web site at `www.communitytheater.org`.

Become a Storyteller

If you enjoy acting, consider volunteering to read stories for children at your local public library. Many public libraries sponsor some type of children's storytelling hour, usually on the weekends or after school. Because you can't just read a story out of a book and expect children to pay attention, you often have to act out the different roles with exaggerated voice and body gestures.

Storytelling can teach you how to vary your speech patterns and emphasize certain points with your inflection alone, giving you practice in using your voice to communicate ideas and emotions. If you can keep a squirmy group of 6-year-olds riveted to what you're saying, you should have little trouble acting in front of a squirmy group of adults as well.

Many special interest groups, such as Pacific Islanders, Native Americans, or people who enjoy recreating medieval or Civil War scenes, can use storytellers to entertain audiences with tales or myths, such as telling Civil War tales to tourists visiting Gettysburg. You can get paid to tell stories and dress up in a period costume to act out your role as a storyteller from another era. (For more opportunities to get involved with period acting, see the section, "Volunteer at Your Local Museum," later in this chapter.) Also, many nursing homes may be open to storytellers who can entertain the residents, and the blind community has a need for people who can tell stories and read books, newspapers, and magazines to the blind.

If storytelling appeals to you, visit the National Storytelling Festival Web site (`www.storytellingfestival.net`) for more information about the national storytelling festival that you can attend as an audience member or as a storyteller.

Join an Improvisational Group

Improv is all about spontaneous play in front of a live audience, so if you enjoy the thrill, danger, and excitement of performing without a script, join or start an improv group today.

Improv groups range from the top professionals who appear on television and in major venues, such as Las Vegas, all the way down to beginners and intermediate improv players performing for their own amusement in a tiny neighborhood theater.

Many improv groups teach classes to raise money and recruit new members. So before signing up for an improv class, find out whether the instructors perform on a regular basis, and about the possibility that you could perform with the improv group when you get good enough.

Visit the Improv Encyclopedia (`www.humanpingpongball.com`), which provides various games and exercises to help you sharpen your improv skills.

Volunteer at Your Local School Drama Department

The drama departments of high schools and colleges often accept volunteers who are willing to put in time to help make the production work a little more smoothly. In exchange for volunteering, you may get the opportunity to perform onstage in bit roles or fairly major roles, depending on the play.

Like working in a community theater, volunteering for a school drama department can expose you to the whole realm of theater production, from creating sets and making up costumes to working the lighting and sound equipment. Unlike community theater, the larger university drama departments can afford to produce more elaborate plays, such as musicals, Shakespearean plays, or plays that require period costumes and sets.

Who knows? By working in a school theater department, you may be able to help guide and instruct the future superstars of tomorrow. At the very least, you can socialize with other actors and perform to keep yourself amused.

Put on a Play for a Charity

Charity organizations often have problems soliciting donations and providing much-needed social work. If you're a member of such a charity, consider combining your acting skills with the organization's need for publicity by creating a play that dramatizes the charity's overriding message.

Rather than presenting a boring lecture, putting on a play that dramatizes the need for the charity and highlights the type of work that it offers can be very effective. Such plays can be especially useful for performing at schools and children's events as a way of explaining to children the problems the charity is facing and what the children may be able to do to help. By presenting the need and purpose for a particular charitable organization in the form of a play, you can use your acting skills for both fundraising and publicity while getting a chance to act at the same time.

Appear in a Student Film

As part of their course work, students studying film or television production often have to produce a short film. This assignment forces the student to become a writer, director, and producer in order to learn all the nuances involved in film and television production, but on a much smaller scale.

Because student films need actors, they often advertise in trade publications, such as *Backstage* or *Variety.* You also can feel free to contact the film department of your local university to find out about student films currently in production. If you love movies, consider joining the American Film Institute (`www.afi.com`), which provides seminars and workshops where famous directors, screenwriters, and actors discuss their past projects and occasionally teach classes on various subjects related to filmmaking. Such classes can put you in touch with the latest batch of student filmmakers and also give you a chance to meet and socialize with famous filmmakers.

Don't expect any pay if you become involved with a student film. The only reward you may get for your effort is a copy of the film or tape, which you can use to demonstrate your acting abilities to potential agents and casting directors or just to keep as a souvenir. (Of course, if your acting in a student film is really awful, you may not want to show it to anyone, let alone an agent or casting director.)

Many student filmmakers eventually become professional filmmakers, so if you strike up a particular friendly relationship with a student filmmaker, they may use you for a professional production later. Who knows? You may get the chance to work with the next Steven Spielberg before he becomes famous.

Work as an Extra

Working as an extra can give you the thrill of being part of a major film or television production without having to spend years clawing your way through countless auditions to do it. Extra work can give you a chance to watch the workings of an actual set from the vantage point of an actor.

Depending on your role, you may have to walk, stand, or perform some other action in the background. If you're lucky, you may even get a chance to perform some action that directly relates to the main characters, such as serving the star a drink or handing the star a telephone. Occasionally, you may even get a chance to speak a line or two, which automatically boosts you into the higher-paying ranks. After you get a speaking role, you may even be eligible for membership into an actors' union, such as the Screen Actors Guild.

Even if you never get a chance to interact with a star on camera or speak a line, working as an extra can give you a chance to participate in a potential blockbuster film or hit television show and work with major stars that many people would give almost anything to meet in person. Extra work may not be particularly glamorous, but given the large number of films and television shows in production at any given time (especially around Los Angeles), you can often work fairly steadily whenever you want. See Chapter 14 for more information about working as an extra.

Even if you pursue extra work as a hobby, you still need to act like a professional. So when you're surrounded by stars on the set, let the stars do their work and don't hound them for photographs or autographs.

Volunteer at Your Local Museum

Many museums need volunteers to conduct tours for schoolchildren or answer questions from visitors. To make this job more interesting, volunteers often dress up in costume and act out the role of another character. For example, in a museum with an exhibition about medieval life, a volunteer tour guide may dress up and act like a medieval squire. In museums dedicated to colonial life in America, actors can dress up like Pilgrims or Native Americans and answer questions from visitors as if they had actually lived through the time period depicted in the museum exhibit.

Such play-acting can make the museum more enjoyable for the public and give them a sense of actually stepping back in time while providing a chance for actors to combine their acting skills with their public speaking and dialect skills.

Although historical museums naturally lend themselves to characters who dress and look like they're from the past, other types of museums can employ volunteer actors, too. Simply dress and play any role that seems appropriate for that particular museum, such as an 1920's aviator, a modern-day astronaut, or an Indiana Jones-type archeologist.

With so many people passing through a museum on any particular day, you just may find yourself acting longer and more often than most professional actors do in the same amount of time.

Appear on Public Access TV

As part of some obscure law, cable television companies have to set aside a public access channel that allows anyone to produce and broadcast almost anything over the air (except for pornography or other questionable material) for free (just as long as you pay for the cost of producing the show yourself). To find out more about producing a show or appearing on a public access channel, contact your local cable television company.

You can opt to produce your own show, but working or appearing on someone else's public access show instead may be easier.

Many people produce talk or variety shows (because they're the easiest types of shows to produce) and need guests or entertainers all the time. Simply contact the producer and ask whether you can act out a scene or appear as a guest.

Public access television isn't likely to make you famous, but it can give you a chance to see how you appear on television and give you an outlet for performing that doesn't require the overhead of a theater. If you get really ambitious, you may even consider starting your own show for broadcast over the public access channel.

Produce Your Own Show on the Internet

For the truly ambitious, consider producing your own Internet show, which can give you the chance to play producer, director, writer, casting director, and actor. (After performing all these separate roles, you may get a better understanding of the types of problems these people face in putting together a show). With a little bit of persistence and fine-tuning, you may be able to create a show that eventually makes the leap to an actual network one day.

Producing a show can be tough, but nothing is more exciting than nursing an idea to completion and releasing your final product for the general public to enjoy. Public access television is still the most obvious choice for broadcasting your show, but with streaming video and the Internet, many producers are skipping public access in favor of promoting and broadcasting their shows through their own Web sites.

Unlike public access television, you can have complete control over your show broadcast over the Internet. (The hard part is getting news of your Web site out to the general public, but that job can give you a chance to play the role of marketing director in addition to the role of producer.)

With the freedom to do whatever you want, you can create a show targeted for niche markets that happen to interest you. For example, many people broadcast Internet shows covering topics that focus on technology, religion, or alternative news. These shows can be humorous, evangelical, or just plain obscure, depending on what you want to do. With the freedom to broadcast anything you want, you can present your opinions to the public without having to stand on a soapbox in the middle of a busy downtown street corner.

To see how other people are using the Internet to broadcast their own shows, visit your favorite search engine, such as Yahoo! or Google, and search for the term *Internet broadcast.*

In show business, nothing is more appealing than any form of success. If you can prove that you're successful in your own show at any level, you stand a much better chance of convincing the show business industry that you can succeed on a larger scale as well.

Index

• A •

• B •

• E •

• F •

• J •

• K •

• L •

• M •

• O •

• P •

• *S* •

• T •

• U •

• V •

• W •

• Z •

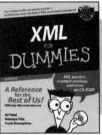

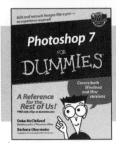

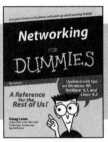